# THE SACRED LIFE OF TIBET

KEITH DOWMAN

# The Sacred Life of Tibet

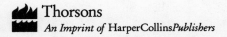

Thorsons
*An Imprint of HarperCollinsPublishers*

*Dedicated to the people of Tibet and their freedom*

Thorsons
An Imprint of HarperCollins*Publishers*
77–85 Fulham Palace Road
Hammersmith, London W6 8JB
1160 Battery Street
San Francisco, California 94111–1213

Published by Thorsons 1997

10 9 8 7 6 5 4 3 2 1

A catalogue record for this book
is available from the British Library

ISBN 0 7225 3375 6

Printed and bound in Great Britain by
Caledonian International Book Manufacturing Limited, Glasgow

# CONTENTS

## PART TWO: RELIGIOUS ORIGINS AND HISTORY

## PART THREE: ART AND ICONS

## PART FOUR: THE YOGA OF PILGRIMAGE

PART FIVE: POWER PLACES

# PREFACE

The sacred life of Tibet takes place in the sacred space of Tibetan Buddhism. This is a transformed landscape, inhabited by gods and demons, Buddhas and bodhisattvas, yogis and magicians. It is a space quite separate from the profane political and social space of Communist Tibet and, perhaps, from our ordinary consciousness.

Part One of this book describes various visionary perspectives on this sacred realm and the manner in which those visions transform the Tibetan landscape. Part Two introduces the Tibetan Buddhist orders and gives a historical view, presenting the chief human players in the mystical drama of the centuries. Part Three introduces some of the divine players as they are represented in art and describes the art forms and where great Tibetan art can be found today. Part Four describes pilgrimage as a devotional exercise and the motivation and practices of pilgrims. Part Five describes the different types of power place, particularly the great sacred mountains, from the pilgrim's perspective.

Today, there are fewer obstacles to foreign pilgrims travelling in Tibet than ever before, but it is still not easy. The domination of the country by a foreign Communist power means pilgrimage is barely tolerated by the authorities and foreigners are viewed with suspicion. Sacred Tibet is still accessible – land-cruisers or buses offer transport to virtually any destination – but on arrival the vibration may not be conducive to worship. The altitude, climate and physical exhaustion may also impede travel. But in so far as experience of the sacred life is an internal journey, no external authority can frustrate the quest. As I hope some readers of this book may verify, it is not always necessary to undergo the physical hardship of pilgrimage on the ground in order to experience the visionary reality of a power place.

Tibet itself, as an ethnic region, does not correspond to contemporary political borders and has not done so since the ninth century. The Tibetan Autonomous Region (TAR) of the People's Republic of China approximates, however, the political area previously ruled from Lhasa by the Dalai Lamas. This excludes Eastern Tibet – most of the old provinces of Kham and Amdo – but sacred Tibet transcends these borders. The Chinese have reorganized Tibet into new administrative districts using names inconsistent with the old divisions. To distinguish between the ethnic and cultural divisions of Tibet I have used the terms 'Western', 'Central' and 'Eastern' Tibet. Western Tibet consists of the Ngari prefecture; Central Tibet includes the prefectures of Lhasa, Shigatse and Lhokha; Eastern Tibet includes the prefecture of Chamdo in the TAR and the old districts of Kham and Amdo, which lie mainly within the Chinese provinces of Qinghai and Sichuan.

# NOTE ON TIBETAN WORDS AND PRONUNCIATION

There is no standard system for transforming Tibetan into phonetic Roman script. The present system is a compromise approximating Tibetan pronunciation but keeping some of the peculiarities of the language. I have retained the Tibetan names of the Buddhas so that their resonance can assist in evoking the mythic realm of Tibet. Some place-names, like Shigatse and Kang Rimpoche, are spelt according to accepted convention.

A final *e* is always pronounced like the French *é*, never silent – thus *dorje*, for example, is pronounced *dorjé*. *Ph* is pronounced with a strong aspiration as in *top-hole*, never like *phantom*. *Th* is always pronounced with a strong aspiration as in *pot-hole*, never as in *think* or *that*. No distinction has been made between *ts* and *tsh* or between *ch* and *chh*.

The first use of a Tibetan term is italicized.

# ACKNOWLEDGEMENTS

I offer my thanks to all those who have assisted me in any way in the completion of this book – with practical help on the ground in Tibet, through the inspiration of the vision of sacred Tibet or through their research. Particularly, I am indebted to Toni Huber for his material on the Labchi, Tsari and Kang Rimpoche mountains; to Charles Ramble for his guide to Bonri and other material on Bon; to Katia Buffetrille for both published and unpublished material on Amnye Machen; to Ian Baker and Hamid Sardar for the material on Padma Ko; to Peggy Day for a description of Nering Senge Dzong and to Steve Leclerc for material on hidden valleys. For the material on Eastern Tibet I am indebted to Tashi Namgyel and also to Gyurme Dorje, who treats Eastern Tibet most thoroughly in his *Tibet Handbook*. I am most grateful to Amely Becker for her generosity and for the assistance of my daughter Ariane and my wife Meryl.

PART ONE

*Visionary Tibet*

# THE LAND AND THE PEOPLE

The Tibetan plateau is one of the most inhospitable regions of the planet. Rugged terrain, extremes of climate, savage weather and high altitude make it a hostile environment. Arctic winter temperatures, searing summer heat and violent temperature change from sun to shade and from day to night stress the human metabolism. Nature is a mean mistress here, withholding rain from the desert lands yet sending it in excess to cause flood and destruction from the rivers in spate, and landslides and avalanches from the malevolent peaks. One minute the summer landscape bathes in brilliant sunlight, the next violent squalls bring sandstorm or hail, both equally damaging to the pitiful fields of barley. Dry storm or rain storm, thunder and lightning cleave across the grasslands, bringing danger to men and cattle. The elements are raw and unmelded in Tibet and the stage upon which they clash is a vast impersonal plateau, dominated occasionally by massive piles of dehumanizing rock that reach up to the clouds.

From the semi-desert of Western Tibet to the grasslands of Kham and Amdo, from the ice-fields of the Himalayas to the steppes of northern Tibet, the plateau is broken by mountain ranges and deep valleys. Only 40 million years ago the Himalayas and the plateau beyond lay under the Sea of Tethys. Since then pressure from the northern-sliding Indian continent has been forcing the plateau upwards, its rivers cutting ever deeper into the rock. The geological youthfulness of the Himalayas, their constant rise and efforts to sort themselves out bring frequent earthquakes. There is little soil anywhere and even where the valleys have broad bottoms the ground is always stony. Only in the valleys of the south-eastern regions, where the altitude is lower and the rainfall greater, can forests clothe the valley sides.

The plateau rises and falls at a mean altitude of about 14,000 ft (4,270m). In Central Tibet the Yarlung Tsangpo Valley has cut down to 11,000 feet (3,350m). In Eastern Tibet the plateau is lower and the river valleys deeper, but even here the altitude is a severe impediment to human activity. The Tibetan people and their animals have adapted to this harsh fact genetically and physiologically. Their red to white blood corpuscle ratio is up to 30 per cent higher than lowlanders. Knowing nothing else, Tibetans consider the thinness of the air the norm. But no one carries heavy loads in Tibet. The pace of a walk, even on the flat, is slow and measured, the gait designed to economize on heat and energy. 'Walking up a hill, proceed at the pace of a child' is an old Tibetan axiom.

The nomads, the *drokpas*, live in tents on the uplands, tending their herds of yaks and sheep; the villagers, *rongpas* or *yupas*, live in cottages of stone in the valleys, cultivating their fields. Whether drokpa or yupa, all Tibetans know the origin myth that explains the relative misery of their human lot and the prophecies that describe the debased nature of human existence – particularly Tibetan existence – at the close of the *kaliyuga*, the butt-end of time, where we now find ourselves. The Tibetan sense of identity is – with a dash of humour – formed by this legend.

The tale runs that when the Buddha Shakyamuni passed into nirvana, Tibet was still an unpopulated wilderness of swamps and deserts between the mountain ranges, a land unfit for human habitation, the abode only of water birds and wild animals. But before he passed away, Shakyamuni blessed the bodhisattva of compassion, Chenrezik, with a self-fulfilling prophecy, and Chenrezik sent a bodhisattva emanation of his heart in the form of an ape to Tibet, while the goddess of devotion, Drolma (Arya Tara), the emanation of one of Chenrezik's tears, projected a rock-ogress into Tibet. These two, monkey and ogress, coupled, and generated male and female progeny who multiplied and peopled the country. So the father of the Tibetan race was an ape, an eloquent speaker of nonsense, and the mother of the race was an ogress with no compassion, delighting in sin and hostile to wisdom.

The descendants of the ape and the rock-ogress were not only gibbering, pitiless and hard, but also barbaric and ruthless savages. This was the human material that the early Tibetan kings moulded into a fighting force that, like the hordes of Genghis Khan, swept into the civilized kingdoms on the borders, pillaging, plundering and destroying. Allowing for some self-deprecation, since he was talking to his spiritual master, the eighth-century King Trisong Detsen could truly say, 'This land of Tibet is a country of cannibal demons, a land of darkness where the buddha-dharma has never been heard.'

The harshness of life on the Tibetan plateau and the absence of influence from higher civilizations contributed to a primitive culture not of noble savages but of feral brutes. Shamanistic priests engaged in human sacrifice for a laity that perceived themselves as descendants of red-faced apes.

The civilizing influence of the high cultures of China and India beginning in the seventh century and the establishment of a monastic system in the eleventh century took the edge off this rudimentary culture. The ethos of Buddhism was assimilated as an ideal and the once ferocious warrior people strove for spiritual accomplishment. But the basic doctrines of Buddhism taught that although they possessed the capacity for self-improvement, human beings, driven by lust and desire, were little better than beasts. The entire scope of human potential was riddled by suffering and there was no release from this human condition except for the fortunate few who obtained the elusive prerequisites for tantric Buddhist initiation and meditation practice.

The monasteries of Tibet, however, became the repositories of a profound religious cultural tradition. Extraordinary yogis, saints and seers were the product of this tradition, and Tibet gained a reputation throughout Asia for its Buddhas and magicians. But the hierarchical social and religious structure left a yawning gap between the monks and the serfs, and between the incarnate Buddhas – tulkus and yogis – and the monks who were monastic servants.

The state of society in Tibet today is indicated by the prophecies that presage the coming of the millennium, the period of degradation of the human condition, of moral behaviour and aspiration, at the end of the kaliyuga. The vision of religious society by contemporary Communists, Chinese and Tibetan, echoes these prophecies and anchors their reality in medieval Tibet, the vestiges of which still exist in Tibet today. According to this view, the religious establishments have since medieval times been inhabited by lamas performing ritual exorcism purely for money, selling tantric secrets and initiation into the tantric mysteries, and accumulating relics and religious treasures; scholars splitting doctrinal hairs and in love with their novice students; monks drunken and pederastic; hermits lounging in the sun awaiting a willing nun or consumed by avarice; and pilgrimage to the power places is simply used as an excuse to trade or for sexual adventure.

As for the laity, the nomads and villagers, the nomads are brigands and murderers and the villagers are sly and deceitful. There is every reason to be wary of such characterizations of nomads by villagers and villagers by nomads, but such statements are so common that not only must they have some basis in reality but they must also affect the Tibetans' view of themselves. Indeed, in the province of Amdo, in the far north-east, for instance, the nomads had a culture of banditry until very recently, and even now Chinese interlopers into their territory are liable to be the target of the Amdowas' wrath. Traders and pilgrims were always fair game to their thieving ways and their bloodlust, and their reputation was supported by hair-raising stories of their cruelty. In order to maintain and fortify their valour, it was commonly believed that they ate the hearts of their captives.

Similarly, the Khampas, the mainly nomadic people whose province lies to the south of Amdo, rejoice in the reputation of wily traders lacking any moral constraint upon their dealings, traders who would and could gladly sell the Brooklyn Bridge many times over if they knew where it was. A sympathetic nineteenth-century Tibetan commentator sums up the Khampa character like this:

> *The people of Kham are great in strength of upright character and they are affectionate to their masters. They are greater in their belief and faith than other Tibetans, and far surpass them in jealousy of their opinions. They behave rudely towards strangers, but are unhesitatingly helpful to their best acquaintances, and they have the fault of being too trusting and naïve.*
>
> WYLIE 1962:104

The devious underhanded character of the village cultivators is perhaps best exemplified by the reputed disposition of the people of southern Tibet. The villagers of the provinces of southern Kongpo and Powo have a reputation as furtive poisoners, weakening their guests, family or travelling pilgrims and traders to extract their money and even murdering them by slow poison to acquire their possessions. This report by a Capuchin monk based in Lhasa in 1741 is perhaps exaggerated and better described the Lopas further to the south, but it represents the reputation of the Kongpo people amongst outsiders:

> The people of this region cannot be subdued, since they are very proud and feed on human flesh. If the missionaries could travel through this province they would greatly reduce the length of their voyage; but they cannot do this without facing the risk of being roasted or stewed and becoming a tasty dish for these people.
>
> RAMBLE MS

It is also held that whereas the nomad peoples, particularly of Amdo and Kham, have a strong sense of honour and loyalty, the valley people have no self-respect and will stoop to the vilest trickery to gain the upper hand in their dealings with friend and foe alike. The Central Tibetans themselves, whose views of provincial nomads and villagers approximate those expressed above, are considered by visitors from the provinces to be shrewd and arrogant, or slavish and mulish, according to their social status. But in general their superior knowledge and practice of the Buddha's teaching are recognized, and this knowledge affects their moral behaviour in a positive way.

Western visions of Tibet and Tibetans, although they have had very little influence inside Tibet, have in the past reflected the above stereotypes. The poet Walter Savage Landor regaled late Victorian society with stories of the Tibetans' cruelty and inhumanity after he had been tortured by local officials in a variety of imaginatively barbaric ways during his intrusion into Tibet. It was widely believed by foreigners that after the nineteenth-century Sikh military adventurer Zarowar Sing had been defeated in Western Tibet the Tibetans dismembered his body and hung up pieces of his flesh in their houses for good luck. Stories told of explorers who had the misfortune to encounter the Amdowas in their Eastern Tibetan territory, never to return, added to this notion of Tibetans as merciless killers.

balance this view, there is a thread of compassionate had its genesis in Kipling's *Kim*, where the Tibetan was a mystic, a lama searching for the nectar of immortality in Indian power places. The commander of the 1904 British military expedition to Lhasa, Colonel Francis Younghusband, gave more substance to this vision when, having seen the soul of Tibet in the indomitable courage of the Tibetans who stood against the British Gatling guns at Gyantse, was blessed by an initiatory experience in Lhasa. Alexandra David-Neel, upon her return from her incognito pilgrimage to Lhasa, told the world that the Tibetan lamas indeed possessed the powers of buddha-realization that the Theosophists claimed for them, but that the common people were bandits and thieves. Perhaps this extraordinary French pilgrim was the progenitor of the view currently held by Western devotees of the lamas, one that whitewashes and idealizes them. This vision has only a tangential bearing upon the inhabitants of the plateau who have never left it, much as Hergé's vision in *Tintin in Tibet* provides only a Shangri-La-type projection of purely Western provenance.

A traveller to Tibet who focused upon an aspect of the Tibetan character – or religion – that is usually overlooked by Western devotees was Professor Guiseppe Tucci, who observed that Tibetans are strikingly lacking in social compassion. The lay Tibetan in his shamanistic religious practice is obsessed with optimizing his good luck and minimizing his bad luck by propitiating the gods and demons that determine his fate, while the Buddhist devotee is concerned primarily with increasing his merit by formal devotions, quite oblivious of the need of fellow human beings who must struggle alone with their unpropitious karma. It is a rare yogi whose meditation has led him to the heart of Chenrezik, the compassionate bodhisattva whose entire being is radiant and active kindness.

The foreign view that has impinged most harshly upon Tibet this century is the Western-originated Marxist view spread through the agency of the Chinese Communists. Nothing in the last thousand years has impacted upon Tibetans and Tibetan culture like the Chinese conquest and suppression. The eradication of the ruling class and the intelligentsia, the closing of all access to high culture and the destruction of the monasteries is the legacy of ruthless Maoist rule and particularly the Cultural Revolution. The crass materialistic ethos of Chinese Communism, the paranoia induced by the destruction of family and religious loyalties, and the reduction of all Tibetan people to a despised and exploited underclass have all contributed to a renewed barbarization of the people. But Tibetan renunciation of traditional attitudes and beliefs has to a large extent been only formal lip-service to the political masters, for above all the Tibetan character is intensely conservative and strongly resilient. The Tibetan propensity to dream dreams and to see visions cannot be eradicated in a single generation of cultural implosion. The reason for these visions – indeed, the necessity for them – as a response to the harsh physical and human environment still certainly exists.

## THE SHAMAN'S VISION

From the very beginning of human habitation in Tibet the main religious preoccupation has been with the hostility of the physical environment. Before Buddhism, with its emphasis on morality, awareness and spiritual liberation, can come into focus, it is necessary to come to terms with the landscape and the elemental powers that inhabit it. Taming the landscape is the principal concern of the shaman. By entering into his vision we enter the mythic realm of sacred Tibet.

The shaman is a magician able to manipulate, to pacify, to control or to subjugate the spiritualistic energies resident in the environment. These energies may be elemental, animal or vegetable, human or relating to the realms of gods, demons and spirits. Through his magic the shaman can influence the elements responsible for rainfall, drought and flood, earthquake, avalanche and landslide, thunder and lightning. He can control the fertility of the soil, assuring bounteous crops and averting famine. He can prevent disease. He can protect the lives of men and women and the lives of their animals, the fertility of their crops and their reproductive potency. He can foretell the future and influence family and political affairs.

The shaman's vision is a holistic one, where the distinction between the outer physical environment and the inner human being is blurred. In the shaman's mindscape there is no radical distinction between outer phenomena and inner noumena. This is a pre-rational mindstate. The development of consciousness that occurred in the Western mind after the Renaissance and the scientific enlightenment with its rational, logical thought processes undermined this holistic vision of reality. As the conceptual capacity of the mind increased, we lost our sense of oneness with the environment. Outer phenomena became separate from us, objects of alienated scientific observation. An acute separation – a dualism – of self and other evolved. Rational consciousness, indeed, depends upon the suppression of the noumena of the holistic mind. But the alienated dualistic mindstate of Western man has now grown like a cancer to the point where we can but rarely gain access to vestiges of the holistic shamanistic vision.

The argument between holistic shamanistic consciousness and rational dualistic mind is not relevant here. But it is necessary to accept the validity of the holistic, mythic vision of the shaman to understand the dimensions of his vision, his spiritualistic terminology, the methods he uses to transform the landscape and its spiritual phenomena, and thereby to enter into sacred Tibet. It may be useful to consider the shaman's vision as a way of 'seeing' that cuts through the duality of ordinary perception where self and other, physical and mental, inside and outside, are separate. So each sensory perception is a totality involving the entire cosmos. This is why it is called 'holistic' – it is entire and complete.

The cosmology of the shaman's mythic realm is best described in the conventional shamanic terms of the three realms of existence. This concept is well known in Tibet, but also in its essence throughout South and South-East Asia. The three realms of existence are the sky, the earth and the subterranean realm. They are inhabited and governed by three distinct categories of beings. The gods live in the sky above, serpent spirits live in the earth below and human beings live on the earth in between. In elemental terms, the sky above is the domain of space, air and fire, the subterranean realm is the sphere of earth and water, and all the elements are present in the middle realm, the domain of human beings. By 'gods' is understood gods (*lha*), demons (*dre*) and the innumerable spirits of various kinds. Serpent spirits (*lu*, *nagas*) are demi-gods and there are also other various spirits that live in the netherworld. The human mind is the stage on which these gods, demons and spirits interact with human beings in the middle realm.

The sky gods include the gods like Brahma of the Hindu pantheon and spirits like the odour-eaters (*driza*), but the sky gods who loom largest in the Tibetan mythic vision are those who live on the mountain peaks, the mountain gods (*noijin* and *nyen*). These most powerful of the entities of the pantheon, male or female, seem actually to be identified with the mountains themselves. They are warrior gods, quick to anger, jealous and violent, and their nature is power. From the human point of view they are trouble-makers, tormentors, terrorists, devils, sitting on their mountain thrones raining down affliction, with little or no cause, upon their human quarry. Their responses are like the reactions of irritable, violent, uptight drunks. Loitering on the passes, unless they are propitiated with offerings they are lethal to travellers – their breath is poisonous. They shape-shift according to their mood and their need. The Indian demon Ravana, who abducted Rama's wife Sita to his Sri Lankan lair, was a mountain god, but he lacks the feral savagery of the Tibetan variety.

The mountain gods are territorial lords – the greater the mountain, the greater their territory. Nyenchen Thanglha, residing on the mountain of the same name in a range that dominates both the northern plains and Central Tibet, can be considered the mountain god-king of the whole of Tibet. The god of a mountain that physically dominates a valley probably rules that valley, as Yarlha Shampo, for example, rules the Yarlung Valley. Every small valley has its own mountain residence of its mountain god.

What ties the human inhabitants most securely to the mountain god and his whims and moods is their relationship of grandson to grandfather. The mountain gods are the original ancestors of the tribes of Central Tibet and they have a certain responsibility to their offspring, although even careful ritual propitiation does not necessarily bring looked-for protection from these irresponsible guardians. They are as capricious as the weather, which is their principal method of cowing and tyrannizing their progeny. Mountain gods are propitiated with complex ritual and offering.

The chief residents of the subterranean realm are the serpent spirits, demi-gods, male and female (*lu* and *luma*). They can be

conceived animistically as the spirits of earth and water and every-
thing that is contained within these elemental spheres. They are
the foot soldiers of a semi-divine natural authority that orders
man-kind's relationship with his terrestrial environment. While the
mountain gods rule with a heavy-handed fickle patriarchal authority, the serpent spirits have allegiance to a thin-skinned, hypersen-
sitive female nature, with a formidable armoury at their disposal.

The serpent spirits live in the earth, in the rock, and in the lakes
and streams. Their usual form is snake-like. They are black, white
or red. They can take human form or shape-shift according to
requirement. They guard the mineral wealth of the earth, including
rock and the soil itself. In a special way they are the guardians of
ecological balance, a highly conservative force inhibiting human
interference with the earth and what is in the earth. Precious stones
belong to them and the magical power of a coral or turquoise stone
is determined as auspicious or inauspicious according to its guardian
serpent spirit's satisfaction with how it was mined and the care that
has been taken of it. To mine iron or gold is to offend the serpent
spirits and is equivalent to stealing from them, unless a pact has been
agreed upon and propitiation made. The low status of iron workers
in traditional Tibet is due to their subordination to the serpent spirits. As rock is protected by the spirits, they object to the movement
of stones from one place to another, and, of course, the hewing of
stone. Propitiation of the serpent spirits precedes any building
activity. Even to dig a hole in the ground is to risk offending them
and to plough the soil is to invade their domain. All agriculture is
therefore dependent upon a working relationship with the serpent
spirits. Trees and plants are also protected by them.

Although any of the gods, demons and spirits can afflict human
beings with disease, either by creating an imbalance through the
element with which they are identified or by acting on human consciousness, the serpent spirits are the chief arbiters of human health.
This power is derived mainly from their affinity to water. As
guardians of springs and water courses they protect its flow and
purity. In the cold Tibetan climate the danger from water-borne
intestinal disease is minimal compared to the peril on the Indian
plains, but the pollution of water sources angers Tibetan serpent
spirits no less than their Indian cousins and their ire afflicts those

who fail in their hygiene. Also, since the body is 98 per cent water, they influence diseases of bodily water imbalance such as abscesses, ulcers, the swelling of the limbs and dehydration. Diseases related to excessive indulgence are also controlled by the serpent spirits, as are leprosy and tuberculosis, sores and itches. Offerings and herbal incense can, however, propitiate the spirits.

The mistress of the legions of serpent spirits is the demoness (*sinmo*) who can be seen in the landscape. The demoness of Central Tibet, for example, lies supine across the central provinces, embodying all hostile elemental powers. Incarnate demonesses or rock-ogresses are original inhabitants of Tibet in Buddhist mythology. They stalk the earth after human prey, combining the chaotic, relentlessly destructive power of the external environment with the savage bestiality of the internally latent female archetype.

The specifically female sky goddesses called sky dancers (*khandromas*, *dakinis*) in their pre-Buddha form share this elementally malign nature and, like the mother goddesses (*mamo*), may eat man's flesh and afflict him through sexual relationship.

The gods of the middle realm, those that live above the earth but are not sky gods, are more intimately related to humans and the daily domestic round than the mountain gods and the serpent spirits. Although these entities are called gods (*lha*), they are very minor gods with specific locations and functions. On a person, the protecting 'enemy god' (*dralha*) sits on the right shoulder, the male and female ancestor gods are in the armpits, and the 'maternal-uncle god' (*zhanglha*) in the heart. Within the house, there is a home god who resides in a main pillar, another god in the main roof beam, another in the hearth and another guarding the store-room. All these have a protective function which includes a sense of family; they may need extra propitiation to allow additions into the family circle. Outside the home, the god of horses presides over all equine concerns and a god of cattle and a god of the fields likewise perform specific functions. The land itself is owned by the earth-lords (*sadak*) and owners of the ground (*zhidak*), rock and earth spirits that must be considered if any special kind of activity is performed within their purview. All these gods may be propitiated with herbal incense.

The terrestrial realm is also populated by various spirits of the dead. Regular ghosts are spirits that have not been able to find rebirth due to an unbreakable attachment to this world, and so wander in the intermediate state attempting to communicate with the living and to influence them. Hungry ghosts (*yidak*) are those whose previous lives were so thoroughly dominated by greed and lust that their karma resulted in a tortured rebirth of frustrated hunger and thirst. They now lurk on the edge of the human realm, sometimes taking a human form. Flesh-eating spirits (*shaza*) also inhabit this realm.

It is very difficult to characterize all the many shades of spirit life and present a unified pantheon showing the relationship between the various noumenal entities and human beings. Only a few of the innumerable categories of inhabitants of the mythic realm are mentioned here. But these spiritual entities need to be recognized before their presence can affect the world of men. They must be named and their specific places of residence identified. In this way the full force of their reality is evoked in the mind of the shaman. He is then no longer a passive witness to the divine drama, but can influence it. Indeed, his religious duty is to assuage the spirits of the heavens and the netherworld. By appeasing them he can maintain an equilibrium of powers in the middle realm and so provide for himself and his community the most propitious conditions for survival in a hostile environment. The rituals by which the gods are appeased once included human and animal sacrifice, but when the influence of Buddhism prohibited blood sacrifice, ritual fire-offering replaced it. Rituals of ransom in which effigies or substances represent the offering to the gods and demons now form a major part of the shamanic rites of propitiation.

## BUDDHA-VISION

In the shaman's vision, the landscape – the universe – is a panorama of spiritual energy described in terms of gods, demons and spirit entities. These are relatively externalized phenomena. Buddha-vision can be described as a process of greater internalization, a deeper penetration of the mind's perceptual and mental dynamic. Here, the nature of mind, inseparable from its sensory field, is experienced as emptiness (*tongpanyi, shunyata*). Awareness rests in the sphere of emptiness and space that is common to both internal mental processes and their seemingly objective referents. In this manner there is no separation whatsoever between internal and external, inside and outside, and out of this awareness of unity arises the visionary realm, the mythic realm, of the Buddhas. With total immersion in the nature of mind, the shaman becomes a Buddha with complete awareness of the totality and a vision in which the external and the internal, the landscape and its life, are part of a holistic vision where all elements are interdependently linked.

Buddhist metaphysicians have described a dynamic structure that acts as a guide to this buddhahood state for neophytes and Buddhist poets have used it to describe partial reflections of it. The fundamental concept is a threefold structure of interpenetrating spheres: the ultimate sphere is of all-penetrating and embracing light and emptiness; within that clear light and emptiness is the sphere of vision; and within the sphere of vision is the sphere of constantly transforming illusion that constitutes the realm of seemingly external appearances. It is the sphere of vision that is all-important to sacred Tibet.

Shamanic consciousness of the gods, demons and spirits of the three realms of existence belongs to a reality separate not only from Western consciousness but also from buddha-vision. The gods and demons of shamanic Tibet must not be confused with the buddha-deities of the tantric pantheon which form a part of buddha-vision. The shaman's reality and the buddha-yogi's reality are identical in so far as the three realms of existence provide the noumenal energy that is the stuff of transformation. The landscape that is to be transformed from a harsh hostile world of gods and demons into a pliable environment that is safe and malleable is the same, but whereas the shaman manipulates the spirit world only marginally, to make the spirit powers less harmful to human beings and to utilize their energy for human benefit, the buddha-yogi effects a complete and radical transformation of the gods and demons, enslaves them and makes them utterly subservient to buddha-mind and to the buddha-dharma.

# Pegging the Earth and the Mountains

Pegging the earth and the mountains is a shamanic ritual taken over by Buddhist yogis to tame the landscape and to bind the spirit powers. The earth is intractable and full of gods and demons. It is mysterious and magical, like a woman's body. It is nature in a seemingly solid and tangible form. To peg the earth is to control it, to make it manageable and submissive. Pegging makes order out of chaos. It binds the gods and demons. It establishes a strong centre with peace and security in the land – and when the pegging is done symmetrically, it makes mandalas out of the landscape.

First, the earth is pegged down by the mountains, which are like nails or ritual daggers (*phurbas*) piercing the earth. The great mountain Kang Rimpoche (Kailash) is comparable to Mount Meru, the *axis mundi*, around which the planets and stars turn, but even in its function as the axis of the universe it pierces the earth and secures it. To fulfil its function and in response to people's need, a mountain may have come from another country, like Amnye Machen *(see p.188)*. A mythic bird may have brought it in its talons, like Tsonying Mahadeva, the island in Tso Ngon (Kokonor) lake. Perhaps magicians brought it, like Tsibri mountain, to the north of the Tingri plain, which was carried up from Bodhgaya to fill a poisonous lake. Even Kang Rimpoche itself is said by some to have originated in another country. Whatever its origin, the mountain pierces the earth and subjugates it.

The mountain itself is then pegged down. To fix Tsibri, four 'nails' in the form of small mountains were driven in at the cardinal points, four rivers were made to flow and four sky-burial sites were established. By laying down a circular path of circumambulation joining the sites of the 'nails' in the cardinal directions, a basic mandala is formed. The mountain is now bound to the earth so that it cannot fly away and the powers that invest it are idealized in a mandala. When the Chinese invaders arrived in Amdo, their coming was interpreted by the nomads as an omen fulfilling a prophecy that in the kaliyuga, the great mountain Amnye Machen would leave for India, for at the end of time 'the high mountains and big rocks appointed by the sky to maintain it will not press on the earth'. In order to keep Amnye Machen in its present location, the gods, it is said, offered a three-dimensional mandala, evidence for which is shown in the sand dunes that surround the mountain within the circumambulatory path, for the dunes are composed of the grains of sand that were sprinkled on the mandala as offering.

Mountains peg the earth on a mythic, macrocosmic, level. On the human level, representations of the mountains bind the earth and its demons. *Chortens*, monuments of brick and stone, are symbolic mountains, 'nails' or 'ritual daggers' that suppress demonic forces beneath them and establish order and create a mandala *(see also p.228)*. The chorten in itself is a three-dimensional mandala. The *gompa* (monastery) *lhakhang* (chapel) mimics the mountain in its ideal structure and also creates a mandala. Stone pillars *(doring)*, that date back to the empire period and are usually engraved with a Buddhist communication or symbol, also pierce the earth and control it. Their ritual status as the *axis mundi* is indicated by the turtle on which some of them stand, for the *axis mundi* is supported at its base by the cosmic turtle. The great masts *(darchen)* that adorn most monastery courtyards are yet another method of binding the earth. In the annual rite of raising the great mast, like the major May ritual at Darchen on the circumambulatory path at Kang Rimpoche, the gods and demons of the earth are secured. Domestic prayer-flag poles mimic this function; so do the flag poles that pierce the cairns on passes or that are built on significant boulders. Likewise, the peak-posts that mark the crests of a ridge tame that ridge or hill through penetration. It is as if the penetration of the rock by the post releases pent up pestilential energy and noxious fumes, allowing the rock to breathe and pacifying it. The peak-posts and the poles that pierce the cairns are the symbols of the earth-lords *(sadak)* and are therefore subject to ritual propitiation. All or any of these pegs may be thought of as acupuncture needles in the body of the earth, balancing and healing the energetic pattern of the entire landscape. The Buchu Sergyi Lhakhang in Kongpo, for instance, is conceived as the acupuncture point through which energetic imbalance in Lhasa may be redressed.

Finally, the earth is tamed by the nomad's tent peg. Each time he pitches his yak-wool tent, he creates a three-dimensional mandala delineated by the pegs. By driving in the pegs, he sanctifies the earth beneath and binds the gods and demons of the earth.

The large formal ritual mandalas of the buddha-deities are likewise pegged in the corners. The pegs are shaped like ritual daggers (phurbas) and the dagger-peg is visualized as a buddha-deity. In the tantric practice of this, buddha-deity Dorje Phurba (Vajra Kilaya), the Indestructible Dagger, the magical power that resides in the 'peg', whether it is a mountain, a mast or a pole, is transformed into the Buddha's enlightened awareness. In the rites of Dorje Phurba, the dagger-peg is used as the agent of binding or even destroying demons, its dynamic energy being the empty awareness that permeates, and thus dominates, all things.

## Binding Gods and Demons

Shamanic Tibet is a land of untamed gods, demons and spirits. Sacred Tibet is a land in which these hostile powers have been transformed, tamed or bound.

The old texts describing the Buddhist conversion of Tibet not only show the nature of the noumenal milieu, the hierarchy and divine pantheon, but also explain the process by which subjugation was achieved. These techniques are as valid today as they were in the period of early Buddhism and are still practised by the lamas to keep the gods and demons bound.

The early Buddhist missionaries to Tibet had first to demonstrate to the shamanic people their control of the gods and demons, for the metapsychological doctrines of Shakyamuni Buddha that showed gods and demons to be the product of mental functions which could be transcended on the path of meditation were not accessible to the unlettered followers of the shamans. Fortunately, it appears that the early Buddhist wanderers in Tibet were tantric sadhus, versed in the highly sophisticated arts of ritual magic developed on the Indian plains, and so were representatives of an ancient and highly developed civilization at the stage that the Tibetans themselves consider the apogee of its achievement.

There is no need to denigrate the efficacy of the rites of the shamans in order to prove the greater competence of the Buddhist tantric yogis. That the shamans were effective in their social role may be deduced from the dynamic vitality of their tribal society. At the time that Buddhism penetrated Tibet, in the seventh century, it was producing a social and military organization that administered a great empire.

The founder of the Tibetan Empire, King Songtsen Gampo, apparently received the first missionaries sympathetically. It is Tibetan belief that he was a thorough-going Buddhist. Certainly he initiated a policy of assimilating elements of both Chinese and Indian cultures that were evidently lacking in Tibet and the 10 virtues of the Buddhist moral code were propagated during his reign. Worship and the meditation practices of Chenrezik, the bodhisattva of compassion, were introduced, or certainly encouraged, and it would appear that the king himself became a devotee of the bodhisattva. He may also have spent time in retreat performing Buddhist meditation. There is little doubt that he built a number of Buddhist temples throughout Tibet, amongst them the 13 missionary temples that bound the great supine demoness of Central Tibet.

## The Supine Demoness of Central Tibet

As we have seen, in the demoness of Central Tibet, who lies on her back, spanning the central provinces, are embodied all hostile elemental powers. We have no representational icon of her from Tibetan sources; nowhere do we find demons represented iconographically. But if we envision her in the form of the Earth Mother, Dhattimatta, a representation of the goddess of fertility as conceived in the Indian cultural sphere, we cannot go far wrong. Dhattimatta lies on her back, naked, her arms by her sides, her knees raised and splayed, her vulva exposed. Specifically, she represents the fecundity of the earth and the fertility of woman, but more than that, she embodies the female aspect of nature. We have no record of whether the supine demoness was recognized as such, and if so, how she was propitiated, before the advent of Buddhism. But to understand what forces were subjugated when she was bound by Buddhist ritual it may be rewarding to look at what she personified in general in shamanistic society.

The earth mothers reveal a primeval strata of religion, a prehistoric era of matriarchy, or, at least, a time when the female psyche, the primordial collective anima of the people, was the predominant religious focus. But before earth-goddess energy is viewed internally as the radical feminine aspect of the psyche, the earth goddess represents nature. Here she is seen as the fecund source of life, the goddess out of whose body grow the crops that sustain life. This benign function, however, is overshadowed by her identification with nature's impersonal destructive powers. She controls the elements and is thus responsible for earthquake, flood, drought and famine, hail and lightning. Although she is impersonal in her dispensation of affliction, an element of personal malice is nevertheless perceived by those she harms. This idea of cosmic malevolence is manipulated by witches and sorceresses seeking to inflict misfortune upon their enemies, for the earth goddess may be prevailed upon to direct her malignity according to her devotees' will and to fortify the curses of her acolytes. So she is the patron and protector of black magicians, particularly witches.

The earth mother is also envisioned as the source of unfettered female sexual energy. In this aspect she is worshipped by newlyweds to arouse their sexuality and to bless their nuptials. She is propitiated to satisfy her devotees' lust for the man or woman of their choice and to facilitate fertility and pregnancy. Nymphomania and orgiastic behaviour are attributed to her malign influence, and irrational and perverse sexual expression is explained as possession by her minions.

The supine demoness, gigantic in size, is herself vast in lust and bestial desire. But as order is imposed upon the chaotic, instinctive and intuitive feminine realm of the psyche by the disciplined intelligence of the masculine Buddhist will, so her desire is tamed. Whenever a chorten is built in Tibet, the demoness is tamed. The following is the original legend of her subjugation.

In the year AD 641 King Songtsen Gampo married the Princess Wencheng, one of the daughters of the Chinese Tang emperor. As part of her dowry she brought a precious Indian image of Shakyamuni Buddha to Tibet. It happened that the chariot carrying the image from China became intractably stuck in the Lhasa mud. Wencheng resorted to the ancient Chinese art of divination to discover the cause of this ill-omen and the solution to her difficulties. Her calculations disclosed that the whole of Central Tibet was 'like a demoness fallen on her back', that the lake in the Plain of Milk in

Lhasa was her heart-blood, and that the three hills rising out of the plain – Marpori, Chakpori and Bonpori – were her breasts and *mons veneris*. The Plain of Milk was the palace of the serpent spirits, who, together with the demons (*dre*), the elemental goddesses (*mamo*), the nature spirits (*tsen*), the hostile earth spirits (*sadra*) and the supine demoness herself, were the cause of all evil and obstructive forces in Tibet. Wencheng's solution was to order a palace built for the king, a lhakhang for her Buddha, a gompa for monks and a park for the common people. The cairn of the demons was to be destroyed and the lake in the Plain of Milk to be filled in with earth and stone.

King Songtsen Gampo and his Nepali queen, Bhrikuti, accepted the dictates of Wencheng's divination. The implementation of her prescription, however, was hindered by Bhrikuti's insistence that construction of the projected lhakhang was her prerogative and that the religious merit generated should accrue to her. The king allowed that Bhrikuti should oversee the work, but at each stage, whenever obstacles arose, usually because Bhrikuti failed to follow Wencheng's stipulated procedure, the Nepali princess deferred to her Chinese sister, obtaining instruction on how to overcome demonic interference. Finally the lake was drained and the foundation of the Lhasa Jokhang was laid, but by this time the king himself had become involved and conceived a grand design to secure the supine demoness forever and simultaneously to convert the Tibetan people to Buddhism.

In King Songtsen Gampo's ideal design, the Lhasa Jokhang would lie at the centre of three constellations of lhakhangs forming concentric squares. The lhakhangs at the corners of each square would tether the demoness at increasingly greater distances from her heart, which lay under the Lhasa Jokhang, and civilize tribes increasingly distant from Lhasa. The demoness was lying with her shoulders to the east of Lhasa and her hips to the west, with her spread-eagled limbs in the border provinces. The four lhakhangs at the corners of the inner square therefore pinioned her shoulders and hips and civilized the four districts of Central Tibet and Tsang. The four lhakhangs at the corners of the intermediate square pinned the demoness's elbows and knees and subdued the provinces of Tibet. The four lhakhangs at the corners of the outer square pinned the demoness's hands and feet and subjected the border areas of Tibet. In practice, in spacial reality, this ideal design was only partially achieved, as none of these quadrilaterals formed a square.

## The Scorpion of Kongpo

The supine demoness of Central Tibet is the principal example of the landscape as subjected demonic being, subjugated by worship at the power places located at the energy points of her body. In her case the locations were determined more by population density and political expediency than by geomancy. In contrast, across the province of Kongpo lies the body of a scorpion. In the natural world the scorpion symbolizes the accidental malignity of nature and in the moral realm the sting of karma, the negative repercussions of sinful actions of body, speech and mind. Kongpo, although relatively close to Central Tibet, has always been considered by Central Tibetans to be a barbaric province, mainly due to the proximity and influence of the Lopa tribes, the animistic peoples of the eastern Himalayas. Songtsen Gampo's missionary temple is located there at Buchu.

The Kongpo scorpion is subjugated by power places located at its vital spots – a cave, a lake and three hills are geomantically and symbolically efficient in binding the giant insect. The presence of Mahadeva (Shiva) and Uma (Parvati), who are protectors of the Buddhist mandala, at Gyala Tsedum removes the malignancy of the scorpion's reproductive organs, while the Lord of Death, Shinje, in its belly has no apparent geographical referent. This description is taken from a New Bon pilgrim guide and there is nothing in it that is at variance with Buddhism:

> At the point of its sting is the Power Place of the Masters and Sky Dancers, Ponse Khandro Ne; in the middle part of the sting is the Orgyen Cave in Uri; at its tail are the three hills that form the triangular offering place of the yidam Shinje and the Mamos; in its mouth is the purifying lake Roden Montso, the Nectarine Lake of Aspiration; to its right and left are Chabkar and Chabnak Gompas to the south of Bonri; the belly of the scorpion is the circle of Shinje; and at its generative organ are the protectors Mahadeva and Uma in consummate union at Gyala Tsedum.

## Subjugation of Gods and Demons by Guru Rimpoche

Tibet's Great Guru, Padmasambhava, known universally in Tibet as Guru Rimpoche, was a Buddhist tantric sadhu and exorcist from the Swat Valley in the ancient kingdom of Uddiyana, now a part of Pakistan, who was invited to Tibet in the eighth century by King Trisong Detsen to establish the tantric teaching and specifically to subdue the gods, demons and spirits. For the Tibetan religious orders who distrust the authority of Guru Rimpoche's lineage, his accomplishment is seen only in terms of exorcism of the land. In their recognition of his achievement in this field, however, his spiritual status as a Buddha is firmly established, for it was his buddha-vision that was effective in subjecting the unfettered spirits of Tibet. The word 'exorcism' is to be understood here not as a process of 'driving out' but as a process of 'subjection within'. And there is no question of *destroying* the gods and demons; Guru Rimpoche's task was to bring them under his control and bind them to the yogi's ritual power for the benefit of the buddha-dharma and all beings.

In this poetic address to the gods and demons while gathering them together to accept a token offering in return for their eternal obedience, Guru Rimpoche asserts the nature of his awareness – his buddha-vision – that has the power either to destroy or give continued existence:

> *My body, speech and mind radiant in a buddha-deity's being,*
> *I overwhelm aggressive demons with my brilliance.*
> *Realizing all mental perception as mind,*
> *I am unafraid of the threats of gods and demons.*
> *Within the mandala of immense space*
> *The four elements' materiality dissolves,*
> *Lost in the vastness and depth of space.*
> *Within the mandala of the empty nature of mind,*
> *The phenomena of gods and demons dissolve,*
> *Lost in the vastness and depth of space.*
> *In the imageless empty nature of mind*
> *No gods nor demons exist.*
> *No matter what magical illusions you project*
> *I waver not nor move a jot.*

*Soon the mind dissolves its forms,*
*So do not disobey me.*

DOWMAN MS

One of Guru Rimpoche's teachers, Shri Singha, pointing a finger at the sky, taught him:

*Ever empty, ever empty; ever void, all void;*
*This crucial absolute truth is a treasure*
*Shining everywhere – above, below, between, in all directions.*

RICARD 1994:257

Guru Rimpoche's buddha-vision is based in the 'deathless' awareness of his body of clear light. This light permeates all reality, including the 'illusion' of materiality, purifying the four elements and making him immune to the 'demons' of disease. The radiance of the clear light, emanating as a 'buddha-deity', permeates the mind-forms that appear as demons and integrates them into the Buddha's holistic vision. Through understanding all mental perceptions as the emanation of the nature of mind, there is no belief in entities external to mind, separate from it, no alienation, and in the acceptance of this holistic vision there is no fear. The mandala of Guru Rimpoche's body of clear light is the mandala of the empty nature of his mind, which is also understood as infinite space, and here no gods or demons exist. The illusion of materiality – including demonic spirit forms – can be reabsorbed into this mandala at his will. Therefore, Guru Rimpoche warns, serve me or you lose your existence.

This vision has been sustained down the centuries by yogis emulating the Great Guru and it is this that transforms the gods and demons of Tibet into servants of the Buddhist yogis. The landscape from which they are inseparable is then tamed and transformed into buddhafields.

The legends of Guru Rimpoche describe in mythological terms his victories over the gods and demons of Tibet and also over the stellar constellations and the planets.

On his triumphant progress from Kathmandu to Samye for the purpose of overcoming the spirits of that place so that a gompa could be built, he was confronted by a succession of the most powerful of

Tibet's guardian gods. Entering by way of the Kyirong river valley and reaching the pass into the Tibetan province of Mangyul, he was confronted by Mutsame, one of the 12 guardians of the passes into the Land of the Snows. Mutsame projected herself into the mountains on either side of the pass and tried to squeeze Guru Rimpoche and his attendants between them. In an enclosed pass with sheer snow peaks at either side, an incipient sense of claustrophobia, intensified by the loss of breath at very high altitude, with inclement weather threatening, does easily develop into the basic fear that evokes the image of 'the crushing hell' and an overwhelming consciousness of the power of the elements. Mutsema actually appears.

The master, however, pierced the rock with his staff and cleared a path. As his party descended from the pass, the goddess became terrified and offered her mantric heart-essence to the master, promising to protect the buddha-dharma thereafter. The master gave her the secret name Indestructible Mistress of the Snow Peaks, Dorje Yubunma.

Piercing the rock with a staff is an image that appears in various guises in the description of subjugation of demons. It induces suspension of belief and the magical ambience in which the tantric magicians operate, but essentially it symbolizes the intrusion of, or recognition of, the all-pervading clear light into apparently external delusory mental forms. The dawning awareness of holistic vision 'clears a path'. The goddess's consequent terror is generated by the loss of her identity inherent in her impending reabsorption into the fundamental spaciousness of the nature of mind. 'Offering her mantric heart-essence' is her gesture of defeat – she realizes that without self-determination, she is only an integral part of the universal illusion. Her mantric heart-essence, a seed syllable, or sound, is her primary mark of identity, her original manifestation out of emptiness. Through this essential euphonic nature, she can be invoked, controlled and commanded.

Finally, the Great Guru gives her a new name, Indestructible Mistress of the Snow Peaks, Dorje Yubunma. The prefix or epithet 'Dorje' indicates that she is now a noumenal entity fixed to the basic mandala by a cord of emptiness, and as such, so long as the ritual act of binding, together with the token offering, is performed by the Buddhist yogi, she will serve the buddha-dharma as a protectress, residing on the snow peaks. And there she remains today, appearing as a malevolent goddess to the traveller who externalizes her, but serving the Buddhist yogi in whose mind she is an integral part of the mandala.

From Mangyul the Great Guru and his party turned north, fording the Raga Tsangpo river and climbing up onto the Tibetan plateau. Crossing the interminable rolling hills of the Northern Sky Plain, Jang Namthang, the White Sky Goddess, Namen Karmo, assailed them with thunderbolts. The White Sky Goddess was a wild-woman demoness (*menmo*). Putting a drop of water into the palm of his left hand, like a droplet on a mirror, the master caught the falling thunderbolts, which appeared as seven dry beans in his hand. The goddess was amazed and frightened and fled into the Pelku Tso lake. The master directed his *mudra* (hand gesture) of threat at the lake, visualizing it as a fiery cauldron, and as the lake boiled the goddess's flesh separated from the bone. The mudra of threat in ritual form has the right arm raised to shoulder height, hand showing the palm, and then the two middle fingers caught by the thumb. This mudra is the sign of ultimate threat, the sign of the dorje. The dorje is a ritual representation of the thunderbolt and symbolizes the empty awareness of the nature of mind. Nothing and no one can resist this mudra when the yogi who shows it is internally composed in the samadhi of nonduality. Again the demoness fled, but the master hit her with his secret dorje-thunderbolt, squashing her right eye. She surrendered to him, offering him her heart-essence, and he bound her with vows of commitment and named her Fleshless White Snow Peak, Indestructible One Eye, Shame Kangkar Dorje Chenchikma.

On the vast northern plains of the Tibetan plateau, the rolling grasslands, the home of yak-herding nomads, there is a sense of human helplessness and insignificance in the face of immense space, an occasional brackish lake and a spine of snow mountains. The belligerence of nature unfolds in freak storms, thunder and lightning. The presence of the White Sky Goddess is revealed by her thunderbolts, neutralized by the master in the pellucid mirror-like water he holds in the palm of his hand. The goddess – her name, space, her weapon, fire – is then confounded with water, where Guru Rimpoche, through visualization, boils her in the crucible of penetrating awareness, separating flesh from bone. In tantric lore, bone symbol-izes emptiness and flesh form. So the goddess is deconstructed and now receives her *coup de grâce* from the master's secret dorje. The secret dorje is his phallus, that in the consummation of awareness and empty form knocks out her dualistic vision, leaving her with the single eye of nondual awareness and inducing her complete sur-render. Her heart-essence, the empty nature of her mind, now an integral part of the holistic mandala, she is bound to serve the Bud-dhist yogi, giving her vow of commitment. Her presence in the landscape is a snow peak on the Jangthang, representing the saving quality of emptiness.

In Central Tibet Guru Rimpoche was confronted by two of the great mountain gods – Nyenchen Thanglha and Yarlha Shampo. The Nyenchen Thanglha mountain range separates the Yarlung Tsangpo river system from the Jangthang plateau. The range rises in the north-east in Nakchu prefecture and continues in a west-south-westerly direction all the way to Kailash. The principal peak of this range, directly to the north of Lhasa and close to the Namtso lake, is the residence of the great mountain god Nangchen Thanglha, one of the four principal mountain gods of Tibet, who gives his name to the range and the peak. His name means 'The Great *Nyen*, God of the Plains', and he is also called Nam Thanglha, 'The Sky-Plain God'. Thanglha challenged the master in the form of a monstrous demon in ravenous mood who would devour the travellers. The master directed his mudra of threat at him, and instantly Thanglha transformed himself into a small child with a turquoise hair knot. In this form he was bound by the master.

Yarlha Shampo was also reduced to service of the master by the art of mudra. He was one of the nine sons of the ancient ancestral Bon god, one of the gods of the original nine clans that formed the nuclear kingdom of King Songtsen Gampo's father in the sixth cen-tury. He was the ancestral god of the clan that inhabited the Yarlung Valley, the cradle of Tibetan civilization. On his approach to Samye,

*Yarlha Shampo projected himself as a white yak on the mountain side. His nose emitting clouds of steam, his bellowing roar resound-ing as thunder, his breath thick like a blizzard, sending down thun-derbolts and hail, he challenged them. The master caught the yak by*

*the muzzle with his hook-mudra, roped its neck with his lasso-mudra, bound its four feet with his chain-mudra, and with his bell-mudra pelted the yak with mud and beat him. The yak immediately changed into a child dressed in silk robes and offered his heart-essence, and was bound by a vow of commitment.*

DOWMAN MS

The yak is usually a gentle beast, shy in the wild and docile in captivity. The exception is the wild he-yak when goaded to protect his life or his cow. Then he is the image of intense savage malignance. So Yarlha Shampo manifests as the archetypal wild yak to Guru Rimpoche in his attempt to protect his domain. But the master catches, tethers, binds and subdues him with four hand gestures indicating functional aspects of his nondual samadhi.

The old legends describe various routes of Guru Rimpoche's approach to Samye. The final place he visited was Medro, 50 miles (80 km) to the north-east of Lhasa, to propitiate a king of the serpent spirits, the most powerful of the elemental earth and water spirits in Tibet and Kham. The pre-eminence of the Medro serpent spirit indicates the dominance of the old shaman order's acute awareness of ecological balance. The kernel of the rite that Guru Rimpoche performs is the burying of treasure for the serpent spirits, an offering in advance to appease them for moving stones and digging the earth that clearing the gompa site of Samye would involve and a thanksgiving for all the gifts of nature that building the temple would require.

At Samye the first fruit of binding the demons became apparent. Shantarakshita, the Indian abbot that King Trisong Detsen had invited from Vikramashila to build Tibet's first gompa, had failed in his mission due to his inability to subdue the gods and demons. The serpent spirits had refused to co-operate, denying the king the necessary wood for the beams and iron for the nails. The owners of the ground (*zhidak*) had created obstacles to the gathering of stone and shaping it, and the walls that the labourers managed to build during the day were destroyed in the night time. The earth-lords (*sadak*) destabilized the foundations and no progress had been made in the construction. Immediately Guru Rimpoche arrived he invoked the gods and demons of Tibet whom he had bound, offering them dough balls in a bowl of *zi* stone. They all appeared at Samye and in return for this offering fulfilled the master's request that they co-operate with the work of construction.

## How Drukpa Kunley Bound Demons

Although Guru Rimpoche subjugated all the major gods and demons of Tibet and the Himalayas, there were areas that he did not penetrate. Particularly, there were valleys in the cis-Himalayas that never received the Buddhist message. It was left to later missionaries from Central Tibet to convert these valleys and to subject their demons. Drukpa Kunley was such a missionary. Born in Tibet in the middle of the fifteenth century, he gained his tantric initiations and instruction at the principal Drukpa Kagyu gompa of Ralung. He is best known in Bhutan, where he spent much of his life per-forming the functions of a wandering Buddhist sadhu and where he achieved the status of patron saint, or, rather, patron tantric adept. A famous biography of the lama, *Divine Madman* (Keith Dowman, Rider, 1980), uses the multi-levelled tantric sexual metaphor to describe Drukpa Kunley's activity, an important part of which was to subdue the demons of the Bhutanese valleys. This is how he dealt with the Demon of Wong in the Thimphu district.

The Demon of Wong, a serpent spirit living high up in an inac-cessible part of his valley, was threatening the village down on the river terraces with extermination. Drukpa Kunley, having eaves-dropped on the demon's minions, detected that on a certain night they would devour the last inhabitant, an old woman. On the night in question he went to the old woman's house. She told him:

> *Once I was wealthy. But since no Buddha or adept has ever set foot in this poor outlandish valley, the demons have run amok and devoured both men and cattle. I myself do not expect to live through this coming night. You are a holy man and need not stay here. Go away while you can or you will be eaten alive.*

DOWMAN 1980:126

The master consoled her and asked her for liquor, which she gave him to drink while he awaited the demons. When they arrived and pounded on the door, the old woman screamed in fear, and Drukpa Kunley grasped his erect penis and thrust it through a hole in the door straight into the gaping red mouth of the demon of Wang, knocking out his teeth. The demon fled for his life and took refuge in the retreat cave of a nun, who explained to him, with chagrin, the nature of that sort of wound and the unlikelihood of a cure, and advised him to return to the lama who had perpetrated it. The demon returned to Drukpa Kunley and prostrated himself before him, saying, 'I'm yours to command. I offer you my life.' The lama placed his 'thunderbolt' on the demon's head and ordained him, binding him with a layman's vows.

Fear of this demon and his minions may be intermixed with the terror of peasant farmers for the bandit bands that infested both Tibet and the Himalayas until very recently. It is possible to perceive the interweaving of an ancient legend of a demonic presence with an actual historical infestation of murderous robbers. The demonic entity is converted by the application of Drukpa Kunley's secret dorje of empty awareness at the same time as the bandit chieftain is converted to Buddhism. The effectiveness of the legend, however, depends upon the spiritual process of infusing the terror-stricken mind with the clear light of empty awareness via the application of the master's sexual organ. The 'secret dorje' has no preference for men or women; its function is to penetrate any seemingly substantial mental entity and to dissolve it into empty form.

When Drukpa Kunley decided to confront the terrible Longrong Demoness, another serpent spirit, on the road to Punakha, in order to subdue her, bind her and to transform her into a protectress of the buddha-dharma, he discovered her in her most fearsome form, floating in a dazzling cloud of spray whipped up by the river. She poured scorn on his Buddhist achievement and demanded to know his spiritual pedigree. In his reply Drukpa Kunley impressed her by his statement of existential authenticity, authority and the promise of buddhahood as a protectress:

*This indigent beggar, this vagrant,*
*Has turned from desire in disgust*
*And speaking whatever enters his mind,*
*Outward show is invested with virtue.*

*Never working, letting reality hang loosely,*
*Whatever arises is the path of release.*

*Longrong demoness, be content as protectress!*
*You, daughter of gods, serpents, devils and demons,*
*Worthy consort, attractive and charming,*
*Insubstantial apparition, follow me!*
*Hold to the blissful path of release*
*With your body, speech and mind*
*And attain buddhahood in this lifetime.*

DOWMAN 1980:113

The demoness changed into a beautiful woman and brought liquor to the lama in a huge crystal urn. She told him of her transformed perception of him – from beggar to Buddha – and begged him to grant her his transformative sexual favours. He purified her through sexual union and she vowed never to harm living beings and thereafter to serve the buddha-dharma.


## Mandala-Vision

In the sphere of buddha-vision, where the nature of mind is understood as emptiness and space, mandalas serve as the infrastructure of awareness. Appearances, such as the landscape, are still in their seemingly chaotic natural order, but within the perception that is a unity of outside and inside, they are mandalas. They are expressed in the symbolic terms of the tantric tradition as three-dimensional models or two-dimensional plans. In those forms the aspiring yogi can visualize them, and through recognition of the reality which the symbols represent, can attain mandala-vision and buddha-vision, mandala-vision being awareness of the underlying purity and perfect symmetry and harmony of every perception.

The simplest of mandalas, the basis of all others, is an empty circle. The Tibetan word for mandala means 'centre-circumference' (*kyilkhor*). The centre of the simple mandala circle represents a point instant of pure awareness of unbounded inner space that is emptiness (*tongpanyi, shunyata*), which cannot be conceived or expressed. It is represented anthropomorphically as a naked blue Buddha, the Primordial Buddha. This emptiness interpenetrates every level of awareness, providing the fluidity of perception and also the transcendent qualities of radiance and fullness that characterize every perception. The fundamental circular mandala also represents an intuitive recognition of the basic building block of experiential reality, the empty nucleus of every moment of experience. Thus, while it indicates the essential element of reality, it also structures 'uncreate', primal awareness in three-dimensional form. Every form that arises in this mandala of mind is empty; all emptiness has form.

The mental generation of a mandala by the yogi is an exercise in structuring the apparent chaos of human experience. Visualization and contemplation of a mandala automatically induce mental calm. The simple mandala circle frames the contents of the mind, giving an essential confining order to what has been unbounded chaos. The empty space within the circumference of the circle evokes the emptiness of its content, the ultimate empty nature of reality. The structure of a complex mandala indicates the essential elements of the mind and its levels of awareness in a point instant of sensory experience. Its imagery and symbolism are usually in the form of anthropomorphic figures – male and female buddha-deities. In order to 'read' a mandala it is necessary to know the structure of the hierarchy of the pantheon and the meaning of the symbols that compose the individual deities.

The internal mandala, crucial to the practice of tantric yoga, describes human interaction with the sensory environment. Implicit in this interaction are the five senses: seeing, hearing, tasting, touching and smelling; the five types of object of perception: sight, sound, taste, touch and smell; the feeling tone that arises with every perception: positive, negative or neutral; the emotional content of the perception: desire, anger, pride, jealousy and fear, and the thought that arises with it; the impulse towards continued sensory activity generated by thought and emotion informing karmic proclivity; and finally the consciousness that greets every perception. Formally, the mandala representing this complex fivefold moment of human experience consists of five circles – a central circle surrounded by four circles in the cardinal directions, all within the confining circle. The five circles are represented by Buddhas of different colour and hand gesture. This mandala, the mandala of the Five Buddhas, is the first level of complexity arising from the simple circle mandala of the Primordial Buddha.

## The Five Buddhas

The Five Buddhas represent the naturally pure five emotions constituting the fundamental components of human emotional experience. In tantric vision they have been developed into a sophisticated pantheon, each endowed with a consort or female Buddha and retinue of bodhisattva 'sons' representing their functional aspects. They are the 'fathers' of buddha-families, or psychological types. Their names and iconography – their colour, their family symbols, the animal that is their vehicle, their mudras and *asanas* (postures) – indicate the qualities of these families and their personal characteristics, showing with which of the five elements and emotions they are associated. Colour and hand gesture provide the immediately apparent element of identification. The inherent nature of the emotions when penetrated by awareness of their emptiness determines their buddha-wisdom aspect.

The Buddha at the centre of the mandala is Namnang (Vairochana), which means 'The Creator of All Appearances'. His symbol is the wheel (*dharmachakra*) of which he is the hub and which he constantly turns, a function echoed by his hand gesture, which is the gesture of teaching (*dharmachakra mudra*). Alternatively his symbol is the trefoil three jewels, representing Buddha, teaching and community. His family is the buddha-family and his vehicle is the lion. His colour is white, the colour of the element ether or space itself. He represents the pure nature of ignorance and sloth which is All-Encompassing Awareness coeval with space and thus also known as the Dharmadhatu Awareness. Namnang represents consciousness which rises to greet every sensory object and his buddha-consort is Dhateshvari, representing the element space.

The Buddha of the eastern direction of the mandala is Mikyopa (Akshobhya), the Immovable. His family is the dorje-family and his symbol the dorje (*vajra*), the adamantine sceptre signifying imperturbable awareness. His vehicle is the elephant with its weight of strength and reliability. He shows the earth-touching hand gesture (*bhumisparsha mudra*) by which the elemental earth spirits and the Earth Mother are evoked to witness and establish enlightenment. His colour is the blue of the element earth and its associated hatred and aversion, which is purified as the Mirror-like Awareness in which the reality of all things is faithfully reflected. Mikyopa represents form, experienced as the objects of sensory activity, and his buddha-consort, Lochana, represents earth and solidity.

The Buddha of the southern direction of the mandala is Rinchen Jungne (Ratnasambhava), the Source of Jewels, the provider of bounty. His jewel-family symbol is the jewel itself, a wish-fulfilling gem. His vehicle is the noble horse, evidence of wealth and plenty. His hand gesture is the gesture of giving or boon-bestowing (*varada mudra*), signifying boundless generosity and liberality. His colour is the yellow of earth and its associated pride, which is purified as the Awareness of Equality, the ultimate sameness of all things. Rinchen Jungne represents feeling, the positive, negative or neutral response to every sensory perception, and his buddha-consort is Mamaki, representing water and fluidity.

The Buddha of the western direction is Wopakme (Amitabha), Boundless Light. His family is the lotus family and his symbol is the lotus of compassion. His vehicle is the multi-hued peacock whose food includes poisonous substances. His hands show the gesture of meditation (*dhyana mudra*). His colour is the red of fire and its associated desire and greed, the essence of which is All-Discriminating Awareness. Wopakme represents the conception that arises with every perception and his buddha-consort, Pandaravasini, is fire and heat.

The Buddha of the northern direction of the mandala is Donyodrubpa (Amoghasiddhi), the Fulfiller of All Wishes. His family is the karma-family and its symbol is crossed dorjes, signifying his all-encompassing transformative capacity. His vehicle is the mythical bird Garuda. His hand gesture shows fearlessness and protection (*abhaya mudra*) and he is canopied by the king of the serpent spirits. His colour is the green of air and its associated jealousy, which in essence is All-Accomplishing Awareness. Donyodrubpa represents the karmic impulse that generates action and his buddha-consort is Samaya Tara, representing the element air, wind and motility.

These associations of the Five Buddhas, the roots of the five buddha-families, are fundamental to an understanding of the practice of tantric Buddhism and also to any articulation of the nature of buddha-vision.

Out of this basic mandala arises the more personalized mandala of the individual yogi. The ruling Buddha of his own 'family' or spiritual type takes the central position of the mandala and emanates a complex dynamic buddha-deity who represents both the transformative function of mind and the resultant vision. This is the *yidam*, whose meditation practice is described in books called *tantras*. Some of the most important yidams of Tibetan Buddhism are Dukhor (Kalachakra), the Wheel of Time; Kye Dorje (Hevajra); Demchok (Samvara), Supreme Bliss; Dorje Phurba (Vajrakilaya), the Indestructible Dagger; and Dorje Phakmo (Vajravarahi), the Adamantine Sow. They are portrayed as wrathful deities due to their powerful dynamic transformative function and are usually represented in sexual union with their buddha-consorts to demonstrate the symbiosis of the basic tantric polarity of compassion and wisdom. They are surrounded by the dynamic forms of the other four of the Five Buddhas and outside that circle are the protectors of the mandala. These protectors, which could be described as buddha-demons, relate directly to the environment, to the landscape, to the elements of experience most difficult to assimilate as factors of buddha-nature. They are usually the old gods and demons of Tibet and their retinues of spirit entities, although some originated as universal elemental energies in India. The manner in which they were transformed and remained bound to the buddha-energy at the centre of the mandala is described above.

## Dewachan, the Pure-Land of Amitabha

Each of the Five Buddhas has his seat in the centre of a pure-land surrounded by a mandala of bodhisattvas and goddesses of offering. A bodhisattva is a supernal emanation of one of the Five Buddhas dedicated to compassionate activity. But it is also a human being whose karma is sufficiently purified that his every action is conducive to the attainment of nirvana. *Bodhi* means 'wisdom' and *sattva* means 'being' or 'hero'. The spiritual practice of the human bodhisattva is twofold: he lives a life of immaculate virtue to purify his karma and he practises meditation (*gom*) in order to identify his awareness increasingly with that of the Buddha, to whom he prays for guidance and support. The virtues he practises are giving, morality, patience and one-pointed endeavour. The meditation is both concentration and awareness meditation. Through this practice he accumulates the merit that results in a better rebirth, providing the conditions that allow greater and greater achievement in the practice of virtue and meditation, until he is born in a pure-land.

Each of the Five Buddhas has a pure-land, but the Buddha to whom most devotees of this bodhisattva path are attached is Wopakme (Amitabha), the Buddha of the western paradise. Wopakme's colour, bright translucent red, signifies his transformation of the base emotion of desire into loving kindness and compassion. His supernal bodhisattva emanation is Chenrezik (Avalokiteshvara), the bodhisattva of compassion, whose primary vow in the presence of his father-buddha Wopakme was to forgo entrance into nirvana until every sentient being had been released from the wheel of rebirth and could accompany him. Wopakme's pure-land is called Dewachan (Sukhavati), the Blissful. For the bodhisattva practitioner of virtue walking the long path of karmic purification through innumerable rebirths to Wopakme's pure-land where the Buddha's enlightenment is made easy, Dewachan is envisioned as only another stage. Not only is it a halting place before the final bodhisattva achievement, it is also envisioned as a world system divorced from the sensory reality of Dzambuling, our own world. This may be a useful didactic ploy to encourage the bodhisattva practitioner to keep his sights on the carrot always dangling just out of reach, but even here the vision of Wopakme is attainable in this lifetime. On the tantric path, where the here and now is the only reality, Dewachan is the Tibetan landscape transformed through the power of compassionate vision.

Here is an excerpt from a classical description of Dewachan given by Shakyamuni Buddha in the form of a discourse to his beloved disciple Ananda:

*The world-system called Dewachan, Ananda, which is the world system of the Lord Wopakme, is rich and prosperous, comfortable, fertile, delightful and crowded with many gods and men. And in this world-system, Ananda, there are no hells, no ghosts, no Asuras, and none of the inauspicious places of rebirth.*

*And that world-system, Dewachan, Ananda, emits many fragrant odours, it is rich in a great variety of flowers and fruits, adorned with jewel trees, which are frequented by flocks of various birds with sweet voices, which the Tathagatas magical powers have magically conjured up. And these jewel trees, Ananda, have various colours, many colours, many hundreds of thousands of colours. They are variously composed of the seven precious things – gold, silver, beryl, crystal, coral, red pearls, and emerald – in varying combinations. Such jewel trees, and clusters of banana trees and rows of palm trees, all made of precious things, grow everywhere in this buddhafield... All around it is covered with lotus flowers made of all the precious things... And from each jewel lotus issue thirty-six hundred thousand kotis of rays. And at the end of each ray there issue thirty-six hundred thousand kotis of Buddhas, with golden-coloured bodies, who bear the thirty-two marks of the superman.*

*There are great rivers there, one mile broad, and up to fifty miles long and twelve miles deep. And all these rivers flow along calmly, their water is fragrant with manifold agreeable odours, in them there are bunches of flowers to which various jewels adhere, and they resound with various sweet sounds...*

CONZE 1959:232–3

The reality of Dewachan in Tibet is focused on two physical locations. The first is at Tashi Lhunpo in Shigatse, where the Panchen Lama resides as an incarnation of the Buddha Amitabha. The second is the Potala in Lhasa, which is the residence of the Dalai Lama, who is an emanation of the bodhisattva Chenrezik. For Indian Buddhists the Potala was located on an island to the south-west of the Indian sub-continent and only transposed to Lhasa when the bodhisattva's incarnation took residence there. The extreme faith and devotion of the Dalai Lama's Tibetan devotees can be comprehended only in the light of his status as an incarnation of the bodhisattva Chenrezik dwelling in his buddhafield.

Since the Dalai Lamas took up residence in the Potala in the seventeenth century, spiritual and temporal power have been united in the person of Chenrezik's incarnation. The Panchen Lama in Tashi Lhunpo, Amitabha in his Dewachan pure-land, is perceived by some, however, as a higher authority since the source of his incarnation is the parent-buddha of Chenrezik.

From the earliest Buddhist period, Chenrezik, 'He who gazes upon the suffering of the world with tears in his eyes', has been the protector of the Land of Snows, and his mantra, OM MANI PADMA HUNG, has been the means of supplication for his blessing upon both individuals and the country. Muttered in prayer while counting the beads of a rosary, carved into boulders on the side of the path or into the rock of a mountainside, printed on prayer-flags fluttering in the wind, or written on rolls of paper and packed into handheld prayer-wheels, or wall-bracketed prayer-wheels, or water-turned prayer-wheels, or wind-driven prayer-wheels, this universally pronounced mantra induces the vision of Chenrezik in his pure-land.

## The Ganden Paradise of the Bodhisattva Jampa

The bodhisattva Jampa is the Forthcoming Buddha. His name, Jampa (Maitreya), means 'Loving Kindness'. Until he descends to earth he resides, like Shakyamuni Buddha before him, in the Ganden paradise, where all bodhisattvas await their rebirth. Ganden (Tushita) means 'The Joyous' and it is the third heaven of the senses transformed into a pure-land by the bodhisattva's presence there. The residents of Ganden live for 4,000 years, a day of which is equal to 400 human years. The height of their bodies is approximately 220 yards (200m). The bodhisattva's rebirth on earth will usher in an aeon of pure buddha-dharma. Not only will this doctrine be taught and practised, but the physical landscape of Dzambuling, our world, will be transformed. Tibetan's harsh mountain environment will become a hidden valley paradise:

> This island-continent of Dzambuling will be quite flat everywhere, it will measure ten thousand leagues, and all men will have the privilege of living on it. It will have innumerable inhabitants, who will

*commit no crimes nor evil deeds, but will take pleasure in doing good. The soil will be free from thorns, even, and covered with fresh green growth of grass; when one jumps on it, it gives way, and becomes soft like the leaves of the cotton tree. It has a delicious scent, and tasty rice grows on it, without any work. Rich silken, and other, fabrics of various colours shoot forth from the trees. The trees will bear leaves, flowers and fruit simultaneously; they are as high as the voice can reach and they last for eight myriads of years. Human beings are then without any blemishes, moral offences are unknown among them, and they are full of zest and joy. Their bodies are very large and their skin has a fine hue. Their strength is quite extraordinary... Only when five hundred years old do the women marry.*

CONZE 1959:238

Dogma asserts that we are now in the aeon of degeneration, the kaliyuga, and that the disease, war and famine that characterize this period will increase in intensity and malignity until the advent of Jampa and the transformation of the world. And yet, in tantric Buddhism, there is an assumption that, through the ritual, devotional and meditative practices of the tradition, Jampa's devotees can experience the aeon of the Buddha's presence on earth, the *dharmayuga*, here and now. In this context, then, aeons of time are the temporal aspects of parallel planes of potential experience and can be accessed through meditative awareness.

For those devotees whose karma obstructs the possibility of attaining the pure-land of Jampa here and now, rebirth into the Ganden heaven, through prayer and virtuous living, is a less demanding and more easily obtainable spiritual goal:

*Yogis and yoginis of all religions can fairly easily attain contemplative trances, in which they can experience the various heavenly realms. And good people, when they pass away, may realistically hope to enter a pleasant heaven realm, though in most of the Indian religions, a heaven can never be a final resting place – only another, rather pleasant, temporary way station in the endless round of rebirths.*

THURMAN 1991:33

The millenarian cult of Jampa has increased along with the ascendancy of the Dalai Lamas' Geluk order, reaching its zenith in the twentieth century. The colossal gilded image of Jampa preserved at the Tashi Lhunpo Gompa in Shigatse, one of the greatest and most costly additions to monastic furniture this century, is evidence of the vitality of the cult. The image, 85 (26m) high, covered in more than 600 lbs (279 kg) of gold, shows Maitreya decked in his bodhisattva ornaments of coral, turquoise and jade. The cult is primarily monastic. The great Monlam Festival, celebrated after the Tibetan New Year, which in the past perhaps provoked more public fervour of devotion that any other religious festival in Tibet, is chiefly concerned with the celebration of Jampa and Ganden is the most common name of Geluk gompas throughout Tibet. The foremost of them is Ganden Namgyeling, near Lhasa, the seat of the order's founder, Je Tsongkhapa. Indeed, the theocratic government of Tibet was called Ganden Photrang, the Joyous Citadel, evoking Jampa's paradise.

## The Five-Peaked Mountain Paradise of Jampelyang

Jampelyang (Manjushri) is the bodhisattva of wisdom. In the popular mind he bestows intelligence and learning. In the lineages of the Universal Buddhist Tradition (*mahayana*), he represents non-discursive intelligence or the Buddha's awareness of emptiness in all things. With the sword that he wields in his right hand he destroys passion-induced mental obscurations, together with attachment to concepts. His principal abode is Wu-t'ai Shan mountain in China's Shanxi province. This most sacred of China's mountains is comprised of five flat-topped peaks rising around a valley system in which innumerable monasteries and temples, mostly the domiciles of Tibetan Buddhist monks, nuns and yogis, have been established over the past millennium. A valley with its surrounding five peaks is the characteristic geomantic feature of Jampelyang's pure-land wherever it is found. The silk route oasis of Khotan possesses this feature and was once a renowned residence of Jampelyang. The Kathmandu Valley, with its surrounding five peaks, is a paradigm of this ideal. The Central Tibetan residence of Jampelyang is Riwo Tsenga, a five-peaked ridge visible from the Kyichu river to the south of Lhasa.

## Shambhala

The legendary land of Shambhala is less of a buddhafield than an ideal intermediary place between samsara and nirvana where the rudiments of the Buddha's vision can be developed through auspicious circumstances at a propitious time. It is to be found in this world, but its exact geographical location is uncertain. It is said to be in the north, beyond Kang Rimpoche (Kailash), perhaps even beyond the Kunlun mountains of Tibet's northern boundary. But those that seek Shambhala's geographical reality enter upon an endless pilgrimage without clear destination, while there are those at home who nod wisely and counsel that it is to be found in states of meditation here and now.

Shambhala is described as a terrestrial paradise, a hidden valley encircled by mountains. A peak rises at the centre of this mandala surrounded by parks and palaces, rivers and temples. The landscape is depicted in terms of an eight-petalled lotus, each petal containing principalities whose kings give allegiance to the King of Shambhala, whose palace is at the centre. The history of the land begins with its first king, Suchandra, who left his kingdom to receive teaching from Shakyamuni Buddha at the famous Shri Danyakataka Stupa in south India. Today the twenty-ninth king of the dynasty rules Shambhala. The thirty-second king, Rudrachakrin, will unleash his armies upon the forces of ignorance and evil and totally destroy them. His victory will herald the advent of a new golden age of spiritual freedom and enlightenment.

The teaching on Shambhala is contained in the literature of the Kalachakra-tantra, the tantra most popular with the Geluk order and the present Dalai Lama. Whereas the Kalachakra-tantra itself details the inner yoga through which the complex nondual vision of the Kalachakra mandala unfolds, the teaching on Shambhala instructs how, outwardly, devotees can be reborn into the paradise where engagement in the process of spiritual realization can become a one-pointed yoga and a complete lifestyle. The late Chogyam Trungpa Rimpoche gave detailed instruction in Western cultural terms on how to reach Shambhala.

## Guru Rimpoche's Glorious Copper-Coloured Mountain Paradise

Guru Rimpoche's charismatic presence dominated the early period of propagation of Buddhism in Tibet, and after the Bon resurgence had worn itself out *(see p.66)* and the second period of intense dissemination began, he was envisioned as a Second Buddha of our era and became an essential figure in the mythic vision of the Tibetan people. His legend describes his departure from Tibet flying from the top of the Gungthang Pass, near the Pelku Tso lake, on the mythical white horse of the buddha-dharma carried by sky-dancing female Buddhas, or khandromas. His destination was Ngayab Ling, an island in the ocean to the south-west of Dzambuling, where his mission was to teach the cannibal-demon inhabitants the transformative path of the tantra. His success in achieving that objective is described in terms of Zangdok Pelri, his Glorious Copper-Coloured Mountain Paradise.

The Glorious Copper-Coloured Mountain is an island-mountain in the cosmic ocean and the periphery of the island defines the circumference of a mandala. Within it are the walls and four gates guarded by the Four Guardian Kings. At the centre is a three-roofed pagoda temple, and between the gated mandala walls and the temple a community of initiates practises the teaching of Guru Rimpoche. In the sky around the top of the temple float male and female sky dancers also practising the teaching. On the ground floor of the temple Guru Rimpoche himself is enthroned, surrounded by his Indian and Tibetan consorts and lama and yogi exponents of his vision. In the centre of the second floor is Chenrezik, the bodhisattva of compassion, and in the centre of the third floor is Wopakme (Amitabha). The relationship between these three Buddhas is defined in Padmasambhava's birth legend:

*Twenty-four years after the parinirvana of the Buddha Shakyamuni, the primordial Buddha of Boundless Light, Wopakme, conceived the thought of perfect enlightenment in the form of the great compassionate one, Chenrezik, and from Chenrezik's heart, I, Padmasambhava, the Lotus Born Guru, was emanated as the syllable HRI, and I came like falling rain throughout the entire world in innumerable billions of forms to those who were ready to receive me.*

DOWMAN 1973:74

Or, as interpenetrating spheres of being, Wopakme is all-pervasive light and awareness; Chenrezik is his pure and compassionate vision; and Guru Rimpoche is the transforming illusion of the lama's sensory fields.

The Glorious Copper-Coloured Mountain Paradise is both a far-away pure-land into which the devotee prays for rebirth so that his meditation practice can mature in the presence of Guru Rimpoche and a state of meditation attainable in this lifetime. Here it can be experienced in actual sensory perception of the Tibetan environment.

The paradise, or more specifically its three-roofed pagoda temple, is sometimes replicated in the gompas of the Nyingma order such as the Lama Gompa near Bayi in Kongpo, at the Jiu Gompa at Tso Mapham lake (Manasarovar), at the Kuthang Gompa in the Kyimolung hidden valley, and at Tarthang and Dodrub Chode in Kham. But at the Chimphu hermitage site a rocky crag, invested with several caves, is called Zangdok Pelri, and in its very lack of symmetry, and lack of formal similarity to the mandala icon, the internal location of the vision and its dependence upon the meditative achievement of the yogis who live there are signified.

### The Mother Tantra Vision

Buddha-vision is a unitary vision of outside and inside, a unification of the objective environment and the subjective mind. The pure-land mandalas and the mandalas of Shambhala and the Glorious Copper-Coloured Mountain describe this vision in terms of a Buddha in his palace at the centre of a purified environment. These are mandalas of form, outer mandalas. Internally, buddha-vision can be described in terms of the focal points of energy in the subtle body of the transubstantiated yogi. The tantras that develop this vision to its optimal extent are the mother-tantras, the tantras that take a female buddha-deity as the principal of the mandala and develop the female aspect of the two-in-one union of tantric metaphysics. The

Demchok (Samvara), Kye Dorje (Hevajra) and Dorje Phakmo (Vajravarahi) tantras are the most popular of this type.

In these tantras the subtle body is described in terms of psychic channels, energy flows and focal points of energy. In a simplified blueprint, the central channel runs from the perineum to the fontanelle. Right and left channels branch off from the central channel below the navel and run parallel to it to the head and then emerge at the nostrils. There are seven energy centres (*chakras*) on the central channel, relating to the anus, the genitals, the solar plexus, the heart, the throat, the head and the fontanelle. Right and left channels join the central channel at the navel, heart, throat and head centres. From the seven energy centres subsidiary channels branch off and, constantly forking at minor focal points, penetrate to every extremity of the body, something like the nervous system. There are various energy flows or 'winds' within these channels, but essentially, in the transformed body of the yogi, the direction of flow, from the central channel into the right and left channels and into the capillary channels, has been reversed, so that all movement is directed into, and up, the central channel, where the energy centres bloom like lotuses of enlightenment. The reversal of energy flow is a metaphor for the unification of duality, a process which results in buddha-vision. The energy centres, major and minor, represent the union of inside and outside.

The subtle body and its focal points of energy are externalized into the landscape as the supine body of Dorje Neljorma (Vajra Yogini), the Khandroma, the essential female Buddha. It is her body that lies across the entire Indian sub-continent, from Cape Comorin to the Himalayas, from Assam to Pakistan, and the major power places of the sub-continent give access to the energy centres of her body. Twenty-four power places are divided into three mandalas of eight places pertaining to the Khandroma's body, speech and mind. The symmetry of these places exists only on the inner, visionary, plane. Two of the original list of 24 are located in Tibet, at the great mountain power place of Kang Rimpoche (Kailash) and at Tretapuri, a power place not far from Kang Rimpoche. But two other important locations were transposed to Tibet by yogis who themselves sanctified the great power places with which they were identified. Devikota, originally in West Bengal, was reidentified with the great mountain of Tsari, with the hermitage called Lhamo Kharchen in Lhokha and also with the lhakhang called Phawongkha near Lhasa. Godavari, in south India, was reidentified with the great Labchi mountain. These transpositions gave Tibetan yogis access to the Khandroma's energy down the centuries.

Most of the 24 power places were originally determined by their geomantic significance and are sacred to all peoples, regardless of their religious tradition. Not only the places in the heart of India, but also Kang Rimpoche and Tsari, which are Bonpo power places too, are sacred in the Hindu tradition. The symbols that represent the goddess Devi – the *yoni* (vulva) – and Shiva Mahadeva – the *lingam* (phallus) – are also found there. This simply stresses the inchoate nature of the energy at these places and the importance of the vision of the individual yogi.

Historically, the 24 power places were first identified as places sacred to Shiva Mahadeva and Devi, his consort, and the Buddhist vision of the manner in which they were transformed, given below, is highly instructive:

> *Towards the end of time, in the kaliyuga, when anger, lust and ignorance were rife, Shiva Mahadeva in his most terrific form, Ugra Bhairava, overwhelmed the earth and took up residence in the form of lingams in the twenty-four power places. At the end of the kaliyuga, Dorje Chang (Vajradhara), the primordial Buddha, resolved in his wisdom to subdue the terrifying gods who controlled the earth. While remaining established in imageless compassion, he manifested as Buddha Heruka, and with even greater wrath than that embodied by Bhairava, in dancing posture he trampled Bhairava under foot and thereby Bhairava attained supreme bliss and complete realization. Buddha Heruka's emanations entered into the lingams that had been Bhairava's abodes and sanctifying them as themselves they dressed themselves in the form of Bhairava and his minions and used their ritual appurtenances as their own and transformed their rituals into the rituals of light and liberation.*

The parable of Rudra describes the subjection or transformation of the inner, divine, ego (Rudra or Bhairava) into an emanation of the Buddha's emptiness and compassion:

*There was once a tantric Buddhist guru who taught that all experience was essentially pure as it arose spontaneously in the mind. The guru had two disciples who were friends. The first, without following after the impulses that arose in his meditation, realized the natural purity in the spontaneous rising and falling of moments of all experience and achieved the detachment of the Buddhas. The second disciple left his guru, and watching the nature of his experience in meditation, he ran after the impulses that arose therein. He built a brothel, gathered a gang of thugs and raided neighbouring villages, killing the men and abducting the women. After some time the two friends met and, surprised by the nature of each other's tantric practice, they sought out the guru to seek his verdict. The guru praised his first disciple and condemned the second, whereupon the brothel owner, unable to bear the knowledge of his own error, unsheathed his sword and killed his guru on the spot. When he died, he was reborn successively as a scorpion, a jackal and other wretched forms of sentient life, until eventually he was reborn in the realm of the gods as Rudra. Rudra was born with three heads and six arms, with fully grown fangs and talons. His mother died at birth and the gods were so horrified by her offspring that they entombed him with her. Rudra nurtured himself on her flesh and blood and when he gained his monstrous maturity he organized the ghosts, ghouls and cremation-ground life into an army and sought to control the heavens, the earth and the underworld. Meanwhile his friend had attained the Buddha's enlightenment and sought to subjugate him. He transformed himself into the Bodhisattva Chakna Dorje (Vajrapani), who in turn became the Heruka Tamdrin (Hayagriva), an emanation of Karunamaya, the bodhisattva of compassion. He entered Rudra through his anus and possessed him with the realization of emptiness and compassion, whereupon Rudra expressed his disillusion and conversion and offered himself as the throne of Heruka at the 24 power places. Buddhist masters intent upon subduing gross forms of ego and attachment to objects of passion, and transforming passion into its pure nature, thereafter took the outer form of Rudra, with his bone ornaments, tiger skin skirt, human and elephant skin shawls, and so on, the form of the wrathful deities of Buddhist tantra.*

This parable is not only important in the understanding of the relationship between Buddhist and Hindu tantra and of the nature of the seemingly demonic forms of the buddha-deities, but also explains the conversion of the great mountain power places of the Himalayan range from Hindu to Buddhist. Kang Rimpoche, Labchi and Tsari were the seats of Mahadeva and his consort Uma long before the advent of tantric Buddhism. Perceived as giant lingams by the Hindus, they were identified by Buddhist yogis as the buddha-deity Demchok (Samvara) in sexual union with his Khandroma consort Dorje Phakmo (Vajravarahi).

The subtle body of the Khandroma is represented at Kang Rimpoche by the three main valleys, Darlung (Flag Valley), Lhalung (Divine Valley) and Dzonglung (Fortress Valley), which are envisioned as the central, left and right channels of the subtle body. The body of the Khandroma can also be found in many places in the sacred landscape of Tibet where the Buddhist tradition has no Hindu antecedents. One of her principal places of residence is Beyul Padma Ko, the Hidden Land Lotus Form, in south-eastern Tibet *(see p.220)*. At Kangri Thokar, a hermitage site to the east of the Kyichu river south-west of Lhasa, she lies supine as the ridge on which the caves and hermitages are located. Two springs generating milky water mark her breasts, the Shukseb nunnery is on her left knee and her vulva is the source of the major stream feeding the northern side of the ridge. Again, the Drikung sky-burial site, or rather the round field of stones where corpses are dismembered, is identified as her navel, while her entire body is to be found in the landscape of the Drikung region.

### The Mandala of the Buddhist Cosmology

Tantric buddha-vision is concerned primarily with the transformation of the here and now of the yogi in his environment into a buddhafield. The mandala is a map of the mind disclosing the nature of buddha-vision and identifying its constituent elements. For the yogi in his cave or hermitage, the centre of the mandala is his seat and he has little concern for geography beyond the geomantic features within his purview. In the descriptions of buddhafields, however, there have been references to their relative location, implying an overall geographical or cosmological schema. Dzambuling is our world-continent, for instance, and the island of the Copper-Coloured Mountain is located in the south-western ocean. These are elements of the cosmological mandala that combine mythic visionary realities with geographical concepts. In this mandala no formal distinction is made between the two, because they are both conceptual supports to enlightenment.

The entire three-dimensional cosmological mandala is shaped like a basin. Ringed by iron mountains, the basin contains the cosmic ocean. At the centre of the ocean is Mount Meru, or Sumeru, ascending in inverted truncated pyramids. This insurmountable mountain has a flat plain at its top. The sun and the moon circle the mountain. Mount Meru is surrounded by seven rings of golden mountains separated by seven seas. In the vast expanse of ocean outside the seventh mountain ring rise four continents in the four cardinal directions. To the east is half-moon shaped Lupak, Noble Body; to the south is Dzambuling (Jambudvipa), trapezoid-shaped (an inverted truncated isosceles triangle), the continent of the Rose-Apple Tree; to the west is circular Walangcho, Rich in Cattle; and to the north is square Draminyen, Unpleasant Sound. Each continent is flanked by two islands identical in shape to the main continent.

At the root of Mount Meru is the indestructible hell that lasts as long as the world system. The hells of temporary rebirth lie around it. Where Mount Meru rises out of the ocean the hungry ghosts live, insulated in their tortured search for sustenance. On the ledges formed by the inverted pyramids structuring the mount the jealous gods live, vainly attempting to climb to the peak. The flat plain at the top of the peak is the mandala of the Buddha's pure-land, populated by bodhisattvas and other enlightened beings with a three-storey temple at its centre. From this rises the inverted conical realm of the gods: the heavens of sensual pleasure in the bottom third of the cone, the heavens of pure aesthetic form in the middle third and the heavens of formless essences in the upper third. The continents are populated by human beings, each with special characteristics. Dzambuling is the continent of the Rose-Apple Tree that grows near the Tso Mapham lake. This is the continent in which Buddhas teach the buddha-dharma and the community of Buddhists practises it.

This mandala forms a basis for geographical interpretation. Mount Meru, for example, can be identified as Kang Rimpoche (Kailash). The southern continent, Dzambuling, can be identified as the Indian sub-continent including Central Tibet, i.e. most of the Buddhist world. The western continent can be seen as western Asia and Europe, the northern continent as the steppe-land of Central Asia, dominated by horsemen, and the eastern continent as China. An alternative interpretation makes the southern continent, Dzambuling, the entire world as we know it. For the Tibetans, constrained by their geographical position in the centre of Asia, a flat world model was serviceable when it came to interpreting this mandala as a geographical map. In Western culture and in the modern world, the concept of the world as a globe not only feeds our need for certainties, but is also a useful model expediting travel across the face of the planet.

As a conceptual support to enlightenment, this geographical mandala, as any other mandala, places the individual at the centre of vast yet confined space that is coeval with the mind, the four continents providing four structured aspects of that mind in the four cardinal directions. Regardless of the relative location of the visionary, his essential identification is with the centre of the mandala, at the point where he is at peace with the seeming chaos of natural appearances.

This mandala is conventionally depicted in a mural in the vestibules of Tibetan gompas, along with the Guardian Kings of the four directions and the wheel of life. It also appears in the design of Samye Chokhor, the first gompa built in Tibet.


## MINOR ASPECTS OF VISION

### Visionary Rock Formations

The buddha-lama's vision transforms each perception as it arises in consciousness into a phantasmagorical dance of illusionary form, with sound effects, and with an infinite potent diversity of taste, smell and touch. Each of these powerful sensory impressions is accompanied by an interpretive visionary consciousness of its symbolic import. Put in another way, each visual image and sound is a dynamic symbol that instructs by disclosing a message supportive to the practice of the buddha-dharma. At its most profound the symbol may be a mandala form with the divinities in explicit manifestation. But on a more superficial level the formation of a rock, the pattern of snowfall or the shape of the skyline may disclose a human or animal outline, the form of a sacred ritual instrument, a Sanskrit or Tibetan syllable, and so on. This interpretive process may be called hallucination or poetic imagination: what gives it significance in the Buddhist context is its grounding in the bodhisattva level of awareness, for, according to tantric dogma, what arises out of an entirely pure perception, undefiled by a sense of self, is motivation that cannot but be beneficial to other beings.

So the Tibetan landscape has been redreamed by its buddha-lamas. What previously appeared as a hillside of shale is now a play of Guru Rimpoche defeating a demon. A bare mountain cliff is the ground of a holographic image of the syllable OM. The leached black juice (*shilajit*) of the mountain makes the pattern of the sacred trident, Guru Rimpoche's *katvanga*. Alarming boulders and threatening crags take the form of protective mythological animals and birds. A cavity in a rock, adventitiously located at the entrance of a cave, is the yogi's skullbowl. Perceived in this manner, the landscape becomes a treasury of symbols that may give succour to the pilgrim overwhelmed by an alien land, provide a constant source of comfort to the resident of a valley, afford a reminder of the goal of the path to recalcitrant monks and nuns, and provide the initiate in solitary retreat high on the mountainside with a source of inspiration and a gauge of the development of his visionary faculty.

The images invoked are not always, or necessarily, of seminal importance, although a mythologically significant reference is usually implicit. At Terdrom, for example, the mountain arising between the rivers whose confluence is at the principal power place is described as an elephant's head, the elephant being a symbol of majesty and dominance. In the description of the circumambulatory path around Bonri mountain in the pilgrim's guide to Bonri, rocks are identified by their similarity to animals or animal parts: 'Garuda's wings' where the Garuda is a representation of a sky god; 'a golden rock that looks like a mother eagle being affectionate to its chick', where the eagle is another sky god, and 'crags which give the impression of scattered vultures' where the vulture is the friend to man that devours the chopped flesh of the corpse at sky burial; crags that resemble a bull, a horse and a wild boar. A rock that 'looks like a tortoise' invokes the tortoise upon which stands the *axis mundi*. Rocks that resemble crocodiles and conjoint animals with the body of a fish and the head of a crocodile likewise invoke the makhara, known for its tenacity of purpose, hanging on forever to whatever it grips in its mouth.

## Sexual Features of the Landscape

As already mentioned, the landscape may be envisioned as the female body. In Central Tibet and its contiguous provinces the supine demoness lies bound by the missionary temples of King Songtsen Gampo while the body of the female Buddha Dorje Neljorma lies across the province of Beyul Padma Ko and other smaller areas.

Specific features of the landscape are identified with the demo-nesses' body parts. This identification of female body parts – head, breasts, nipples, stomach, vulva and limbs – with natural features first of all reinforces the identity of the earth with the female principle and its anthropomorphic representation as goddess or demoness. Then, where the female form represents a buddha-deity, the imminence of that female Buddha is emphasized.

More specifically, rock formations are often envisioned as the female reproductive organs. In the cave system of Drak Yangdzong, for example, it is easy to identify the entire female reproductive system. With more symbolic imagination, any cave can be envisioned as a womb. The symbolic representation of the womb is the triangle, so any triangular rock formation may be seen as the matrix of existence, the womb of the Buddhas, the source of all things (*chojung, dharmodaya*). Such a rock formation is frequently taken to indicate the residence of a protectress. The triangular space at the confluence of rivers, such as the triangular plain between the two rivers of Labchi, is also conceived as the cosmic womb. A spring emerging from a cleft in a rock is another natural symbol for this.

Rock formations evocative of the male sexual organ rarely form the basis of similar visualization. Such envisionment can lead to the Hindu fallacy of the cosmic lingam, a form of Shiva Mahadeva. So the archetypal phallic mountain, Kang Rimpoche (Kailash), is envisioned by Buddhist visionaries as a chorten rather than a lingam. A stalagmite lingam is worshipped in Dzong Khomphu in Drak, but this is due more to its spontaneously manifest nature than its phallic form.

While representations of the female organ evoke the female Buddha as the origin of all things, the womb of the Buddhas, the Great Mother (*Yumchen*), and gain their sanctity from such an identification, features of the landscape that lend themselves to envisionment of sexual union, or appear as poles of that union, refer immediately to the basic metaphysical principle of tantra – the two-in-oneness intrinsic to the vision of tantric reality. The poles of this union are symbolized as male and female Buddhas, and the sexual union of male and female as the inseparable union of this polarity. Thus a sacred mountain is seen as a union of male and female Buddhas (most frequently Demchok and Dorje Phakmo) whether or not there is a basis in the topography for such a vision. Likewise, a mountain alone is viewed as the male Buddha and a lake in its proximity as the female Buddha. Mountain and lake are present at most of the great mountain power places – Kang Rimpoche and Tso Mapham lake, Nyenchen Thanglha and Namtso lake, and Tsonying Mahadeva and Tso Ngon lake *(see Part Five)*.

## Visionary Transformation of Animals

The sacred landscape of Tibet is also inhabited by sacred fauna. The lama gives wildlife the same kind of symbolic value as the inanimate landscape, while for the layman, the animals at power places are the domestic animals of the deities that dwell there.

In the story of Gotsangpa's opening of Yak-Horn Cave, for example, the buddha-lama perceives a wild female yak as the Lion-Headed Sky Dancer, Senge Dongchan. The animal's activity is seen to be divinely inspired and it leads Gotsangpa to the discovery and 'opening' of a power place. Later, in his circumambulation of the sacred mountain, where the path is lost amongst a field of rocks, he enters the state of awareness called the Sky Dancer's Secret Path and immediately sees a pack of 21 wolves ahead of him. Interpreting them as emanations of the 21 forms of the female bodhisattva Drolma, Arya Tara, the Saviouress, sent to guide him, he follows them to the top of the path on the northern side of Kang Rimpoche and there they magically vanish. This was the origin of the name of that pass, Drolma La, and wolf paw marks in the rock there are said to have been made by the fabulous wolves.

Animal imagery is also used to show the fears the 'soul' is assailed by in the intermediate state between death and rebirth. Tigers, lions, crocodiles and serpents all appear, and although the images are those of the jungle and seemingly terrifying, their nature, as described in the *Tibetan Book of the Dead*, is peaceful. They are terrifying masks, their actions frightening, but they are really friendly helpers along the path.

The tameness of animals in Tibet, particularly at power places, has been remarked upon by many Western travellers. A recent English pilgrim to Bonri, Dr Charles Ramble, after sleeping in the forest on its eastern side, wrote:

*I left the cave the following morning and after a short time stopped to watch the sunrise from a clearing that afforded a fine view of the Tsangpo Valley far below... Birds began to come into the clearing. Among them were various species, ground thrush, shortwing and rose finch; picas – tailless mouse hares – also appeared from their burrows. They all went about their business of foraging closer and closer to where I sat, until the birds settled on my shoulders, head and knees, and even on my outstretched hands, and the picas ran across my feet. Animals and birds are not in the habit of clustering around me and I attribute their companionability on this occasion not to a few fugitive moments of Grace, but to the place itself, whose wild creatures have doubtless learned over hundreds of their generations that they have nothing to fear from solitary people who are sitting still.*

RAMBLE MS

Sitting still, however, is doubtless only part of the equation. If the mind of the solitary motionless human is in a fearful, turbulent or angry state then animals and birds, whatever their conditioning, will be deterred from approaching. If, on the contrary, the hermit's peaceful vision is based on the passive awareness common to all life forms, then animals and birds will be free of fear. From this may be deduced the possibility of influencing the mindstate or behaviour of animals, or indeed human beings, through cultivation of vision, a notion that is accepted without reflection by the Tibetan people.

PART TWO

# Religious Origins and History

The original spring that issued from under the bodhi tree in Bodhgaya in India after Shakyamuni Buddha's enlightenment was the source of all Buddhist streams. But wherever these streams flowed they were to water diverse religious cultures and nurture widely differing Buddhist traditions. Original Buddhism was recast in the lands to which it migrated, due to their unique cultural environments. Tibet, one of the last Asian countries to accept Buddhism, was steeped in a shamanic religion, whose measure of success may be gauged by the degree of loathing with which the new religion was regarded in the eighth century. Buddhism gained sway by assimilation of the old shamanic practices and its later evolution, the successive establishment of new religious orders, was a reforming process in which the old shamanic ways were gradually purged. Still, Western travellers to Tibet in the nineteenth century, knowing only the southern Buddhism of Sri Lanka and Burma, could not even perceive the Buddhism in Tibetan religious practice. Their perspective was entirely superficial, but it does indicate the profound difference between the Buddhist traditions founded on early, southern Buddhism, and later, northern, tantric Buddhism.

The Universal Buddhist Tradition (*mahayana*), imported from India, is the basis of Tibetan Buddhism. The overt ritual forms are indigenous developments. The distinctive characteristics of Tibetan Buddhism developed as a response to the indigenous shamanism.

There are four chief orders of Tibetan Buddhism. All are based in the physical and moral discipline, the philosophy and metaphysics, and the yoga and meditation that evolved out of the Buddha Shakyamuni's teaching in India, but each order is characterized by a separate path. They were established at different periods, with different Indian lineages as their antecedents. These Indian lineages were the original sources of the orders' diverse paths. Although the original variations have become blurred to some extent, still the four orders are quite distinct, and, more important, are seen by their adherents to be different. However, their paths are all said to lead to one end – the Buddha's enlightenment.

The fifth major Tibetan religious order, Bon, has original myths that are home-grown rather than Indian in origin and tend to dwell on the conflict between good and evil. The metaphysical terminology is different and the pantheon has a different structure with different names. However, the mindset of the modern Bonpo is indistinguishable from that of the Buddhist.

The following portraits of Bon and Buddhist orders focus primarily upon their origins and their early history. The originators of the spiritual lineages, like the 'ancestors' of Chinese Taoist worship, became mythic figures in Tibetan vision and both the early and the later periods of dissemination of Buddhism are perceived as golden ages. A profound veneration for lineal predecessors is built into daily devotions. Every Tibetan yogi can recite the initiatory names of his lineage, beginning with its Indian root-guru, or perhaps Shakyamuni Buddha himself, all the way down to his personal teacher. Authority, power and blessing are derived from this practice, but the downside is a political and social conservatism derived from the notion of progressive decline from the golden, mythic, period.

## BON: THE INDIGENOUS TIBETAN TRADITION

In early historical times Bon was Black Bon, a barbaric shamanism. It was proscribed in the eighth century by the Buddhist King Trisong Detsen and for political reasons the Bonpos were exiled into the provinces. In the sixteenth century the Geluk theocracy ran a pogrom against the Bonpos in Amdo. These days, apart from enclaves in the Nepali Himalayas, Black Bon has become New Bon, a doctrine that has assimilated elements of all the Buddhist orders until its ritual and meditative practices have become superficially indistinguishable from Buddhist practice. The contemporary Bon monk practises a monastic discipline and learns logic and philosophy through the practice of debate in his pursuit of a *geshe* degree just like the Gelukpa monk *(see p.78)*. The Tibetan cultural basis is the same and the ultimate goal of Bon religious practice, Dzokchen, differs little from the Dzokchen of the Nyingma order *(see p.68)*.

The process of assimilation was not, however, a one-way street. While Bon was absorbing Indian elements from the Buddhist Nyingma order, the Nyingmapas were absorbing indigenous Bon elements until there was little distinction between them. The Nyingma pantheon of gods and demons is mostly Bon in origin and the Bon tradition of treasure text (*terma*) revelation began at the same time as the Nyingma practice. The Nyingmas also felt the force of the sixteenth-century pogrom. These days Guru Rimpoche is evoked in the Bon liturgies and his image is found on Bon altars, as indeed is the Dalai Lama. Only recently the Fourteenth Dalai Lama formally accepted the Bonpos into the fold of Tibetan religion.

The source of the Bon tradition was the master Shenrab Miwo, the Perfect Priest, the Great Teacher. His home was in Olmo Lungring in Takzik. Takzik was located in the Persian cultural sphere and we may presume that it was the Tibetan name for Bactria. Olmo Lungring is, however, a semi-mythical pure-land very similar to Shambhala. Its mandala design is described in detailed geographical terms and its original location in Takzik is indisputable, but at the same time it is a pure-land that remains indestructible in the final conflagration at the end of time.

Shenrab Miwo made several missionary journeys from Takzik to Zhangzhung in Western Tibet to teach his doctrine. In the centuries – or perhaps the millennium – before the rise of the Yarlung Valley culture of Central Tibet, Zhangzhung was the heart of Tibetan civilization. Its centre was at Kang Rimpoche (Kailash), it had a written language and a literature, and had cultural and political connections with India, Persia, Khotan and China, but we know virtually nothing else about it. It collapsed after King Songtsen Gampo's conquest in the seventh century and little remains today except the cave city of Khyunglung, its old capital near Kang Rimpoche, and fragments of texts in the Zhangzhung script.

Shenrab Miwo taught his doctrine to the people of Zhangzhung and he also travelled to Bonri, the sacred Bon mountain in Kongpo. Olmo Lungring, his pure-land in Takzik, was transposed to Kang Rimpoche. At the centre of the Olmo Lungring mandala is a mountain called Yungdrung Gutsek. Yungdrung is the swastika, the Bon symbol of indestructibility and eternal dynamic activity. Gutsek means ninefold. Nine and 13 are the most significant numbers in a numerology that is one of Bon's gifts to Tibetan Buddhism. The ninefold mountain represents the nine ways of practice of the Bon tradition and it is this mountain that is identified with Kang Rimpoche. From its base four rivers flow into the four directions. Hundreds of cities, temples and parks, constituting the inner area, surround the mountain. The intermediate area has 12 cities, four in the cardinal directions. Beyond the outer area, crossed by rivers and spotted with lakes, is the outer ocean, and beyond the ocean is a ring of snowy mountain peaks. Mundane access to Olmo Lungring and Yungdrung Gutsek may be as easy as a pilgrimage to Kang Rimpoche, but spiritual access is not so simple. Shenrab Miwo shot an arrow through the encompassing mountain wall, creating a great tunnel obstructed by gorges and cliffs, where wild beasts lurk in the dark. It takes nine days to negotiate the tunnel, but the location of the entrance is covered in secrecy.

This Bon mythology and the legends of Shenrab Miwo were gathered together during the dissemination of Buddhism in the heady renaissance of Tibetan culture in the eleventh and twelfth centuries. The old Bon shamanism, Black Bon, had by then been virtually eradicated by Trisong Detsen's expulsion of the Bonpos from Central Tibet and by the pressure of the Buddhist ethos. By the fourteenth century Bon had assimilated much of the Buddhist teaching, its categories and practices, and the exposition of the Nine Ways of Bon, all attributed to Shenrab Miwo, formed a synthetic mixture of all the doctrines taught and practised in Tibet at that time – a statement which is in no way meant to denigrate the Bon tradition. These nine paths all lead to buddhahood, *sangyepa*, the same term with the same meaning used by the Buddhists. Shenrab Miwo is a Buddha.

Of the Nine Ways of Bon, the first four are paths of ritual magic that include the old Bon rites practised in the pre-Buddhist period. This ritualism constitutes a valid path to buddhahood because it is altruistic activity benefiting sentient beings and harmonizing the spiritual environment so that the spontaneous thought of enlightenment and a naturally pure and illuminated state of being can arise. The first path includes methods of prognostication to clarify the elements of any present situation and to predict the future – divination, astrology and medical diagnosis. The second path is the way of evocation, propitiation and subjugation of the spiritual powers of the environment – gods, demons and spirits – that can also be conceived as archetypal elements of the mind. The ritual practices of this path include purification through exorcism, suppression of demonic forces, ransom of human spirits from the hold of noumenal powers and the propitiation of the gods of luck.

The Bonpos are, *par excellence*, ritualists who keep the old Tibetan gods and demons and their spirit minions favourably inclined towards human activity. Before Buddhist adepts turned the gods and their retinues into slaves of the buddha-dharma, the Bonpos were propitiating them and using their power to facilitate human activity and maximize human 'luck'. Through the Buddhist example they assimilated the Indian doctrine of karma, but rather than follow the thorough-going Buddhists who attributed every situation and its result, including 'acts of god', to the previous activity of the human agent, the Bonpos believe that fully 50 per cent of the causative factors of any given situation and its result are determined by the influence of independent noumenal powers. This divine power is embodied particularly in the earth-lords (*sadak*) and the serpent spirits (*lu*) who control the fertility of the fields, the bounty of the harvests, the fecundity of cattle, human political status, the extent of personal human power, and so on. The rites subjugating and propitiating these gods and spirits are held to be of supreme importance, even amongst the Bon bodhisattvas, because human beings benefit thereby. The priests who perform the rites, the *shen*, have the highest status within the community.

The third Bon path is concerned with the ritual extermination of enemies. Although the rites to cause the death of human beings are subject to abuse by priests whose motivation towards the Buddha's enlightenment is immature or corrupt, if motivation is pure then benefit to sentient beings may accrue by the elimination of intractable enemies of the tradition or of the teacher. Buddhist tantra also includes such rites.

The fourth path is concerned with assisting beings in the intermediate state between death and rebirth, the *bardo*, and leading them to liberation from the wheel of rebirth. These ritual practices, like many of the rites included in these four lower paths of Bon, are shared by the Nyingma order. They became one of the sources of the doctrines of the *Tibetan Book of the Dead*.

The four higher ways of Bon are all Buddhist derivative. The fifth path is the way of the virtuous layman who takes the 10 vows to refrain from karmically negative activity of body, speech and mind, and who practises the 10 perfections of social morality and meditation. The sixth path is the monastic path of the monk, or ascetic (*drangsong*), who practises a strict monastic discipline, very similar to the Indian-derived Buddhist discipline, but including vows and rationales for those vows that are Tibetan in origin. The seventh and eighth paths correspond to the creative and fulfilment phases of tantric Buddhist meditation. The creative path is 'the way of pure sound' – mantra – by which the mind is reconditioned as a mandala. Fulfilment meditation is 'the way of the primeval *shen*', practised with a consort, in which the nondual mandala arises spontaneously. This meditation is supported by practice of seemingly crazy, unpredictable, behaviour like that of the Kagyu order adepts called *nyombas*.

The ninth path is the supreme path, the way of Dzokchen, the Natural Great Perfection. Dzokchen is a causeless path; in other words there is nothing that can be done to develop or facilitate it. Why? Because any thought about it or any aspiration towards it are the delusive flickerings of its mental emanations. It is the natural state of being and arises spontaneously and immediately like the heat of the sun with the sun itself. It is pure awareness and informs every movement of body, speech and mind. It is clear light and emanates a continuum of transforming illusion that is our everyday reality. The entire experience of Dzokchen is infused with bliss. It is innate buddhahood and spontaneously natural enlightenment. This Bon Dzokchen is virtually identical to the Dzokchen of the Nyingma order, except the Nyingmapas have a highly developed gradual approach cultivating the conditions wherein the natural state of being can be recognized. The Bonpos believe that their Dzokchen was a teaching of Shenrab Miwo and that it is an indigenous Tibetan yoga; that it has no Indian source in common with the Nyingma variety; and, indeed, that the Nyingmapas learned of it from Bon adepts.

Since Bon was proscribed by Trisong Detsen it was cast in an adversarial role *vis à vis* Buddhism, and the Bonpos saw themselves as outcasts, while at the same time they strove for acceptance by assimilating the Buddhist ethos and aspects of its creed. The original method by which this was achieved was through the revelation of treasure texts, a method employed contemporaneously by the Nyingmapas after the tenth century. Indeed many treasure-finders (*tertons*) discovered both Bon and Nyingma treasures. The early revelations were mostly texts that had been written in the empire period and hidden during the time of persecution. Later revelations had their provenance in a mystical sphere identical to the mind of Shenrab Miwo and such Buddhas as Drenpa Namkha, a great Bon adept and a disciple of Guru Rimpoche. The reformation of Bon in the fourteenth and fifteenth centuries, associated with the prominent figure of Nyame Sherab Gyeltsen, brought them closer to the Buddhist fold, but not close enough to avoid persecution by the unifying Gelukpas during the Great Fifth Dalai Lama's war on unorthodoxy in the seventeenth century. After that, like the Nyingmapas, the Bonpos established monasteries so that by the eighteenth century when a further reformation, led by Sangye Lingpa, resulted in the establishment of the New Bon, there was little formal distinction between Bon and the Nyingma traditions.

Down the centuries the Bon separation from the Buddhist mainstream was not only a doctrinal matter. It was also geographical. First, the main source of lay practice, priesthood and patronage has been the nomad pastoralists. This has always set them apart from the sedentary farmers, inhabitants of the valleys, where the great monasteries, particularly the Geluk monasteries, were built. Secondly, the persecution emanating from Central Tibet had the least effect on the border peoples, whom the cultured Central Tibetans consider barbarian tribals, and amongst these people Bon has thrived. Thirdly, Bon kept a deep hold in Amdo, the province to the far north-east of the Tibetan ethnic area, which has always had strong separatist tendencies. The principal areas of Bon strength were and still are in the Himalayan regions, particularly in Dolpo and Lo, in lower Kongpo and south to the Himalayas, in the Jangthang northern plains and in Amdo. Some of the great Bon power-place mountains are Kang Rimpoche (Kailash), Bonri mountain in Kongpo, Ritse Druk, the Six-Peaked Mountain, in Khyungpo, Amnye Machen in Amdo and Gyelrong Murdo in Sichuan. The important Bon monastic academies, however, were located in Tsang province, where several great Bon families lived, although they were supported by the nomads of the north. Menri Gompa, founded in 1405, was to thrive until 1959 and was the principal Bon monastic centre in Tibet.

## THE NYINGMA ORDER: THE OLD ORDER OF GURU RIMPOCHE

The shamanic religious culture of Tibet was only slowly infiltrated by the buddha-dharma. Before the Tibetan political ascendancy in Central Asia starting in the seventh century, there was little cultural contact with the surrounding Buddhist countries. The silk route passed Tibet by to the north and anyhow the vast spaces of the Jangthang, the northern plains, separated the oasis settlements of the silk route from populated Tibet. To the south the climate and the jungles were an effective barrier to contact with the Indian plains. The harbingers of buddha-dharma were the Indian Buddhist sadhus who, like their Hindu counterparts, climbed the Himalayas on pilgrimage to the sacred mountains and for meditation retreat, and then wandered beyond the divide onto the Tibetan plateau and found a civilization in Western Tibet in Zhangzhung and a budding culture in Central Tibet. Perhaps the third-century king of the Yarlung Valley Lhatho Thori had a connection with such wandering sadhus, although legend relates that the first Buddhist texts known in Tibet were magically transported from India to land on the roof of his Yambu Lhakhang palace.

In the seventh century, with the rise of the Yarlung Valley in Central Tibet as a military power, Tibet's borders were opened by conquest and the Buddhist tradition formed part of the imported cultural wealth. King Songtsen Gampo, after conquering the Tibetan territories surrounding Yarlung, including the kingdom of Zhangzhung, attacked the Kathmandu Valley and the Chinese Tang empire. The prowess of his horse-riders was so feared that both the Tang Emperor and the King of Nepal acceded to his request that they send princesses to be his wives. The Chinese princess Wencheng Kongjo brought the Chinese classics with her, and the sacred sciences of astrology, geomancy and medicine began to be assimilated as the Tibetan nobility learned the Chinese language. The Nepali princess Bhrikuti opened the doors to the high Indian Buddhist culture of the Kathmandu Valley. So, during this springtime of Tibetan power, foreign cultural influence flowed into Yarlung for the first time. Songtsen Gampo understood the value of the Indic and Chinese cultures as civilizing tools in his land of cannibal demons. The Tibetan alphabet was also introduced at this time, employing a Sanskrit script as a base, and the first few of thousands of Buddhist Sanskrit texts were translated into the Tibetan language. Songtsen Gampo had the missionary temples built *(see p.21)*, including the Lhasa Jokhang, and the worship of Chenrezik and his wrathful emanation Tamdrin (Hayagriva), the horse-headed buddha-deity, was initiated at this time. The king also propagated a civil code based on Buddhist social values, indicating how high Buddhism stood in his estimation.

During the following 250 years the Tibetan kingdom and its empire flourished, and so did the Bon establishment. Buddhist influence continued to invade Tibet and worship of the Buddhas persisted, but the royal priests were Bonpos and the ancient tradition of sacred kingship continued, each king abdicating as his son reached the horse-riding age of 13. Although there were urban centres where artisans could produce their fine quality bronze, silver and gold artefacts, the court was nomadic, housed in a city of tents. Tibetan culture was a martial, horse-riding one. The Tibetan cavalry rode to Bodhgaya in India to collect Buddhist relics, confronted the Muslim onslaught in Turkestan, garrisoned forts on the silk route in subjected Central Asia, plundered the Tang capital of Xian itself and, briefly, set up a puppet Emperor.

The turning-point came in the middle of the eighth century with the great King Trisong Detsen, who instigated a cultural, political and religious revolution. First, he attempted to unseat the Bon priests from their position of power and replace them with Buddhist monks. In this he was partially successful. He invited the Bengali abbot and scholar Shantarakshita to Central Tibet to establish a monastery at Samye. Shantarakshita was unable to overcome the opposition of the Bonpos, so the king invited a tantric mendicant yogi to reinforce the Buddhist presence. This yogi was Padmasambhava, who later became known as Guru Rimpoche, the Precious

Guru, and he succeeded where the monk had failed: the Samye monastery – Tibet's first gompa – was built, the first monks were ordained by Shantarakshita and Guru Rimpoche initiated the first tantric lineages in Tibet. While attempting to convert his court to the new faith, the king invited scores of Indian scholars to translate Sanskrit Buddhist texts into Tibetan and to teach the buddha-dharma. Meditation communities were organized, the monasteries were supported by taxation and a pillar was erected at Samye proclaiming the establishment of a Buddhist state.

This first period of Buddhist propagation was dominated by Guru Rimpoche, an exemplar of the tantric method who may not have figured prominently in the annals of the great Indian adepts, but who was to be perceived in retrospect in Tibet as a Second Buddha and the root-guru of the Nyingma order. He was not, however, the only major figure of this period. The Chan (Zen in Japan), the school of meditation that taught sudden enlightenment without recourse to karmic reconditioning, was a powerful force, led by the Chinese adept Hwashang Mahayana, while Vimalamitra led an Indian Dzokchen school teaching a similar but more thorough-going nondual vision supporting meditation practice. Meantime the orthodox Indian teachers of the monastic Universal Buddhist Tradition naturally had the inside track, because it was – and still is – recognized that the monastic community forms the crucial basis of any Buddhist society. The philosopher monk Kamalashila was the principal mouthpiece of this faction.

For nearly a century Central Tibet was a cauldron of religious change. Trisong Detsen's successors continued his policy of buddhification before the last of these Buddhist kings, Repachan, was assassinated by his brother Langdarma, who stood for the Bon counter-revolution. Repachan's Buddhist agenda, particularly his propensity to fill the court with Indian scholars, had pushed the declining Bon authority to the edge of its tolerance and in a bloody reaction Buddhism was suppressed. The consequences of this were the loss of the empire and the fragmentation of power.

During the subsequent century of Bon counter-revolution, monasticism was quashed and Buddhist practice was conserved by tantric householders, some of whom had assimilated Dzokchen and Chan influences. These laymen coexisted with the Bon shamans and were naturally affected by them. Guru Rimpoche had converted the Bonpos by demonstrating his capacity to subjugate and exorcize the Tibetan spiritual powers and employ their energy in rites of magic. His successors incorporated aspects of shamanic ritual into the Buddhist tradition. This represented an Indian current of tantric practice in which every aspect of human being – with no exception – was manifestly expressed in order to realize its buddha-nature. When, during the second period of dissemination of Buddhism in Tibet in the eleventh century, monastic discipline and bodhisattvic morality were reintroduced, however, these laymen were chastised for ritually acting out the propensities to take life and to indulge sexuality.

Despite the criticism and the successive waves of reforming influence to which this tradition was subjected down the centuries, these Buddhist shamans became the foundation of the Nyingma tradition. They transmitted their lineal tradition to their sons or nephews living within established communities, although some of them undoubtedly resorted to the cave, the better to hone their meditation practice. They were village lamas, married yogis, with the reputation of adepts in magical rites and display, all derived from the higher culture to the south.

With the rise of monasticism in the eleventh century and the flourishing of new Tibetan orders, there were important developments in the Nyingma tradition that elaborated the mystical tendencies of its tantric base. At the expense of the other masters of the empire period, the Great Guru was elevated to the status of a buddha-lama embodying the entire tradition. During his sojourn in Tibet he had travelled throughout the land concealing treasure texts, which were available only to his incarnate emanations, who were one with his buddha-mind. This buddha-mind could be reached through meditation and the guru's revelations imparted to those ready to receive them. The tradition of treasure-finders reinvigorated the Nyingma order and strengthened its status in the villages, for many of the treasure-finders were village lamas, and although plenty of them revealed liturgical texts replicating the visions of their predecessors, amongst them were great mystical poets with original vision, steeped in the Tibetan rather than the Indian heritage and dedicated to the existential welfare of their parishes.

Nyingma lineages are the carriers of Dzokchen, the tradition of the Natural Great Perfection, which provides the most thoroughgoing nondual vision and meditation in Tibetan Buddhism. The quintessence of the highest tantras, Dzokchen's particularly efficacious meditation practices, on a short-cut path to buddhahood, transform the material world into a vision of lightform and the yogi's body into a rainbow. The attainment of the fruit of Dzokchen is evinced in the rainbow body that spirals away at the time of death, leaving only body hair and finger and toe nails behind it. Dzokchen doctrine was synthesized from the oral instruction passed down from spiritual father to son and from the revelations of the treasure-finders by the great polymath Longchen Rabjampa in the fourteenth century. The Great Fifth Dalai Lama, a scion of a Nyingma family, was a Dzokchen practitioner and sympathetic to the Nyingma order. Under his seventeenth-century reforms, when gompas became the political tool of the centralized lamaist state, the Nyingma order was monasticized and two important Nyingma gompas – Dorje Drak and Mindroling – were developed in Central Tibet. These were the home gompas of the northern and southern traditions of treasure-revelation.

The Nyingma order has been fortunate in that it has never gained the wealth that forms the stepping-stone to political power and its temptations. Until the seventeenth century its lineages were held by sedentary village lamas, their itinerant brothers called *ngakpas*, and the yogis (*neljorpas*) of the caves and hermitages. The ngakpas, recognizable by their red long-sleeved gowns (*chubas*), their dreadlocks and ritual possessions like dorje, phurba and monkey drum, still travel from village to power place to village, performing magical rites for the benefit of laymen. A white shawl will identify the ngakpa as a Dzokchen yogi with either married or renunciate status. Relative to the other orders the Nyingmapas have suffered less under the Chinese.

# THE KADAM ORDER: THE MONASTIC VISION

The foundation of all Buddhist societies is the monastic community. This is proven historically by the disappearance of Buddhism in India and in the Central Asian oasis states after the monasteries were destroyed by the Muslims. Without a monastic centre the lay community loses the source of its inspiration, and tantric meditation and ritual practice lose their specifically Buddhist character. Without a lifeline to the institutions that are the repositories of sacred treasure and power objects, the libraries of sacred texts and the houses of monks demonstrating the efficacy of Buddhist psycho-physical discipline, Buddhist lay society retreats into mere worship of the gods.

In Tibet, the cave or hermitage power place is a higher adjunct to the gompa. The gompa functions as a preparatory school for the hermitages and acts as a provider of material support for the ascetics in the caves. The gompa also plays crucial economic and political roles in the lay community that it dominates.

The second period of propagation of Buddhism in Tibet began with the return of fully-ordained monks from Eastern Tibet and the re-establishment of monasticism.

In the eleventh century stability was attained in Tibet under the noble families that ruled from their rock fortresses (*dzongs*) in every district of the country. Political stability permitted cultural resurgence under the patronage of wealthy families and the re-establishment of Buddhism was the chief result. The way was led by a monk called Lume, who was amongst 10 Central Tibetans who went to Kham to receive ordination into the lineage that had been sustained by Khampa *gelongs*, the fully ordained monks, since the flight of monks from Central Tibet in the ninth century. Upon his return Lume built some lhakhangs in Central Tibet. But the event of the century was the arrival of a monk from Bengal, where in the great monastic academies tantra had been given a very firm base in the philosophy of the Universal Buddhist Tradition (*mahayana*) and also in monastic discipline, or, to put it another way, sutra and tantra had been wed. The monk's name was Jowo Atisha and he comes across as a kindly if somewhat austere patriarch instructing his children in the easy but slow method of transforming Tibet into a buddhafield. Jowo Atisha was invited first to the thriving kingdom of Guge in Western Tibet by the King of Guge, who had to expend his own weight in gold in the political process. The ground for his stay had been prepared by a Western Tibetan monk called Rinchen Zangpo, who had studied for years in Buddhist Kashmir before returning to Western Tibet to build what we now call the Rinchen Zangpo Gompas: Alchi and Lama Yuru in Ladakh, Tabo in Spiti and Tholing in Guge. Then, travelling via Kang Rimpoche (Kailash) and across Tsang, Atisha arrived in Central Tibet to the five-star treatment offered him by some brilliant young men who were to become his disciples and the founders of the lineages of the Kadam order.

In Jowo Atisha's perspective, the raw tantra that was the legacy of Guru Rimpoche lacked the foundation of discipline and study that is necessary for an understanding of tantric methods and therefore proper practice. Whether it was because of this view, eloquently expressed in his sermons and lucidly written in his books, or the personification of the superbly honed Buddhist culture of Bengal, or the allure of his charisma, his mission was met with unqualified success. After the master died in 1054, students poured into the Lhasa valley and the valleys of Phenyul and Jang to the north of Lhasa from all over Tibet to study with his root disciples at the gompas they built. Dromton, Sharapa, Potowa, Neuzurpa and Puchungwa were some of the masters to found gompas where, according to Atisha's precepts, the tantras were given a secondary role and study of the sutras of the Universal Buddhist Tradition in a strictly disciplined monastic environment became the path to the Buddha's enlightenment.

Jowo Atisha's legacy was the Kadam order that is synonymous with monastic discipline and study. He showed the Tibetans the monastic mindset and gave them the vision of the monastic community which was to become the cornerstone of Tibetan Buddhism and Tibetan theocracy for the following 900 years. But the method of the Kadampas was not to last. It lacked the tantric mysticism of Guru Rimpoche's followers; it lacked the allure of high spiritual power and ecstasy that Milarepa's tradition offered *(see below)*; it did not relate sufficiently to the gods, demons and spirits that filled the minds of ordinary Tibetans; and it did not create a political power base to counter the developing Sakya and Kagyu orders. Despite an enormous contribution to Tibet's religious life, at the end of the twelfth century the Kadampas were overtaken by the extraordinary renaissance of religious culture channelled into the Kagyu order, which was successful in uniting monasticism with mystical yoga.

## THE KAGYU ORDER: ASCETICISM AND POLITICAL MASTERY

The underlying ethos of the Kagyu order has always been renunciation and asceticism. The image of the Kagyu yogi sitting immovable in his cave for 12 years, covered only by rags, subsisting on nettle soup, was established by Jetsun Milarepa in the eleventh century. The lucid biography of Milarepa and his collected songs published a couple of hundred years later etched that image into the Tibetan imagination. Here was a Tibetan peasant who accomplished as much as his Indian lineal forbears in the attainment of buddhahood. He was indeed a Tibetan Buddha and proved forever that the Tibetan consciousness was capable of the ultimate achievement on the tantric path. Milarepa was the meditator *par excellence* and exemplifies the yogi on the one-pointed search for enlightenment through tantric meditation. The meditation he practised is the two-phase yoga of creative and fulfilment meditation, the creative phase conditioning the mind to a vision of reality described in terms of the deities of a mandala, and the fulfilment phase concerned with the dissolution of those forms, and the dynamic psychic processes that they represent, into the awareness that permeates all experience. The method that Milarepa took and made his own was called the Yoga of the Inner Heat (*tummo*). A fire was envisioned in the stomach that melted the concrete focal point of energy in the head centre so that a stream of ambrosia poured down the central channel, energizing the successive chakras at the speech, mind and activity levels.

Milarepa's achievement is described in terms of the great magical powers of walking through rock, flying in the sky, perceiving with the single eye of nondual awareness, eating stone, and so on. The

Kagyu tradition developed a highly poetical and mystical manner of describing events on the level of buddha-vision that had its origin in the Indian songs called *dohas* sung by the early holders of the Kagyu oral tradition.

'Kagyu' means 'lineal oral instruction' and the order prides itself on the strong unbroken transmission of the essential yoga and meditation instruction by word of mouth from master to disciple. The main lineage originated with the Indian adept Tilopa, a mythical character inseparable from the archetypal guru who appears in a dream or vision and instructs in a non-discursive manner. Naropa, his heart-disciple, was a scholar turned wandering yogi, whose practice was a 12-year search for his spiritual master, then a short successful experience of creative and fulfilment yogas. A Tibetan disciple of Naropa, a householder yogi, Marpa the Translator, brought all of Naropa's lineal teaching back to Tibet and passed it on to several disciples, the chief of whom was Milarepa. Milarepa was famous and his reputation attracted several extraordinary characters to him. One was the unconventional yogi Rechungpa and another was the scholar Je Gampopa Dakpo Lhaje. Gampopa transmitted the oral instruction governing uncompromising ascetic yoga to two extraordinary students – Drogon Pakmodrupa of Densathil and Karmapa Dusum Khyenpa of Tsurphu. The ascetic Drogon Pakmodrupa's great achievement was to produce three masters of status equal to himself – Drikung Kyabgon of Drikung, Taklung Tashi Pel of Taklung and Tsangpa Gyare of Ralung in Tsang – but his lineage at Densathil became mired in a political swamp.

The main five independent gompas, however, became the seats of four of the five principal Kagyu orders that have survived to this day – the Karma, Drikung, Taklung and Drukpa Kagyu. With the astonishing growth of these gompas and with increasing Kagyu political preoccupation, the spirit of Naropa and Milarepa was diluted by monasticism, but the ideal of retreat to a cave on the snowline robed in cotton cloth and subsisting on nettle soup survived the tendency towards academic study, and the Kagyu tradition has continued to produce yogis of remarkable calibre.

The Karma Kagyu became the most successful of the Kagyu orders in the political arena, but it still maintained its yoga traditions. It instituted the system of consecutive incarnation of its chief hierarch, the Karmapa, as the means to assure continuity of authority. Both the Drikung Kagyu and Drukpa Kagyu orders assimilated much of the Nyingma tradition and maintained a strong inclination for the hermitage. The Taklung Kagyu, strongly influenced by Kadam monastic discipline, became renowned for its monastic purity but was a casualty of the Great Fifth Dalai Lama's reorganization in the seventeenth century. The Kagyu orders suffered politically at this time; however, the tradition continued to thrive, particularly the Karma Kagyupas in Kham.

All these lineages, transmitting Milarepa's instruction, concentrate upon yogas of control and manipulation of the subtle energies of the spiritual 'body' in order to resolve its inherent dualities and to attain Mahamudra, where the oneness of the Buddha's enlightenment is achieved.

The potency of Milarepa's example and the ongoing practice of his tradition is proven by the history of meditation retreat at the three great mountain cave sites down the Great Himalayan range: Kang Rimpoche (Kailash), Labchi and Tsari. Although all the Kagyu orders participated in the tradition of sending off monks from the home gompas in Central Tibet to the hermitages of these three great mandala mountains, the Drukpa and Drikung gompas were fully immersed in the ascetic renunciate ideal. During the twelfth and thirteenth centuries the caves and hermitages, where the founders of the Kagyu orders had meditated, were established as major power places and small meditation centres grew up. This tradition was perpetuated at least into the seventeenth century, but it seems to have been negatively affected by the Great Fifth Dalai Lama's centralization, after which the meditation communities in the Himalayan borderlands went into decline. Still the tradition is maintained, though at a low ebb, until today, and meditation-adepts (*gomchens*) are still to be found in the mountain hermitages.

Another dimension of the Milarepa legend that was copied and developed was that of the peripatetic yogi, the ascetic renunciate who wandered from power place to power place, from cave to hermitage, servicing the villagers' and nomads' need for ritual exorcism in its various forms and, perhaps, teaching the basic Buddhist doctrine on the way. Drukpa Kunley, a yogi of the Drukpa order, demonstrates this mode and strengthens the notion common in

Buddhist Himalayan villages, that the Buddhist sadhu is a deflower-er of maidens and a life-line to old maids. Some of these homeless wanderers lived from the offerings made by the villagers and nomads like Milarepa himself. But most were patronized by their home gompas or by wealthy individuals associated with the spiritu-al – inseparable from the political and the economic – fortunes of the monastery.

There have been many, many remarkable exponents of the Kaygu tradition, including the Sixteenth Karmapa, who in 1959 emerged from Tibet into exile and the Western limelight.

## THE SAKYA ORDER: TANTRA AND SCHOLARSHIP

Today, the Sakya order of Tibetan Buddhism has the lowest profile of all the Buddhist orders and so it has been for several centuries. A strong monastic order with an emphasis on discipline and scholar-ship, the Sakyapas were established in the first phase of the second wave of dissemination of Buddhism in Tibet, and at their inception they combined elements of the old and the new. From the original Nyingma tradition, they took many of the tried and tested tantras, such as that of the buddha-deity Dorje Phurba (Vajrakilaya), and they inherited the old guardian protectors such as Dorje Lekpa. In the old manner, the tradition was transmitted within the family, first from father to son and then, after the Sakya hierarchs became celibate monks, from uncle to nephew, the nephew taking the full celibate monastic ordination while his married brother begat his successor. From the new lineages transmitted from India, the Sakya order received the tradition of full monastic discipline, together with the systematic philosophical and logical analysis that more than any other feature was to characterize the order. New tantras, particularly the Kye Dorje (Hevajra) tantra, and new translations from Sanskrit to Tibetan provided an added dimension to the schol-arly tradition and also to its ritual and contemplative aspects.

The root Indian guru of the new tantric lineages of meditation practice and study was the great adept Birwapa (Virupa), one of the 84 tantric buddha-adepts, whose example, like that of Naropa for the Kagyu order, was to remain as a guiding star for his Tibetan successors in tantric practice. The most popular icon of Virupa shows the great adept sitting, pot-bellied, dressed in his tiger-skin loincloth, his right hand raised, a finger pointing at the sun, which remains arrested in its tracks while Birwapa finishes a mammoth drinking spree. The tantric tradition of Birwapa was transmitted to Tibet by the translator Drokmi Lotsawa, who taught it to Konchok Gyelpo, the scion of an old land-owning family, who had been schooled by Nyingma teachers. In 1073 Konchok Gyelpo established a monastery at Sakya ('White Earth') in the province of Tsang, to the south-west of Shigatse on the trade route from Shigatse to Nepal, not far from the Nepali border. So while the Kadam order, inspired by the Bengali abbot Jowo Atisha, was setting Central Tibet on fire with the monastic and scholarly tradition of Bengal, the Sakyapas were disseminating an equally potent blend of Buddhist traditions in Tsang. The Kadampas and the Sakyapas met in Central Tibet at Sangphu Neuthok, 'The Source of All Learning', where their scholarly traditions were sustained and developed in parallel curricula in colleges of study and debate.

At Sangphu Neuthok and other Sakya gompas established in Tsang and also to the south of the Yarlung Tsangpo river valley and to the west of Yarlung, teachers like Lama Dampa Sonam Gyeltsen, Rendawa and Rongtonpa created a reputation for Sakya scholarship that has led the order to claim that all Tibetan monastic orders are based firmly in their philosophical method and logical analysis. The principal teacher of Je Tsongkhapa, the fourteenth-century reformer of the Kadampa and founder of the Geluk order, was Rendawa, the Sakya polymath.

Not that the Sakyapas are merely scholars. Their mystical tantric tradition, based in the Kye Dorje mother-tantra, teaches psycho-sexual yoga and the *summum bonum* of their tantric practice is a nondual discipline called the Path and Fruit (*lamdre*). Derived from Birwapa and containing a thorough-going nondual vision similar and equal to that of the Nyingma order's Dzokchen or the Kagyu's Chakchen (*mahamudra*), the efficacy of this short-cut, tantric, path to realization of the Buddha's enlightenment is demonstrated by the Sakya masters' legendary displays of magical powers.

The Sakya order was the first of the monastic orders to gain political ascendancy over all of Tibet. The Sakya lineage began with five extraordinary masters, the product of the eleventh and twelfth-century Tibetan religious genius, who over 150 years expanded and developed the Sakya tradition. The first of the six was Konchok Gyelpo, who founded Sakya Gompa. The second was his son, the Great Sakya Sachen Kunga Nyingpo, who gained a systematic mastery of the old tantras and the new Indian learning. His reputation brought power and wealth to Sakya. Sachen's sons were Sonam Tsemo and Drakpa Gyeltsen, who developed the tradition and transmitted it to Sakya Pandita, Drakpa Gyeltsen's nephew. Sakya Pandita's reputation as a lama of scholarship, awareness and power was even greater than his forbears', and it was this reputation as chief of one of Tibet's major gompas that led to the Sakya order's entrance into the international political arena.

In 1207 the military genius Genghis Khan began his genocidal conquest of Central Asia with his horse-riding Mongol shamans. In that same year his envoys appeared in Central Tibet demanding Tibetan submission. The abbot of Tsel Gungthang, the Kagyu gompa near Lhasa, negotiated a treaty with the Mongol envoys that was to define the relationship between Tibet and the Mongols, and later the Ming and Manchu dynasties, down to the twentieth century. This treaty is perceived to have exchanged Tibetan religious protection for Mongol and Chinese political protection, establishing Tibet as a tributary state of the Mongol and later the Chinese empire. It was called 'the priest–patron relationship' and it provides evidence of the meteoric rise of the Tibetan lamas' reputation as the high-priests of Central Asia. The treaty was not immediately enforced – perhaps the wealth of the Central Tibetan gompas was too juicy a plum for the Mongols to ignore, for they plundered the important Kadam gompa at Reteng in 1239. But soon after, Sakya Pandita was invited to the Mongol court of Ogadai Khan's son Godan, where he impressed the Mongol shamans with his Buddhist knowledge and power sufficiently for him to return to Tibet as Regent. His nephew and successor Chogyel Phakpa emulated his uncle in both scholarship and lama-ship. Invited to Kubilai Khan's court, he defeated all-comers in debate and magical display and re-established the lamas' ascendancy at the Mongol court. He was imperial preceptor in 1260 and returned to Tibet as Tishi, Viceroy. He was the last of the great Sakya hierarchs.

The Sakya political ascendancy was maintained into the middle of the fourteenth century and with it the dominance of the province of Tsang. It ended with the rise of Phakmodrupa in the Yarlung Tsangpo valley. Then it was the turn of the Kagyu order to assume political power in its shift from Tsang to Central Tibet. However, although stripped of national political influence, the Sakya order continued to thrive. The fourteenth-century polymath Buton at Zhalu Gompa was one of the most remarkable monks of his day. Many of the original Kadam gompas were adopted by the Sakya order during the latter's period of political ascendancy. New centres of Sakya spirituality arose. In 1429 an extraordinary Sakya monk called Kunga Zangpo founded the Ngor EVAM Choden Gompa, which became the centre of a Sakya sub-school with subsidiary gompas throughout Tibet. In the fifteenth century an extraordinary lama called Tsarchen founded another lineage in Tsang at Dar Drangmochen. Later, when the reformist Gelukpas dominating Tibet, the Sakyapas suffered little, and their tradition of monastic discipline and tantric scholarship were sustained until the Chinese suppression.

## THE GELUK ORDER: MONASTICISM AND THEOCRACY

The Sakya and Kagyu monasteries dominated Tibet spiritually and politically until the middle of the fifteenth century, but by then there was enough corruption in these monasteries – probably induced by the worm of political ambition – to give space for one of Tibet's great saints and scholars to launch a reforming movement. Je Tsongkhapa was born in Amdo in the far north-east and came to Central Tibet, like so many Easterners down the centuries, to study in the gompas of the heartland. He sat at the feet of Kadam, Sakya and Kagyu masters, and gained a reputation second to none as a scholar and debater. When he began to teach in his own right he applied the Kadam ethos and method not only to study of the sutras but also to four of the principle tantras – the Jikje (Bhairava),

Demchok (Samvara), Sangdu (Guhyasamaja) and Dukhor (Kala-chakra). He systematized his analysis of the spiritual path in his *magnum opus*, *The Great Exposition of the Stages of the Path* (the *Lamrim Chenpo*), which provided perhaps the clearest and most inclusive analysis of the Buddhist path that had yet been written. Je Tsongkhapa's voluminous commentaries on every imaginable topic relating to the path presented the largest and most integrated corpus of scripture produced by a Tibetan mind.

Thus the Geluk order was born. It started as a purist, reformist movement stressing monastic discipline and study of the basic tenets of Buddhist philosophy as the foundation of tantric practice. The important place of debate and examination in the system indicates the movement away from the cave and from ritual activity and back to basic philosophic education. Twenty years of study leading to the academic degree and title of geshe is required of Geluk monks before yoga and meditation practice in the tantric tradition are permitted. Develop the rational mind, create discipline and order, give the gompas a central social function and an ideal Buddhist society evolves!

Tsongkhapa was an idealist and a theorist and during the first centuries of the development of the Geluk order, while the purist principles he espoused were effective in curtailing the excesses of the politically dominant Sakya and Kagyu orders, the Gelukpas were indeed the order of virtue and merit. But perhaps the order was too successful in its appeal, not only to the Tibetans looking for a reformed tradition but also to the Mongols, who after their acceptance of the Geluk tradition played a major unwanted and disastrous part in Tibetan politics. With a centralized monastic system and both spiritual and secular power effectively in the hands of the Geluk hierarchy, a theocracy was created governing a unified Tibet. Without forgetting the virtue of Tsongkhapa's spiritual tradition, it is this political aspect that is important, particularly as it bears upon the contemporary destiny of Tibet.

After Je Tsongkhapa's death in 1419, the gompa he founded, Ganden Namgyeling, to the north-east of Lhasa, together with Drepung and Sera, both close to Lhasa, established by his disciples, attained an overwhelming hold on the Kyichu valley area, while Tashi Lhunpo in Shigatse began to threaten the Kagyu dominance in the province of Tsang. Ganden, the seat of the Ganden Tripa, the Ganden Throne-Holder, head of the order, gradually became the nucleus of a centralized monastic system including all Geluk gompas in the country. The old Kadam gompas were absorbed into the new order. Then, in the sixteenth century, the Qosot Mongols were successfully converted by Sonam Gyatso, the abbot of Drepung, and the Gelukpas acquired a vast new constituency. Altan Khan, the Qosot leader, bestowed the title of Dalai Lama upon Sonam Gyatso, retrospectively exalting his two predecessors, Gendun Drub of Tashi Lhunpo and Gendun Gyatso, abbot of Drepung, to the same rank. Thus Sonam Gyatso became the Third Dalai Lama. The Fourth Dalai Lama was discovered as a grandson of Altan Khan and the Mongols were thereby inexorably pulled into the Tibetan political arena.

To distinguish the new spiritual and political power in Tibet from the old unreformed orders, the Chinese gave them the label 'Yellow Hats' as opposed to the unreformed 'Red Hats', the type of hats and their relative status being an old obsession of the Chinese that the Tibetans had absorbed during the earlier period of Mongol domination.

The Red Hats' authority was dispersed amongst their great gompas, but they were entrenched amongst the nobility, particularly in the province of Tsang, where in the late sixteenth century the princes were virtually kings of Tibet. The conflict between the Yellow and Red Hat orders can actually be seen in terms of a continuing rivalry between Central Tibet and Tsang. The Pakmodrupas had ruled for a century from Yarlung, but by the end of the sixteenth century, power had again moved to Shigatse. The victory of the Gelukpas was finally to establish Tibet's seat of power at Lhasa in Central Tibet.

A political giant was then to enter Tibetan history – the Great Fifth Dalai Lama, Lobsang Gyatso, who was born in Chongye in 1617. A highly learned man, prolific in his writing on sacred topics and conscientious in his religious duties, he reformed the reintegrated state and its finances; with tact he expropriated run-down Red Hat gompas and restored them. Under his rule, a census was taken, penal laws were promulgated and trade prospered.

However, reform and centralization came at a price. The Karma Kagyu jealousy of the Gelukpas' rising political power, translated into military force, would probably have proved effective had not the Great Fifth invited a foreign army in to secure Geluk supremacy. The Qosot Mongol general Gusri Khan was his instrument. In 1642 the Mongols defeated and slew the King of Tsang at Shigatse, sacked the Karma Kagyu gompa at Tsurphu and killed many monks. Rampaging from Kham to Ladakh, they defeated every opposition to the central Geluk power with the exception of the Drukpas (the Bhutanese), who alone amongst the Tibetan peoples retain their independence today. Gusri Khan gave ultimate authority over the realm to the Great Fifth, but imposed a lay regent as his representative. In 1679 the Dalai Lama elected his spiritual son, Sangye Gyatso, to the position of Regent.

The Great Fifth's death in 1682 was concealed by the Regent Sangye Gyatso to avoid a hiatus in government, but in the absence of a genius at the helm of Tibetan affairs even Sangye Gyatso could not prevent the repercussions of Mongol intervention in Tibet. The untimely recognition of the Sixth Dalai Lama, a poet and sensualist, was the signal for a renewed Mongol invasion. Lazang Khan, the Qosot ally of the Chinese Manchu Emperor, invaded Lhasa in 1706, killed the Regent, burnt many gompas, kidnapped and assassinated the Sixth Dalai Lama and installed his son in his stead. Then in 1717 the Qosots' rival Mongol clan, the Dzungars, took advantage of the Tibetans' disillusionment with Lazang Khan and after killing him, plundered and terrorized Central Tibet for five years.

Peace was restored by a Chinese Manchu army that brought the new incarnation of the Dalai Lama to Lhasa in 1723. The lay-regency was abolished, future Regents being monks responsible for government only during the Dalai Lama's minority. For 20 years thereafter a capable Tibetan minister, Polhane, successfully arbitrated between the Manchus' stranglehold on the country and the Tibetans' animosity towards this new army of occupation.

After Polhane's death, the Chinese Emperor's representatives, the Ambans, maintained an influential presence in Lhasa for 150 years. They gave Tibet peace and prosperity, but the seclusion imposed on the country by the Manchus, supported by various conservative factions in the large Geluk gompas in and around Lhasa, sustained Chinese influence. In Lhasa a succession of Regents favourable to the Ambans' dictates retained power through the expediency of assassinating the Dalai Lamas by poison before they attained their majority. Further, during this period when the Eighth to Twelfth Dalai Lamas died young, the Panchen Lamas of Tashi Lhunpo at Shigatse, who were equal or even superior to the Dalai Lamas in spiritual status, were played off against the Geluk establishment in Lhasa, thus exploiting the old rivalry between Central Tibet and Tsang.

It was not until the end of the nineteenth century, when the Manchu Qing dynasty in Peking, and also in Lhasa, had weakened, that a Dalai Lama was installed who had attained his majority since the Chinese occupation. In breadth and depth of vision, this Dalai Lama, the Thirteenth (1876–1933), stood head and shoulders above his monastic contemporaries. The Geluk establishments in the great Lhasa gompas had atrophied in a pro-Chinese stance, ignorant of and uninterested in world developments, particularly in the Western influence in Asia led by the British in India. Colonel Younghusband's military expedition to Lhasa in 1904, designed to open Tibet to trade and to exclude both Russian and Chinese influence from the country, gave the Tibetans, however, a glimpse of the European culture – a culture that by way of Marxism was finally to swallow their ancient traditions and politically engulf them.

## THE TIBETAN CULTURAL SHIFT

Since the tenth century there has been an apparent drift in the focus of Tibetan culture from the west to the east of the Tibetan ethnic area. Beginning with Rinchen Zangpo and the rise of the kingdom of Guge, then with the dominance of the Sakya establishment in the province of Tsang and the Kagyu ascendancy in Central Tibet, followed by the Geluk theocracy centred on the Lhasa valley, the political and cultural hub of the country moved from west to east. Some people see this movement as the result of a climatic change, particularly as a decline in rainfall. The oases of the Tarim basin declined during the same period, probably due to the reduction in run-off from the Kunlun mountains.

In the absence of statistics it is impossible to prove this climatic shift, but what is certain is that there are far fewer trees in Western and Central Tibet than there were 1,000 years ago. The Guge area is virtually treeless today and we know from early Western travellers' reports that the Tsaparang valley was once partially forested. Forests that take thousands of years to develop are destroyed by armies out of enmity and by local populations out of greed, and probably both these factors were operative in Western and Central Tibet while rainfall was decreasing. The great gompas of Central Tibet required massive amounts of wood in their construction and then the large numbers of people there made gradual depredations upon the trees that remained. The first gompas were constructed of wood from local forests. Later they were made of wood imported from the Kongpo forests and stone. The various Mongul invasions must also have resulted in significant despoliation of trees and we know certainly that the half million soldiers of the Chinese People's Liberation Army living off the land since 1959 have made serious inroads into the forests that remained. Chinese economic exploitation of the Eastern Tibetan forests, from Kongpo through Kham, has also destroyed a large proportion of the Tibetan remaining forests, but this destruction is only 20 years old.

Central Tibet and Tsang gave birth to most of the schools of Tibetan Buddhism and during the period of the rise of the gompas (eleventh to fourteenth centuries), the energies of the Tibetan people were concentrated there. Many of the individuals responsible for founding the great gompas, however, were Eastern Tibetans, who had come to Central Tibet to study and meditate. Many of the scholars who gave those gompas later renown were also from the east. But after the establishment of the Yellow Hat sect as the dominant Buddhist order in the Fifth Lama's time, the centre of vitality and creativity appears to move to the east. The brilliant exponents of the Buddhist tradition from Eastern Tibet no longer came to Central Tibet, but stayed in their homelands. Central Tibet was still revered as the original source of spiritual power, but the gompas of Kham and Amdo and their lamas dominate the Tibetan spiritual scene.

# KHAM AND THE ECLECTIC MOVEMENT

The most important development to occur in Kham was the eclectic (*rime*) movement, which united the Red Hat sects in a renaissance of aspiration and systematization in the nineteenth century. This movement is the most recent major development in Tibetan religious culture and it was still in full swing when it was cut off by the Chinese Communists.

The chief figure in this resurgence was Jamyang Khyentse Wangpo of Lhundrub Teng Gompa in Derge. He was an initiate of both Nyingma and Sakya lineages. His brilliant disciple Jamgon Kongtrul Lodro Thaye was responsible for gathering and editing both Sakya and Nyingma texts into important collections, saving them from inevitable loss. Choling Rimpoche was another participant of this non-sectarian Red Hat movement. Khyentse Chokyi Lodro and the late Dilgo Khyentse and lamas like Mipham Namgyel continued this development into the last generation.

The eclectic movement was effectively destroyed in its place of origin by the Cultural Revolution and the major beneficiaries were to be the Western students of the Eastern Tibetan lamas amongst the refugee community in India and Nepal.

# THE LATE TWENTIETH CENTURY

The Thirteenth Dalai Lama proclaimed his country's independence and after the ousting of Chinese troops from Lhasa, had turned his own troops on the conservative gompas that had supported the Chinese. But his attempts at modernization were foiled by the continuing strength of isolationist and traditionalist sentiment, and it is probable that in the end he died of poison administered by his unyielding enemies. With his death in 1933, at the early age of 57, Tibet's opportunity to enter the world stage as an independent political and cultural entity was lost.

Although British influence in Lhasa was consolidated by a series of sympathetic and able Residents, the regency of the young Reteng Rimpoche merely sustained the status quo. When Reteng resigned to return to spiritual retreat, a successful conspiracy led to his death in prison and thereafter no strong or even competent hand was available to defend Tibet against the Communist invasion that followed the defeat of the Chinese Republic. With British withdrawal from India in 1947, Tibet lost its only friend. In 1951 an unfortunate choice of general led to the surrender of the flower of the Tibetan army at an unassailable position near Chamdo in western Kham, and the People's Liberation Army, at the height of its power and self-confidence, flooded across the Tibetan plateau, seeking to consolidate Chinese territory at the greatest extent of the Manchu empire. An indication of the confusion existing in Lhasa at the time of invasion was the directive of the State Oracle to install the 15-year-old Fourteenth Dalai Lama as head of government.

By 1959 Tibetan indignation at the humiliation suffered during eight years of Chinese rule led to a spontaneous popular revolt known as the Lhasa Uprising. In the wake of its failure, the Dalai Lama fled to India and the 100,000 Tibetans who followed him were reduced to the pitiful status of refugees.

The merciless suppression of the Lhasa Uprising by Chinese artillery positioned on the flanks of the Lhasa valley was merely a foretaste of the suffering that Tibet was to endure in the following 15 years. Tibet was reconstituted as the Tibetan Autonomous Region (TAR), theoretically with some independence but in practice under the heel of the Chinese military. Of the remainder of the Tibetan ethnic region, the eastern part of Kham became an autonomous prefecture of Sichuan province while north-eastern Tibet, including Amdo, became Qinghai province. In all Tibetan areas the gompas were forcibly dissolved and agriculture was communalized. Later, with the advent of the Red Guards, with the exception of monuments of historical importance specifically named by Prime Minister Chou En-Lai, every defensible building in Central Tibet, most religious buildings and most structures with more than two storeys were destroyed. Dissenters against Maoist thought were executed, imprisoned or brainwashed by means of the infamous *tamzin* system, as indeed was the case throughout China. Artificially aggravated famine, loss of menfolk to enforced labour camps and the futile attempt at Mao's order to turn grazing land into arable fields and to replace barley and wheat with rice cultivation led to widespread death from starvation in the villages,

The south flank of Kang Rimpoche: Asia's most sacred mountain at daybreak.
*Brian Beresford*

The north flank of Kang Rimpoche with the Jampelyang and Chenrezik hills from Driruphuk.
*Brian Beresford*

Amnye Machen: The great massif in Amdo province. *Katia Buffetrille*

Amnye Machen: Mural of the Machen Pomra Palace mandala in Guru Gompa.
*Katia Buffetrille*

Nangchen Thanglha and Namtso lake with Tashi Do bodhisattva rock. *Katia Buffetrille*

The Guru Rimpoche cave and lhakhang at Tashido, Namtso lake. *Ahmano*

The Guru Rimpoche image of
Nedong on the Tenth Day
walkabout. *Ahmano*

The head of the 'talking' Shelkar
Guru Rimpoche. *Ahmano*

Ceiling painting of the Five Buddha-Deity Demchok mandala. *Ahmano*

Mural of Korlo Demchok in the south of the mandala, Demchok Mandala Lhakhang, Tsaparang. *Brian Beresford*

An Amdo dakini prostrating at Tsurphu Gompa. *Mani Lama*

A Khampa devotee performing endless prostration around the Lhasa Jokhang Barkhor. *Keith Dowman*

Yogi with thighbone horn and monkey drum in Kham. *Thomas L. Kelly*

conditions unprecedented in Tibetan history. Guerrilla activity throughout Tibet, chiefly waged by the Chuzhi Kangdruk, proud individualistic Khampa warriors, kept Tibetan nationalism alive but provoked the Chinese to even harsher policies of repression.

Relief, indeed reprieve, came with the death of Mao, the disgrace of the Gang of Four and liberalization under the relatively liberal leadership of Deng Zhao Ping. In the 1980s, although there were no Tibetans in important decision-making positions in Lhasa, the Tibetan Communist cadres in the valleys were often generous nationalistic Tibetans intent upon developing the country economically. These officials have overseen the reconstruction or restoration of some structures in many gompas, financed by small grants from the central government and by donations from overseas, and supported by the free labour of the villagers. In the process of liberalization, communes were given the choice of dissolution and return of property to the families of the original owners or maintenance of the status quo. It is indicative of Tibetan conservatism and the rigid hold that the Communists had achieved in Tibet that a small proportion of the communes chose to maintain the status quo, like the commune at Sakya in Tsang, where reactionary Maoist cadres continue to impede implementation of religious freedoms.

In the 1990s, at the close of the era of Deng Zhao Ping, the Tibet freedom movement, focusing on the person of the Fourteenth Dalai Lama, with wide sympathy in the West and backed to some degree by European and American governments, is applying pressure upon an intractable Chinese government to give Tibet its political freedom, or at least to allow the real autonomy that the Chinese constitution provides. The effect of this pressure has been to impede the process of political and religious redevelopment in the TAR that is permitted under the new rules. Redevelopment is well advanced in the Han heartland and also in the Tibetan areas of Sichuan and Qinghai. Geluk gompas associated with the Dalai Lama, however, have been particularly repressed and monks and nuns showing the least support for their spiritual leader are imprisoned. The numbers of young boys entering the gompas for a Buddhist education are severely restricted. What is most pernicious in the political, economic and religious destiny of the Tibetan people is the influx of

Han into the TAR, which has made Lhasa a Chinese city and the Tibetans a minority in their own country.

So has ended the dream of a Buddhist Tibet guided by pure monastic exemplars. It may be argued that theocracy – the union of spiritual and temporal powers – is an attempt to marry good with evil and can never be successful in governing human affairs. It could be claimed that centralization, while expediting political goals, has a long-term negative effect on the spirit of the people of the marginalized provinces. Was it pride that motivated the conversion of the Mongols? Was it pure Machiavellian thinking that led the Great Fifth Dalai Lama to promote the Mongol invasion of Tibet to crush the Red Hat opposition? Does the atrophy of the great Geluk gompas – Ganden, Sera and Ganden – by the twentieth century prove the superiority of decentralized, smaller monastic institutions with no political axes to grind? What happened to the teaching of Atisha and Tsongkhapa? The examples of Guru Rimpoche and Milarepa have certainly long been excised from the body politic. How did the gouging of eyes, stretching on the rack and other medieval methods of torture, even within the precincts of the Dalai Lamas' most hallowed power place, the Potala Palace itself, relate to the theocratic ethic? But perhaps in the time of moral and spiritual degeneration, the kaliyuga, no political system, not even theocracy, is adequate to expedite the Buddha's enlightenment in all sentient beings.

# PART THREE

# Art and Icons

# SACRED ART

Tibetan art is almost entirely religious in form and meaning. The mystic realm of buddha-vision is described in shapes and symbols which provide the motifs for religious artefacts and domestic decoration. Houses are decorated with religious symbols and furniture is painted with designs that have religious meaning. It is difficult to find examples of secular art, except sometimes in carpets and textiles whose designs originated in China and also, these days, in paintings and prints representing Communist subjects.

In the gompa compound the decoration and ornamentation are designed to support religious practice by presenting to the mind an image or symbol of the Buddhist tradition. The architecture of the gompa buildings and chortens all has symbolic significance. But in the lhakhang, the house of the gods, an entire range of the best and most sacred of Tibetan fine art is displayed. The walls are covered with murals of the pantheon of lamas, Buddhas, bodhisattvas and protecting deities, all in their buddhafields, with depictions of offerings above and below. Sometimes the walls are covered with murals of mandalas. Hanging on the walls are painted scrolls, *thangkas*, of cotton or silk, depicting the same subjects framed in brocade. Sometimes the thangkas themselves are woven in brocade, or in the *kosu* weaving technique, or done in appliqué.

On the altar, the focus of the lhakhang, are sculptured symbols of the Buddha and other power objects. The large buddha-images may be clay sculptures with a wooden frame within, or part repoussé and part cast bronze. The smaller images will be bronzes cast in the lost wax (*cire perdue*) technique. Sculpted wooden images are rarely found on the altar. If there are large reliquary chortens there then their ornamentation will be done in repoussé and the jeweller's art will be evident in the inlaid semi-precious stones. The small chortens will be done in cast bronze. The art of the metal carver is demonstrated not only in the finishing work on the bronzes but also in the power objects such as dorjes and ritual daggers that are carved out of blocks of iron, sometimes meteoric iron.

All these paintings and sculptures were made to last. But there are other works of art no less striking and no less demanding in their execution. These are the butter and tsampa sculptures. These temporary forms, sculpted with the hands, are either made entirely of butter or of a dough of roasted barley flour mixed with molasses and butter. They are called *tormas* and although most are thrown out of the lhakhang as offerings to humans, animals and spirits during the ritual in which they are employed, those that depict buddha-deities may remain until they begin to fall apart. Another form of temporary art is the sand-mandala, created by sprinkling sands and chalks of various colours down a narrow tubè onto a large outline done in chalk.

Behind the altar, or perhaps to its sides, are the texts of the Buddhist canon. These texts, with the carved wood of their covers showing Buddhas and bodhisattvas in relief, the sheets of rice paper frequently covered in blue paint (lapis lazuli or indigo), the wood blocks carved with the orthography in reverse from which the texts are printed, the painted illumination of the most valued texts, and the printing itself, are entirely works of art. Other art forms made of wood are the masks used in the lama dances, but these will be usually hidden away in a store room.

Stone sculptures are rarely to be found in the lhakhang. The stone sculptor's art is revealed, however, on the paths for circumambulation as relief rock carving of images or sacred syllables, or in the round in the images in caves. The quality of this carving is such that the credulous devotees can imagine only that it was the work of the gods, or perhaps that it manifested spontaneously out of the rock as an image of natural perfection produced by the pure inborn buddha-quality of the natural world.

In shrines in the wilderness the art of the woodblock carver is also demonstrated by the designs on the cotton prayer-flags. Woodblock prints of Buddhas and protecting deities are also found in the amulets hanging or tied to the bodies of devotees, together with their mandalas printed on rice paper.

Art is not sacred by virtue of its quality but of its content. So the decorative ornamentation of buildings, furniture, carpets and so on is religious in nature but not sacred in the sense that representations of the Buddhas, texts and all chortens and their images are sacred. Buddha-images and power objects, scriptural texts and chortens are sacred in so far as there is no distinction between the work of art and the reality it symbolizes. Sanctity is added by formal rites of consecration in which sculptures in particular are filled with sacred substances and written mantras, and paintings are blessed by the mantric syllables written on their reverse side. Informally, a living Buddha's blessing is particularly effective in endowing an object with his meditative vibrations. These can then be transmitted to the devotee who worships it. All such works of art, therefore, are to be worshipped by prostration, by bowing and touching them with the forehead or by making offering.

For the lay devotee and the non-initiate, images of the Buddhas are a source of blessing and a support to their devotion. For the tantric practitioner, they have a special function. In the creative phase of his meditation the yogi practises the invocation of the Buddhas through visualization, and in the early stages of that practice sculptured images and paintings can provide models for visualization. Although the Buddhas are represented in human form, the images are a constellation of symbols that have the power to evoke buddha-attributes in the yogi's mind. Thus the complete image is a symbol of an archetypal deity, and the mood, the posture and gesture, the ornamentation and clothing, and the symbols the Buddha holds in his hands all support the creation of a mind-state, a samadhi, in which the yogi is identified with the buddha-archetype. The individual manual tokens that the Buddha holds are symbols that in their own right have the power to evoke their deep meaning: the dorje, for example, evokes the immutability of empty awareness, and the sword the power of radiant awareness to cut through obstructions on the path of meditation. The proportions of the buddha-figures are created according to the Buddhist canon of aesthetics to approximate an ideal form that can arise spontaneously in the mind of an adept in his realization of the buddha-nature. Colour is also symbolic and there can be no deviation from the conventional code. In the latter stages of the yogi's practice, once the visualization arises easily and completely, there is no difference between the external representation and the actual inner mindform which is the reality of the buddha-deity. Thus the art form is no longer a two or three-dimensional design of form and colour, but a reflection of buddha-mind, an ideal state of enlightenment.

In so far as a painting, for example, is a support to meditation, the nature of the entire composition, and each motif in the picture and, each line and colour, is the result of 1,000 years of practice in creating the ideal buddha-image. For this reason there is very little room for imagination in Tibetan art. The buddha-representations are technical blueprints to be used by the yogi in designing his own mind-state. The artist has very little latitude for imaginative innovation and self-expression. By intruding his own personal inspiration into the art he may even create obstacles for the yogi seeking the impersonal instruction of generations of adepts who have refined the blueprint. The quality of Tibetan art is to be judged first by the degree to which the artist has followed the traditional strictures of his craft and only as a secondary afterthought by the quality of his inspirational treatment of the details of his composition. Of course, it is the latter that excites the untutored Western eye.

## ICONOGRAPHY

The Tibetan Buddhist pantheon is vast and impossible to list here in its entirety. So there follows a description of the most common forms that the pilgrim will see on the lhakhang walls and on the altars of the power places.

### SHAKYAMUNI, GAUTAMA BUDDHA

The Buddha of the present aeon who taught in central India does not have the primary place of worship in the lhakhangs that one would expect. His place was superseded by subsequent adepts, or Second Buddhas, whose tantric teachings were more relevant to the religious climate of Tibet. However, the depiction of Shakyamuni's '12 acts' form a common theme for lhakhang murals.

### THE 16 NETEN OR ARHATS

These are the formalized group of Shakyamuni's disciples who attained the ultimate realization of the original teacher's meditative goal. The cult of these 16 or 18 neten or arhats came from China at the beginning of the second dissemination of Buddhism in Tibet. The two extra arhats are the Chinese Dzokchen master Hwashang Mahayana and the travelling scholar Dharmatala. In the portrayal of these Indian saints in murals or sculpture Chinese Taoist influence is usually evident.

## THE TRIAD OF PAST, PRESENT AND FUTURE BUDDHAS

These are a common adornment in sculpture in the centre of lhakhang altars. On the left is the Buddha of the previous aeon, Dipankara, who shows the gesture of protection. In the middle is Shakyamuni, who shows the earth-touching gesture to demonstrate his enlightenment under the bodhi-tree in Bodhgaya. On the right is Jampa, the Buddha who will teach in the next aeon, showing the gesture of teaching. All are in lotus posture.

## LAMAS AND ADEPTS

In tantric Buddhism, the lama is held to be the first object of refuge, before the Buddha, his teaching and the community of bodhisattvas, because without his kindness in bestowing initiation, instruction and blessing, the door to the path of liberation remains closed. The first lama of the lineage and one's own personal teacher are held in particular veneration and identified as Buddhas. Guru Rimpoche Padmasambhava, Jetsun Milarepa, Je Tsongkhapa, Kunkhyen Longchenpa and others are Second Buddhas.

Guru Rimpoche, Tibet's Great Guru, is especially venerated and his image is invariably found on the altars of the Red Hat order, in clay, in repoussé or cast bronze. Je Tsongkhapa is likewise always portrayed on the altars of the Geluk order, as was the Dalai Lama until politics intervened.

The founding lamas of the various orders are very frequently depicted in murals with their principal disciples, creating triptychs. Guru Rimpoche is flanked by the abbot Shantarakshita and the king Trisong Detsen, or by his two consorts; Tsongkhapa with Khedrub Je and Gyeltseb Je. Guru Rimpoche is always unmistakable with his hat of victory with an eagle feather stuck in the top, his heavy Tibetan robes, his trident (*katvanga*) in the crook of his arm, representing his female consort, holding dorje and skullbowl, and with one leg extended. The five great Sakya lamas are often portrayed in a group. Early in their history the Sakya order initiated a tradition of portraiture when depicting their lamas in sculpture or paint which adds greatly to Western appreciation.

The identification and character of the lineal lamas are usually shown iconographically or by a single stylized characteristic like a beard or a gesture. The word 'lama' means teacher and priest, and although the lama is usually a monk wearing the robes of his order, perhaps holding a book in his scholarly hand, he may also be a yogi, an adept wearing the cotton cloth of the renunciate with his hair in dreadlocks.

## THE ADIBUDDHAS

The adibuddhas are the first, the original, the primal Buddhas, who are identified with the founding lamas of the lineages. Kuntuzangpo (Samantabhadra), the All-Good Buddha, naked, blue, is the adibuddha of the Nyingmapas. Dorje Chang (Vajradhara), the blue Buddha holding dorje and bell in arms crossed over his heart, is the adibuddha of the other orders. Dorje Sempa (Vajrasattva) is a representation of the visionary aspect of the guru-lama and while Kuntuzangpo and Dorje Chang always sit at the top of the depictions of the 'lineage tree', Dorje Sempa, white, holding dorje and bell, the ritual instruments of all tantric lamas, will sit below them.

## THE FIVE BUDDHAS

Nampar Nangdze (Vairochana), Mikyopa (Akshobhya), Rinchen Jungne (Ratnasambhava), Wopakme (Amitabha) and Donyo Drubpa (Amoghasiddhi) have been described as the basis of all mandalas (see p.33). Their importance cannot be exaggerated. But except in tantric mandalas the five are rarely portrayed in their seminal form of unornamented Buddhas. Rather, they are displayed in their visionary bodies, arrayed with silks and ornaments, like bodhisattvas, and here they are called *tathagatas*. In this form they are shown seated in their pure-lands and are to be recognized first by their colour and secondly by their gesture. They are to be seen frequently on lhakhang walls.

The three great spiritual bodhisattvas of Indian Buddhism were brought together in Tibet to form a protective triad. These bodhisattvas are Chenrezik (Avalokiteshvara), Jampelyang (Manjushri) and Chakna Dorje (Vajrapani), who protect speech, mind and body respectively. Their three forms, the first two peaceful and the third wrathful, are common subjects of relief sculpture in rock, mural painting and bronze sculpture.

Here is a list of the bodhisattvas most often encountered in Tibetan art:

*Chenrezik*, 'He who gazes upon the suffering of the world with tears in his eyes', is certainly the most common representation in Tibetan art. He is the bodhisattva of compassion and not only the protector of buddha-speech but also the primary protector of the Land of the Snows. He is most usually portrayed in lotus posture with four arms, the upper right holding a rosary, the upper left holding a lotus and the lower two in prayer gesture holding a wish-fulfilling gem at his heart. He is the image of compassion. Another common form is the Eleven-Headed Chenrezik, the Great Compassionate One, who stands with his thousand arms in a circle around him and his heads piled up on top. This form represents the multiple skilful means that the bodhisattva employs in his work of assisting all sentient beings.

*Jampelyang*, Sweet Voice, is the bodhisattva of wisdom, wielding aloft in his right hand the sword of pure awareness with which he destroys the darkness of ignorance. He is the patron of learning, which makes him popular with schoolchildren, and muse of the arts, which makes him popular with all artists.

*Chakna Dorje*, Dorje-in-Hand, is the prototype of all wrathful deities. He stands with his pot-belly protruding, one leg aggressively outstretched and bent, the other rigidly retiring, his face a mask of anger and belligerence, his hair piled wildly on top of his head, wearing a tigerskin around his waist. This representation of the buddha-dynamic, unconstrained energy and one-pointed concentration upon the transformation of emotional poisons and thought-patterns into buddha-awareness protects from sickness and also from hostile spirits.

*Jampa*, Maitreya, is the Future Buddha, and as such he has the attributes and form of a Buddha. But until his coming to earth he is also a bodhisattva, a Buddha-to-be, the bodhisattva of loving kindness, and here he sits in Western style, his feet on the ground, his hands in the gesture of teaching. Colossal images of this bodhisattva are common, particularly in Geluk gompas.

*Drolma*, Arya Tara, the Saviouress, the bodhisattva of devotion and service, is the principal female example on the bodhisattva path, and is almost as commonly depicted as Chenrezik. She appears in two forms, in two colours. The White Drolma, seated in lotus posture, holding a lotus in her right hand, is the passive, contemplative saviouress, while the Green Drolma, one leg extended for swift response, holding an identical lotus, is the active form of this female role model. She is a common subject for bronze sculpture and can also be seen everywhere in rock, paint and stone.

BUDDHA-DEITIES AND MANDALAS

The buddha-deities (yidams) are representations of the dynamic enlightened mind as described in the tantric texts and as such are usually to be kept from the eyes of the uninitiated. Each of the tantras focuses upon a different buddha-deity in the centre of his or her mandala, which usually gives the tantra its name, like Dukhor (Kalachakra), the Wheel of Time; Demchok (Samvara), Supreme Bliss; and Dorje Phurba (Vajrakilaya), the Indestructible Dagger. For reasons of secrecy, these deities, the most complex and symbolically varied in the pantheon, are rarely depicted singly in their glorious power forms as murals, although they can be seen in miniature in the centre of their complex mandalas on lhakhang walls. As support to his meditation the individual yogi may possess a thangka or a bronze of his personal buddha-deity and thangkas and bronzes are sometimes displayed in the lhakhangs. The buddha-deities are usually depicted in sexual union with their consorts (*yabyum*) and this overt sexual show is another reason for their veiled display, for young monks may be sexually aroused and the uninitiated, monks or laymen, may misconstrue the symbolism. The union of male and female Buddhas here describes the indissoluble union of perfect insight and compassion, and has only an indirect link to mundane sexual congress.

The mandala murals that form the wall decoration in many lhakhangs usually depict a cycle of mandalas revolving around a particular deity. A central mandala will show the buddha-deity himself and the remainder will show subsidiary circles of his retinue, sky dancers or protectors *(see below)*, for instance. In order fully to appreciate these works of art, which often show the climax of an artist devotee's technical mastery, some knowledge of the symbology of the mandala frame and also the retinue of the deity is required. In this way the esoteric significance of this art is kept hidden.

### THE KHANDROMAS, DAKINIS, SKY DANCERS

The Khandromas are female Buddhas, and while they are the equal partners and consorts of the buddha-deities, they constitute a separate class of Buddha in which the female element is distinct. The consort of Demchok, for example, is Dorje Phakmo and the union of these two buddha-deities represents the holistic totality of buddha-mind. But standing alone, Dorje Phakmo represents the totality in terms of its constantly transforming illusory reality. She is the source of empowerment and initiation, she is the yogi's muse, inspiration and guide on the path, and she is also a fearsome protectress. She stands in dancing posture, one leg bent and one raised to her crotch. She holds a skullbowl to her heart and wields a hooked knife in her raised right hand. Her skin is red and she is adorned only in silks. Apart from the sow's head extruding from her skull, this is the archetypal form of the Khandroma Dorje Neljorma (Vajra Yogini), recognized by all orders and tantras, but there are many variations in iconography. Like the buddha-deities her representations are secret, mainly employed in the form of thangkas and bronzes by the yogis who aspire to a spiritual union with her. But she can also be seen in murals on the lhakhang walls.

### THE 100 PEACEFUL AND WRATHFUL DEITIES

These deities of the Nyingma order constitute a pantheon including all the elements of an entire hierarchical order. In the murals and thangkas that depict them, Kuntuzangpo, the All-Good adibuddha, sits at the apex, above Dorje Sempa. Bodhisattvas and lineal lamas are shown on the sides. Mandalas of the Five Buddhas constitute the peaceful deities, and mandalas of their five wrathful emanations show the buddha-deities. The Khandromas stand below; the protectors of the tradition are below and to the sides. Circles of the peripheral retinues of the wrathful deities show these beings to be spirits of the mythic realm, some with animal or bird heads. The 100 peaceful and wrathful deities are the manifestations of mind that appear to consciousness in the intermediate state between dying and rebirth.

## CHOKYONG: PROTECTORS OF THE TRADITION`

The protectors are a rich and variegated group of gods and demigods who have been commandeered by the yogis to be guardians of the gompas, their treasuries, monastic communities and particularly the buddha-dharma. Iconographically, they are very similar to the wrathful deities – indeed, some of them are taken as buddha-deities for meditation purposes – but close examination reveals that their proportions are different. They are slightly dwarfish, smaller than the wrathful deities. They are usually angry, showing belligerent mask-like faces, but sometimes they are armed warriors with peaceful faces and sometimes they are positively seductive.

The place of power where these protecting deities are invoked and propitiated is the *gomkhang*, a secret, dark and sinister chamber, usually forbidden to the casual visitor to the gompa and full of sculptures, murals and power tokens of these dark lords, but their forms are also found on the murals on the gompa walls. In murals and thangkas the protectors are frequently depicted in a golden line on a black background. They are portrayed in many different ways and only the common forms are described below.

*The Four Guardian Kings* guard the gates of a mandala as they guard the four directions of a lhakhang. They are Mongol in origin, as their dress and armour reveal, and must have originated as Buddhist protectors after the invasion of Genghis Khan. Painted in Chinese style, they hold sword, victory banner, lute and chorten. They are found in the vestibule of virtually every gompa lhakhang.

*Gompo Chenpo*, Mahakala, the Great Black One, is one of the great all-purpose protectors, most fierce and all-powerful. His representation, usually Chakdrukpa, the Six-Armed One, although there are many variations upon the theme, is found at the back of most Sakya, Kagyu and Geluk lhakhangs, lurking in the dark, the gilded elements providing a fearsome outline, intimating the impotency of the enemies of the tradition in the face of such enlightened righteous wrath.

*Pelden Lhamo*, Shri Devi, the Protecting Mother Goddess, with her roots in the all-powerful Indian goddess Durga Devi, is the great female protectress of the Geluk order and the state, and also the Kagyu and Sakya orders. She is a nightmare hag, naked, wielding a sword and a human heart, riding a galloping mule with an eye on its rump, a die tied to her saddle.

*The Dzokchen protectors* are Relchikma (Ekajata), who is a one-eyed, one-breasted hag protectress, aggressive, her face frozen in a mask of wrath; Dorje Lekpa (Vajrasadhu), riding a snowlion, wearing a broad-brimmed Mongol hat, who was a vow-breaking layman bound to serve the buddha-dharma; and Rahula, the naga-serpent lord, who arises out of a triangular box in a whirl of serpentine fury, a face in his stomach and heads piled on his shoulders, eyes in his arms and a crow of ill-omen in his hair.

## A HISTORY OF STYLE

Tibetan art has its own unmistakably Tibetan style, but the best way to analyse it is through the outside influences that produced it.

The Tibetans have never been a people who have invested aspiration and energy into refining a rich sensual culture, and their artists were never given social status higher than craftsman. Besides, the painters seeking the mineral constituents of some of their pigments and the bronze casters working in metal had to pay a high price to the spirit-guardians of the earth. Also, the Tibetan nomadic tradition stood in the way of a developed culture of fine art, for artefacts had to be constantly transported by yak.

The arts of painting and bronze-casting arrived in Tibet with the Indian Buddhist tradition that required that religious practitioners possess representations of the Buddhas for worship. During the first period of dissemination of Buddhism in Tibet, the empire period (600–850), the stylistic influences came from the Kathmandu Valley, from the north Indian plains, from Kashmir, from Khotan and the silk route, from Sassania in the west and finally from China. During this period, and through successive periods, all these regions were to provide elements that, fired in the crucible of Tibetan religious culture, produced Tibetan style. During the empire period, the Kathmandu Valley, then in the throes of its magnificent Licchavi period of artistic achievement, particularly in sculpture, was the strongest influence on Tibetan bronze casters, although there are only a few examples to demonstrate it. The wood-carving on the lintels of the Lhasa Jokhang indicates that Newar craftsmen from the Kathmandu Valley were called to work there.

The Lhasa Jokhang, Trandruk Gompa in Yarlung, Samye Chokhor and the Kachu Gompa in the Won Valley were all founded in the empire period and all have structural elements dating from that time. Kachu is most remarkable for its wonderful clay buddha-image that is believed to date from an influx of Khotanese refugees in the eighth century and to demonstrate Khotanese influence.

In the second period of dissemination of Buddhism in Tibet, the early monastic period (1000–1250), different influences worked on different regions of the country. In the west, in the kingdom of Guge, in Spiti and Ladakh, the primary influence was from the great Buddhist culture of Kashmir, with a secondary influence from Khotan and the silk route oasis states. The so-called Rinchen Zangpo temples, named after the Tibetan who travelled to Kashmir for his Buddhist education and who had these temples built upon his return, notably at Alchi and Lama Yuru in Ladakh, and Tabo and Tholing in the Guge kingdom, date from this period. Most likely the murals of these lhakhangs were painted under the direction of Kashmiri master painters guiding journeyman artists from Kashmir and the silk route states and local artists. The overall concept and style were Kashmiri, but other influences were also assimilated, so that the result is unique to these temples.

The masterwork of the Rinchen Zangpo temples is reflected in the cave lhakhang at Dungkar, north of Tsaparang, in the old Guge kingdom. This great domed grotto, decorated with the Nampar Nangdze (Vairochana) mandala, probably dating from the eleventh century, has murals dominated by the Kashmiri style. But there are unmistakable elements of Khotanese style and motif here that are evocative of the Buddhist mural remnants from the oases of the silk route. Perhaps they were introduced by journeymen or refugee artists from Central Asia.

There may be further examples of early monastic period painting of the Dungkar variety in undiscovered caves in Western Tibet, but nothing else is left to illustrate the Western Tibetan mural style except the monastery lhakhangs of the Tsaparang fortress, the castle of the Guge kings. The murals of the White and Red Lhakhangs at the base of the fortress were painted in the fifteenth century and the Mandala and Yidam Lhakhangs within the fortress in the sixteenth century. All illustrate how the artists of Guge fully assimilated foreign elements to produce an indigenous style of undeniable power and beauty. These murals are some of Tibet's greatest artistic treasures.

Western Tibetan bronzes began in the early monastic period as crude copies of Kashmiri originals, but in the late monastic period (1250–1650) ateliers evolved a separate style and were capable of producing finely cast, wafer-thin bronzes with copper and silver inlay in the eyes, lips and nails. These beautiful bronzes continued to be made into the sixteenth century, but thereafter the tradition declined along with the religious culture of Western Tibet.

During the early monastic period in Central Tibet, the principal influence extended from eastern India, Bangala, where the patronage of the Pala dynasty had caused a flowering of Buddhist tantric art. Bangala and the Kathmandu Valley were the destinations of aspiring Tibetan monks and yogis who sought instruction from the Indian masters, and close ties were developed with these regions. Certainly these students and pilgrims brought back bronze images that could be used as models for indigenous Tibetan artists, and although no Indian thangkas exist – and it is uncertain even that this form of painting was ever undertaken in India – Indian Pala painting styles were certainly known at this time. Whereas the bronzes of the period had a strong Indian stylistic bent, however, the thangkas, which are most of what remains of the painting, are characterized by inseparably entangled elements of Bangala and Kathmandu Valley style. Great thangka masterpieces were painted during this period of brilliant cultural outpouring and were preserved in the gompa treasuries until the Cultural Revolution.

There may have been Indian artists working in Tibet throughout this period, along with the Newars from Kathmandu, who had much easier access along the trade routes from Nepal to Central Tibet. But the two sites that provide the only remaining evidence of clay statuary and murals from that time indicate that the style of Kashmir and the silk route states still wielded a significant influence, although those lands had all been invaded and their Buddhist culture destroyed by the Muslims. A mixture of strong Indian Pala influence with Kashmiri and silk route style is shown at Yemar (Iwang), where three unroofed lhakhangs remain, their clay statues left desperately open to the weather. The murals from this period are confined to some extraordinary paintings in the Drathang Gompa in the Yarlung Tsangpo valley. The well-preserved murals on either side of the space where the central Buddha sat in the lhakhang show the same strong Kashmiri and Khotanese influence.

By the late monastic period, when the building of the great home gompas of the newly founded Kagyu and Sakya orders reached its height, Buddhist Bangala was no more, the silk route was Islamified and Tibetan art was increasingly dominated by the Newars from the Kathmandu Valley. It was during this time that a brilliant Newar artist called Aniko was invited to Sakya to paint murals. He so impressed the great Sakya lama Phakpa that he took him to Peking, to the court of Kubilai Khan. It appears that Aniko established a brilliant atelier of Newar/Chinese art there, attended by Tibetans. These artists later returned from Peking to Tibet and established the first truly Tibetan school of art. Their early product can be seen in the murals of Zhalu Gompa, near Shigatse. The mature work of this school, done 100 years later, is preserved on the walls of the Gyantse Kumbum and Tsuklakhang. The murals of Riwoche Kumbum in western Tsang, the only major *kumbum* chorten besides Gyantse to escape destruction at the hands of the Communists, show a rough local development of this style *(see also p.255)*. In parallel to this, after the strong Indic influence on bronze casting of the early period, by the fifteenth century Tibetan sculpture had assimilated the Newar/Chinese style of the Yuan dynasty to produce a powerful home-grown Central Tibetan style.

With the political ascendancy of the Geluk order in the seventeenth century and the consequent loss of artistic patronage in the Red Hat gompas, a new style of painting came to dominate Central Tibet. In the theocratic period (1650–1959) the Newar influence was minimal, although workshops in Kathmandu and Patan continued to turn out large quantities of bronzes and paintings for the pilgrim market. The style that typifies this period is the Chinese-influenced Khyenri/Menri style. The roots of this style go back to the fifteenth-century masters Menthangpa Menla Dondrub and Khyentse Chenmo. In the seventeenth century a master called Choying Gyatso further developed the same stylistic tendencies and his school became known as the New Menri school. The Khyenri/Menri style is to be seen at its best in the great Geluk gompas of Drepung, Sera and Tashi Lhunpo, in the Potala and also at Samye. Later developments produced the ubiquitous style found in most lhakhangs painted during the last 300 years. Khyenri/Menri murals and thangkas are characterized by Chinese facial features of the Buddhas, by a landscape environment, and thus a larger spatial concept providing greater depth, and by the dominance of green in the palette. In general, Khyenri/Menri is considered by Western critics to lack the creative flair of both early and late monastic periods. The same applies to the later bronze sculpture, which was a sorry continuation of the Central Tibetan tradition that was firmly established by the seventeenth century. This is not to say, however, that Tibetan artists have produced nothing of mastery during the theocratic period.

The artistic tradition of Eastern Tibet has been influenced primarily by Chinese style. But the earliest form of sculpture, rock carving dating back to the empire period, shows Indian and Kathmandu Valley influence besides the Chinese. Bronze casting is strongly Chinese influenced, but the various ateliers and styles are difficult to identify. Some of the gompas of Kham are as old as those of Central Tibet, but the murals, almost without exception, have been destroyed. What remains are the thangkas, frequently painted in the distinctive Eastern Tibetan style called Karma Gardri. This easily recognizable style originated in the sixteenth century and was associated with the travelling court of the Karmapas. Contrary to the Newar and Indian influenced styles that cover every square inch of the canvas with decoration, Karma Gardri painting leaves the subjects, Buddhas or lamas, hanging on the canvas, giving a transcendental sense of space and light.

The doctrine of revealed treasure can shed some light on the creative process of the Tibetan artist. Revealed treasure consists primarily of treasure texts, but it also includes *objets d'art*, clay and bronze images, wood carvings and power objects. It may be that such objects jumped spontaneously out of the dynamic space of clear light, but another way to say it is that they are the works of yogi-artists inspired by a spiritual identification with the image they were creating. Such images are also called *thongdrol* objects, those that can produce liberation from the wheel of rebirth merely by the devotee setting his eyes upon them. Precisely prescribed form and immaculate execution combine to produce an image of the Buddha that has an automatic effect of liberation on the mind. Such inspiration is evident in individual works throughout Tibetan art history.

A very large proportion of Tibetan art, particularly bronzes and thangkas, was destroyed, of course, along with the gompas, during the Cultural Revolution. Another significant proportion was carted to China by the Communists or looted by the Red Guards. Some bronzes and thangkas were officially garnered from all sources to become collections in the museum gompas, particularly Tashi Lhunpo and the Potala. Some were carefully hidden from the despoilers and, like revealed treasure, have been unearthed recently to adorn local gompas. The walls of most gompa lhakhangs that were not destroyed display some remnants of Khyenri/Menri style murals. But apart from the artefacts that are now found in the gompas or were stolen by the Chinese, a significant but small proportion of the hundreds of thousands of objects that once filled the gompas have found their way to Western museums, private collections and Buddhist altars. Although Tibetans are forbidden by the lore of the lamas to trade in sacred art and icons, in this difficult political and economic period both laymen and monks have found it propitious to exchange power objects for the hard cash that can feed their families or restore their gompas. Meanwhile, as the Dalai Lama has said, the West gains the privilege of possessing these objects of power and benefiting from their presence while preserving them in a manner that is impossible in Tibet today.

Since the rehabilitation of Buddhism in the 1980s, restored gompa lhakhangs have, to some extent, been repainted, and rebuilt lhakhangs freshly painted. Some of the artists are Chinese, sent from Peking or Chengdu for the purpose, some are native Tibetans, some refugee Tibetans returned and some Bhutanese. The style is in general Khyenri/Menri and the quality of the work is highly variable. Frequently good faded or damaged original work has been covered by indifferent new work. Concerning metal sculpture, to the small quantity of old bronzes that have been returned from storage in China has been added the products of foundries in Chengdu and Shigatse and also commissions made by refugees in Patan, Nepal. Much of this work is at least as good as the creations of the theocratic period and is indistinguishable from it.

PART FOUR

# *The Yoga of Pilgrimage*

Pilgrimage as a yoga and a devotional exercise is as old as Buddhism itself. The pilgrim may be a layman intent on accumulating merit for a better rebirth, to obtain a mundane boon, to improve his luck or to expiate a sin. For him pilgrimage is still as much a part of his lifestyle as a summer holiday is in Europe, although he will leave his village or nomad encampment only when the cycle of agriculture or pastoral pursuits allows him. If he is a monk he may have come from the provinces to pay homage at the power places associated with the great lamas of his religious lineage and to obtain their blessings. If he is an itinerant yogi he may have taken constant peregrination from power place to power place as his path to buddhahood, or perhaps he moves from place to place meditating for a few weeks or months at each power place. Whatever the motivation, the physical exertion and the sensual feast that are an integral part of pilgrimage in Tibet can become the means of attaining the Buddha's enlightenment.

## BUDDHAHOOD

The karmically blessed, fully committed yogi will find a cave or hermitage and spend 12 years or more in a single place, practising the meditation his lama has prescribed to attain buddhahood, the Buddha's enlightenment. The renunciate lifestyle and one-pointed meditation of the yogi in his hermitage cave are considered the *summum bonum* of religious practice.

For the monk who is still at the stage of study and basic mind-training, developing physical and moral discipline in the monastery, full focus and uninterrupted concentration upon his agenda are required. The great Indian yogi Naropa disparaged 'simple fools who wander about the country from power place to power place'. For him pilgrimage was a devotion for people who cannot meditate in seclusion for their lifetime or practise the disciplined living of the ordained monk. But such opinions are surely directed to encourage

the aspiring yogi or monk to stay where he is and develop his meditation practice to the height of his potential.

The tradition of pilgrimage as a tantric yoga was founded in
India by the great adepts who sought buddhahood through the
techniques of Mahamudra. In their vision the great power places,
particularly the 24 places that were the abode of the buddha-deity
Demchok (Samvara), were the external geographical references of
the 24 focal points of energy in the subtle body of tantric yoga. The
energy of these points can be realized, and the direction of the energy flow through them reversed, by either internal meditation practice or by the external yoga of pilgrimage.

Examples show the effectiveness of pilgrimage. Jogipa was an
Indian tantric initiate with so little intellectual acumen that he was
unable to understand even the tantric precepts that his teacher gave
him and with such weak powers of concentration that he could not
sit still long enough to meditate. His teacher substituted pilgrimage
for meditation, instructing him to walk to the 24 great power places
while chanting the mantra of the buddha-deity Demchok. After 12
years of pilgrimage he had purified the defilements of his mind and
attained the state of buddhahood called Mahamudra. Another Indian adept, Udhalipa, attained magical powers through a yoga of pilgrimage. He was instructed to visit the 24 power places and to recite
the mantra of the resident dakini (sky dancer) of each place. After
collecting all the dakinis' elixirs, through an alchemical process of
assimilation he attained the ability to fly. Buddhahood is called 'the
ultimate achievement'. Attainment of magical powers is 'the relative
achievement'. The ability to fly in the sky, to walk through rock and
to run at incredible speeds over vast distances, together with knowledge of the language of animals and birds, the ability to read other
people's minds and so on, are some of the relative magical powers.

After buddhahood has been attained, pilgrimage becomes a
skilful means of benefiting other beings. Guru Rimpoche himself,
after demonstrating the way of tantric meditation practice while
wandering from power place to power place and finally attaining
the Buddha's enlightenment, spent the rest of his life on pilgrimage
in Tibet, a large part of it with his Tibetan consort, Yeshe Tsogyel,
meditating at the power places. This lifestyle became a paradigm of
practice for the Tibetan yogi who, after 12 years in a cave maturing

his meditation, wished to share the substance of his achievement and also for lamas who felt that the monastic environment, with its politics and intrigue, was not the best place to serve all sentient beings. Take Zhabkar Rimpoche, Tsokdruk Rangdrol, one of the most renowned lamas of the nineteenth century. Born in Amdo in 1781, he started young and at the age of 16 completed a year's retreat. Then he found his root teacher, whose meditation instructions he practised during eight years of solitary retreat, and he attained buddhahood. Thereafter, for more than 20 years, he was on constant pilgrimage from place to place, spending time in meditation at each of them and also teaching the buddha-dharma to whomever he could. Much of Zhabkar's pilgrimage took place in Central Tibet, the home of most of the lineages of Tibetan Buddhism, and in the high Himalayas where Milarepa and many other cave-dwelling yogis spent their lives.

In the early years of the twentieth century a lama from Riwoche Gompa in Kham, Kanjur Rimpoche, followed much the same agenda, emulating Zhabkar in his extended pilgrimage to the heartland. The great Khyentse Wangpo and Situ Rimpoche, scholarly types from Eastern Tibet who did pilgrimage to the famous power places of Central Tibet with large entourages, wrote guide books for use of Khampa and Amdowa pilgrims who visited Central Tibet with the same itineraries.

Since 1980 and the selective granting of permits to refugee lamas to return to Tibet, the tulkus have been strongly motivated to return to their home gompas and make pilgrimage to the power places associated with the great names of their tradition. The late Dilgo Khyentse, one of the teachers of the present Dalai Lama and of the Queen Mother of Bhutan, made three land-cruiser pilgrimages through Central Tibet in the 1980s in notable exhibitions of compassionate Buddha-like activity, bestowing blessings upon thousands of laymen and giving initiation and empowerment to those who were ready.

# LAY MOTIVATION

Realized yogis, though they may appear as beggars, and the high lamas, though they may appear as glorified mannequins, are on pilgrimage with intent to serve the Buddhist teaching and all sentient beings. What of the ordinary lay pilgrim of today, who is, perhaps, a Communist functionary or an illiterate nomad? First, if he is aware of the rudiments of the Buddhist doctrine, his intention will be to attain merit or to gain some specific spiritual advantage. Secondly, he may be travelling to power places to increase his luck or for some mundane boon.

The merit, *sonam*, that is sought in devotional activity, and pilgrimage in particular, is a peculiarly Buddhist concept. There is actually no precise equivalent of the Tibetan word in English. Sometimes it is simply translated as 'virtue', but there are better words in the Tibetan language for virtue. Merit is the product of positive or virtuous activity. The karmic effect of a virtuous action is to reinforce the tendency to repeat that action in the future; merit has this same tendency. The feeling that should arise in the wake of a virtuous action is a pleasurable glow of self-satisfaction; merit evokes this same feeling. But merit is also quantifiable. It accumulates like savings in an account in the karmic bank. The product of virtuous activity is credited to the account and negative or vicious activity results in a debit.

The 10 chief meritorious actions are: restraint from killing, thieving and inappropriate sexual activity; refraining from lying, worthless chatter, cursing and sowing discord; and suppression of covetousness, malice and opinionatedness. Committing such activity creates demerit. All kinds of devotional exercise create merit, especially offerings to the Buddha, the teaching and the community. Pilgrimage, as already noted, is a major merit generator.

Merit is invested primarily to ensure a better rebirth. The higher the karmic bank balance, the better the rebirth. A substantial balance guarantees a rebirth in the upper realms of the gods, the jealous gods or the human realm. A negative balance results in a low rebirth, in the realms of the animals, the hungry ghosts or the denizens of hell. A large store of merit at death is the result of a lifetime of prudent and careful living. For as soon as merit has been generated, the temptation will arise to exchange it for a consumer product – a mundane boon, a guarantee of certain success in any enterprise, financial, sexual or social.

As for pilgrimage, the more potent the power-place destination, the greater the merit accumulated. The great sacred mountains, such as Kang Rimpoche (Kailash), Labchi and Tsari, are the most powerful merit generators. Just the intention to make pilgrimage generates merit and when even a first step is made towards a power place, the meter measuring the merit begins to run.

A major source of merit is circumambulation, one of the main devotional activities on pilgrimage:

> *The benefits [or merit] for anyone who takes a step with the intention of performing circumambulation around a reliquary shrine of the Buddha, with faith in mind, are as great as making a donation of one hundred thousand ounces of gold.*

HUBER 1993

The merit generated by a single circumambulation of Bonri mountain is 700 million times that of any ordinary circumambulation. The year and month of the pilgrimage also affect the quantity of merit produced. If circumambulation is performed in the horse, sheep, bird or monkey months, the merit is multiplied 1.3 billion times. Even meritorious actions on the Bonri pilgrimage – saving the life of an animal, for example – result in an automatic 10,000-fold increase in the merit accumulated. Likewise, according to one of the guidebooks, 'Whatever sins or demerits you commit will become as vast as Mount Meru or the cosmic ocean.'

Evidently, with these vast amounts of merit in the offing, major changes to the pilgrim's habitual state of consciousness and his karmic patterning are possible. There is seemingly a threshold in the accumulation of merit above which transcendence is achieved, along with the Buddha's enlightenment or liberation from the round of rebirth, the wheel of life. According to doctrine, it is required that both merit and meditative insight into the nature of reality are optimized before this liberation is accomplished. The tradition, particularly in the guide books to the power places, is quite explicit that merit is optimized by pilgrimage to the great sacred places. Also, there is the assumption that insight into the nature of reality will also be increased to meltdown point, or at least that a radical change in the nature of consciousness will occur. As many pilgrims will affirm, awareness *is* involuntarily heightened at pilgrimage destinations. So, the guide book to Kang Rimpoche, quoting Guru Rimpoche, assures the pilgrim that:

> *Whoever visits Kang Rimpoche, the omphalos of the world, will achieve liberation within three lives. Whoever circumambulates Tso Mapham lake with sincere faith will spontaneously attain buddhahood.*

RAMBLE 1995:98

Or, at the very least, the 'doors of the six realms will be closed' to the pilgrim after death and at the end of the bardo, the intermediate state between death and rebirth, if the transient principle of consciousness has remained in fearless equilibrium, it will resist the beckoning lights of the wombs of rebirth into the upper and lower realms and find itself in the pure-land of one of the Five Buddhas or in the Copper-Coloured Mountain Pure-Land of Guru Rimpoche, in Shambhala, or in the Land of the Orgyen Khandromas.

If the merit that is accumulated is not quite sufficient to produce buddhahood, or liberation from the wheel of rebirth, it may nevertheless be enough to induce magical powers or supersensory insights. The ability to fly in the sky or walk through rock, or knowledge of the language of animals and birds, the ability to read minds and so on may be attained, particularly at the power places where the sky dancers dwell. It is they who bestow such powers. The guide book to Tsari mountain, one of the gathering-places of the sky dancers, promises that if you make any offering to the Buddhas there, you will achieve special powers. Likewise, if you meditate only for a short time without moving on the rock called Amoliga at the Bon mountain of Kongpo Bonri, you will enter samadhi, which will blaze up in you like a fire, and the memory of your past lives will be awakened.

The pilgrim with the right intention will, at least, and automatically, be cleansed of sin. Sin (*dikpa*) may be defined as ignorant acts of thought, word or deed, acts only partially understood, because of lack of awareness or stupidity, acts producing demerit, acts conflicting with moral standards or codes imposed by society, by the lama or by the individual. Whatever the cause of sin, demerit is the result, together with the karmic propensity to repeat the sinful activity. Purification and absolution can be achieved by various methods, according to the spiritual maturity of the sinner. A lama's blessing may be sufficient. Meditative absorption can be effective. Ritual confession in meditative concentration is the monk's method. For particularly intractable cases, pilgrimage is a last resort. Pilgrimage purges the mind of the demerit and the propensity to repeat the action, and absolution is obtained at the power place.

> *Because of the blessings bestowed by the three great knowledge holders, just by visiting that holy place [Bonri] your impurities will be purged. It is sufficient merely to set foot upon that flowery place…If you drink from this water and wash in it, your defiled sinful condition will immediately be purified and you will receive spiritual benefit and immeasurable wisdom…Whoever drinks from the blue lake of Tso Mapham will purge the sins of his successive lives.*
>
> RAMBLE MS

The most intractable of sins are the five boundless or so-called 'inexpiable' sins. They are the sins of killing one's father or mother or a lama, creating a schism in the religious community and maliciously causing a Buddha to bleed. At death such a sinner falls immediately into the deepest of hells, without any opportunity for release in the bardo. But even these so-called inexpiable sins can be eradicated through pilgrimage. Circumambulation of Kang Rimpoche will certainly expiate them, according to the guide book. There are also specific power-place destinations that guarantee absolution for particular sins. Chorten Nyima, near the Sikkim border, for instance, is the destination of those who must expiate the sin of incest.

The power of the water of sacred sites to purify sin is mentioned above. The virtue of bathing in these waters is seldom spoken of, however, since bathing is traditionally taboo in Tibetan society. The reluctance to bathe is based on a valid concern for health; the veneer of fat and grease covering the body is necessary to retain heat in the extreme cold and the water of the body in extreme heat. Loss of body heat causes disease; loss of water through perspiration causes dehydration. Perhaps the ritual of bathing for purification is derived from the Hindus, in whose culture and climate bathing is a rite of worship and crucial to good health. At least drinking the holy water is offered as an alternative in Tibet, but there is indication that bathing results in rebirth in the paradise of sensually absorbed sky dancers: 'Those drinking or bathing in the waters of Tso Mapham lake will go to the sky dancers' paradise of great bliss.' Sacred waters also have the power to cure disease and pilgrimage is frequently undertaken to this end:

> To the south of Bonri, there flow nine streams which heal leprosy, sores, deafness and the hundred and four types of ailment. Nearby, there is a stream of purifying nectar which cures dropsy and leprosy.
>
> RAMBLE 1995:53

As already mentioned, the attainment of liberation from the wheel of rebirth immediately, at death, or in three lifetimes, magical powers, rebirth in a buddhafield, the purging of sin and negative karma, and healing are all benefits that may accrue to the devout lay pilgrim whose intention or prayer it is. Undoubtedly pilgrimage benefits those best equipped to receive its effects, that is, pilgrims with a developed meditation ability, a responsiveness to the inner world and a receptive vision. But what proportion of Tibetan pilgrims today have this karma?

It may be that the ratio of the spiritually mature and immature in any given culture remains more or less the same regardless of the political or social regime. Perhaps in times of adversity – and Tibet has rarely experienced such misfortune as in the last 30 years – faith and devotion and craving for spiritual solace increase. It is difficult to register to what extent the radical diminution of institutional religious education affects the aspiration of the people, though it is certain that Tibetans have had less of that input in the last generation than any time in the last 1,000 years. In Tibet, as in the whole of Asia, there is evidently an increasing fascination with technology and the material culture of the Western world, and the materialistic propaganda of the Tibetans' political masters, the Chinese Communists, has also made a deep impression.

Regardless of these external conditions, what is certain is that the motivation of a large proportion of Tibetan pilgrims is mundane and has always been so. The pilgrim wants his yak herd to increase, or more specifically he wants Drolma, his yak, to calve this season. He wants promotion within the commune so that his pasture rights are assured. He needs the price of butter offered by the dairy collective to increase so that he has the extra cash in his pocket to buy a radio. He, and his daughter, need protection from the Chinese cadre whose face he blackened and who wants him in jail. He has that little bronze Buddha that his father gave him and for which the Khampa trader offered him 100 qwai, but maybe, tomorrow, 200. He wants the girl who is on the same pilgrim truck. He wants the weather to change.

He is a Buddhist and he will recite the MANI PADMA mantra, and the refuge in the Buddha, and make offerings to the lamas and the Buddhas to increase his merit on this pilgrimage. Perhaps the merit will be sufficient to obtain his goal. But he has no knowledge of the arcane doctrines of tantra or the mysteries of the lamas, who are like gods to him, and while he lives in awe and fear of the great buddha-deities and protectors, his faith is focused more on the local gods, the mountain gods, the elemental spirits, the spirits with whom he feels at home and to whom his father prayed and devoutly made the calendary rituals. The lamas who did not flee to India when the Chinese suppression began were murdered or imprisoned. Where was their vaunted power of protection then? They could not save his uncle from death in the labour camp building the great road or his grandmother from death by starvation. The gods of the fields and the cattle, the fierce gods and goddesses who lived on the mountains and their minions of the rocks remained unchanged during the hard times and, although outward ritual was forbidden, prayers to them still seemed to be answered. His luck has not been so bad in the last few years. Yes, it all comes down to luck.

The concept of luck, or *tashi*, is much older than that of karma, which came from the south, from India, with the Buddhist missionaries during the empire period. Luck was always the preoccupation of the nomads and villagers and shamans. It is the gift of the gods and spirits, who are not influenced by virtuous conduct or social morality. They require recognition through offering and ritual –

even token notice is enough – and through such recognition a balance is created, an ecological balance and an equilibrium of man within his environment. If recognition is withheld and offering and ritual omitted, then their displeasure will be revealed as a disequilibrium of man and nature and ill luck will ensue. Disease of men and cattle is the chief symptom of chaos in the three realms – the heavens, the earth and under the earth. The gods' anger shows in unseasonable and inclement weather – hail, sandstorm or drought – causing destruction to crops and cattle. In personal affairs illluck will attend sexual liaisons, business enterprises, trade and, of course, dice.

While the doctrine of karma is easy to grasp in theory, it is difficult to see how the acts of the gods are determined by personal moral behaviour and impossible to know how conduct in past lives is influencing the present. Luck and ill luck, on the other hand, are the impersonal dispensation of the gods and spirits who may be influenced by ritual offerings. A better rebirth in the next lifetime is, of course, much to be desired, but rebirth is an abstract concept, far away. Luck, on the contrary, is here and now; it is tsampa and butter tea and good health; it is sexual conquest and one in the eye for the enemy; it is money in the pocket and a transistor radio on the shelf; it is a healthy thriving herd of yaks and a good crop of barley. So, the ordinary pilgrim to the power places will be seeking to re-establish or secure a line of communication with the gods and spirits of the place in order to gain their favour, to increase his prosperity and his luck.

There is another issue that looms large in the minds of many contemporary Tibetan pilgrims, regardless of whether their aspiration is spiritual or mundane. This is the matter of Tibet's political status. Only a very few Tibetans do not find the Chinese occupation burdensome and wish for relief from it. The notion of Tibetan freedom, *Bokyi rangtsen*, is now universally known in Tibet, and although few Tibetans are aware of the geopolitical realities, they devoutly wish for a change. On pilgrimage, at the power places, this will be articulated as a prayer for the retreat of the Chinese into their own lands, or a prayer for the long life of Yishi Norbu, the Fourteenth Dalai Lama, and for his return to the Potala in Lhasa as the head of state. Even if the wish for independence is not explicitly verbalized, it will certainly be implicit in the pilgrim's prayers to Chenrezik, the protector of the Land of the Snows. It will also be implicit in prayers to the fierce guardians of the tradition, to the mountain gods and their retinues who are bound to protect Tibet, its inhabitants and the Buddhist teaching.

## THE PILGRIM'S DEVOTIONAL PRACTICE

Involuntarily heightened awareness, the psychedelic aspect of the pilgrimage experience, can be seen as the effect of automatic, reflexive purification. Through a process of purging and repurging body, speech and mind, the pilgrim may experience euphoria, a vision of the landscape transformed, internal apocalyptic vision, a sense of weightlessness and slow motion, and a singular gaiety and bonhomie – none of which has any significance beyond the gnostic awareness that gives rise to it.

The body is automatically purified by the exertion to the point of exhaustion that is inescapable at most power places. The Western pilgrim's constitution is capable of less exertion than the Tibetan's, but the effect is the same. Fatigue purges the body and renders the psycho-organism more susceptible to the vibration of the power place. Physical exposure to extremes of weather – the sun, the snow, the wind, at high altitudes – has a similar purging effect. If just getting to the place does not induce the requisite exhaustion, then prostration and circumambulation certainly will.

Speech and vibration are purified by external sound, rushing water or sighing wind, which may become objects of meditation, and also by incessant recitation of mantra and prayer *(see p.127, p.132)*. Once a mantra is set in orbit around an internal energy centre, a chakra, it will spin automatically, producing the sound that purifies psychic energy, its subtle vibration and articulated speech. And the mind, through concentration upon an object of meditation, a mantra perhaps, or its accompanying visualization, is also naturally purified. The blessings of the lama, the power place and power objects purify body, speech and mind as well.

The mind can be spontaneously reconditioned to the Buddha's reality by synchronistic circumstances that leapfrog the process of karma, and pilgrimage appears to offer such opportunities. But in the relative world nothing whatsoever can be accomplished without faith. This the pilgrim has in abundance. Pilgrimage itself is a demonstration of faith and so are the devotional exercises, the prostration, circumambulation, offering, prayer and recitation of mantra, that all pilgrims practise at the power places. Faith is the belief, confidence and then conviction that heartfelt aspiration, sublime or ridiculous, can be realized. No faith, no realization. Nothing can happen without it:

> In those who lack faith
> Nothing positive will grow,
> Just as from a burnt seed
> No shoots will sprout.
> RICARD 1994:172

Faith is also the key to the transformation of the landscape from an elementally savage scenario into a mandala vision:

> People with pure karma can see these outer places of Heruka as pure lands; those with impure karma see them as ordinary geographical locations...When you walk around places such as Bonri in Kongpo, since they are receptacles that have been blessed by an enlightened teacher, you should imagine that, while performing your circuit, you are walking round the enlightened one. It is not merely a matter of making prostrations and circumambulations while bearing in mind the local genii, territorial gods and swastika of these places: whatever sacred receptacle you visit you should consider that it is this or that enlightened one and be reverent and rejoice. This is what is important.
> RAMBLE 1995:55

It is certainly impossible to enter the mythic realm, whether the objective is to attain buddhahood or to manipulate spiritual phenomena for personal advantage, in a state of rampant egoism. In fact there is no possible purpose of pilgrimage that does not demand certain loss of ego. The Buddhist definition of ego loss implies a diminution of the sense of 'I' as a separate person and a corresponding increase of a consciousness of the interdependence of all existence, inner and outer. Total loss of the sense of a substantial self in both oneself and others and simultaneous arising of the knowledge that nothing exists in the outer world independent of the mind that perceives it is a definition of buddhahood. Much of yoga and meditation technique has loss of ego as its aim, and all tantric meditation liturgies begin with the basic technique of ego reduction – homage and prostration. The pilgrim makes verbal homage and physical prostration whenever suitable objects of obeisance appear. Indeed, the opportunity that pilgrimage offers for prostration is one of its most potent blessings.

## Homage and Prostration

Verbal homage to the higher power may be one of the time-honoured Sanskrit formulae – NAMO BUDDHAYA, NAMO AVALOKITESHVARA, etc. – or it may be in the Buddhist formula of refuge *(see below)*. The attitude of obeisance is physically expressed in the namaste mudra, palms pressed together at the heart centre. It may be useful to remember the popular Indian interpretation of this gesture – 'I bow to the divine within', whether it is a person, an image, a rock or a mountain that is addressed. But the sentiment of obeisance is better expressed physically as prostration, lost in India but seen everywhere in Tibetan devotion and pilgrimage. With palms together at the heart centre, first touching the forehead, the throat and again the heart, the common half-prostration involves touching the ground with seven points of bodily contact – toes, knees, palms and forehead. The full prostration consists of an extension of this so that the arms are outstretched, the palms touching and the body lying prone full length on the ground.

Obeisance and prostration are performed before symbols of buddha-body, speech and mind. An image of the Buddha is the best representation of his body, but the devotee on pilgrimage in the sacred landscape finds symbols of his body in mountains and rocks. Books of scripture represent buddha-speech, but single mystic syllables carved into the rock symbolize an entire canon of scripture. Chortens represent the buddha-mind and are to be found at most pilgrimage destinations. The lama himself is an embodiment of buddha-body, speech and mind, and provides the superior object of prostration. To the mindstate of devotion and receptivity that is the immediate effect of prostration, the lama can add his blessings.

The object of obeisance can also be visualized. For the pilgrim who performs full-length prostrations counting his outstretched body-lengths, from toe to finger tip, from his home to his pilgrimage destination, his mental yoga is to visualize the Buddha or a buddha-deity in front of him. The same applies to the devotee who prostrates around a *khorra* circuit, a circumambulatory path.

The advantage of full-length prostration is explained by the Fourteenth Dalai Lama:

> When you walk a circular pilgrimage route, such as the one around Mount Kailash, your feet touch the earth with big paces between them, but when you prostrate, your whole body connects with the sacred ground to close the circle.
>
> DALAI LAMA 1990:132

## Offering

In a mindstate of devotion and humility the visionary realm is accessible. The ritual procedure now required for a dynamic interactive relationship with the noumenal forces of this realm supports and develops the process of ego-loss already begun. This ritual gesture required here is offering (*chod, puja*). The full ritual of offering – seven outer sensory objects and the inner experience of those sensory impulses – is required only if a simple token gesture is ineffective. The image of a child making a gift of a flower provides the paradigm of such a token offering. The gift is offered in innocence; it has no intrinsic value; there is no thought of advantage. The result is a communicative bond between the giver and the recipient. When the devotee makes an offering to the spiritual energy of a power place, if the devotee's attitude is sufficiently strong, then the bond is an integral union. At least, a bond is formed, which provides a conduit for a two-way flow.

A white flaxen scarf (*katak*) is the conventional offering made to a lama as a token of respect, but the katak is also offered to an image or to a Buddha or buddha-deity seen in an aspect of the landscape. Kataks piled on the lap of an image, or on top of a shrine or a rock, are signs of pilgrims' devotion.

A butter lamp is the symbolic offering of light, both sunlight and the inner light of vision. Pilgrims and devotees at the great gompas and temples will walk from shrine to shrine carrying a kettle of melted butter or oil, pouring a ladleful of liquid into each of the giant butter lamps that are never allowed to run dry. The offering of a butter lamp may also be made by the priests of a place upon a small payment. Electric lights in front of images on altars have now begun to augment the butter lamps as permanent offerings of light.

The offering of incense, providing sweet-smelling fragrance for the divine presence, visible or invisible, together with the medicinal effect of many kinds of Tibetan incense, also gives pleasure to the deity. Flowers delight the deity's eye and nose, while food or drink please the sense of taste, and a part of the offering returned to the giver contains the deity's blessing. Roasted barley flour (tsampa), the staple of Tibetan diet, is the usual offering of food, though rice is beginning to replace it.

Now that paper money has become common in Tibetan society it is very frequently given as an offering. Money represents not so much the currency of mammon as a precious item difficult to come by and hard to part with, and so more meaningful as an offering. The final recipients of all offerings that have some intrinsic value or use are, of course, the priests, the monks or the lay officiants at the shrine, and money is best received by them. The final destination of the offering, however, is of little concern to the pilgrim. The function of the offering is to create a relationship with the divine presence and the ritual giving itself is the point of the exercise. Yet waste in the form of offerings is less evident at Tibetan shrines than at many Indian power places, for example, where a less hard-headed and less practical attitude prevails.

Another category of offerings to the Buddhas is personal effects. A piece of clothing, a shirt, a sock or an old shoe will do. A hair band or a safety pin that has been in touch with the body will also serve the purpose. Pilgrims will leave strands of hair, or indeed the complete cropping of the head, from the living or the dead. The intention of such an offering is to leave tangible evidence of the pilgrim's presence to remind the deity of his prayer, particularly when he is passing through the bardo between dying and rebirth.

Wherever there is an altar – in a domestic shrine-room, in a gompa, in a hermitage or cave – a formal ritual of offering is one of the first actions of the day. The object of the offering is the Three Jewels – the Buddha, his teaching (dharma) and the community of practitioners (*sangha*). The tantric practitioner will also have the Three Roots in mind – the lama, the khandroma and the yidam. A single buddha-image can embody all of these. If there is no image or representation of a Buddha, then a buddha-recipient is visualized. The symbolic offering is made in the form of water, preferably water brought from a power place, poured into seven bowls. The first is water for the Buddha to drink, the second is for washing his hands and feet, the third represents flowers to adorn his head or hair, the fourth represents incense to please his sense of smell, the fifth represents a butter lamp to please his eyes, the sixth represents perfumed water to sprinkle on his body, the seventh represents food to please his sense of taste. Sometimes an eighth is added to represent music to please his ears. The bowls are drained and stacked in the evening in readiness for the morning rite.

On pilgrimage, perhaps the most common form of offering is that of perfumed smoke or *sang*. Sometimes a raised hearth built into a chimney is provided for this purpose, such as those on the Barkor in the four directions of the Lhasa Jokhang. If there is no ritual hearth, then the offering can be burned in the open. Leaves and twigs of fragrant shrubs such as juniper and rhododendron are most favoured by the Buddhas and their guardian retinues. But what is crucial is that perfumed smoke should rise into the sky and be received. Prayers are offered to the Three Jewels, the bodhisattvas and the buddha-deities, but the recipients uppermost in the prayers of the layman are the guardian protectors such as the mountain gods and the protectors of the tradition and their retinues of minor spirits to whom some karmic debt is due.

Offering, or ritual giving, is generally the most vital purpose of the pilgrim at the power place. As the single most effective ritual gesture that creates the intimacy with the divine presence, it is the precondition for any advantage the pilgrim may gain. So offering is made as obeisance and as thanksgiving; as a token requiring reciprocal response from the deity; as propitiation averting hostile influences; and as a means of accumulating merit towards a better rebirth. The meaning of the offering is determined by the relationship between the giver and the recipient.

## Circumambulation

Circumambulation, or walking around an object of reverence, called *khorra* in Tibetan, may appear as the simplistic devotional practice of a credulous devotee. Indeed it is. The Tibetan devotee performs circumambulation of a chorten, a lhakhang, a sacred rock or a holy person without a shadow of doubt as to the efficacy of the practice and without any rationale to support his action. And yet this practice is not the province of the layman; even the most exalted lamas and yogis perform it.

Any sacred object may be used for circumambulation and merit will be gained whatever its nature. The most meritorious circuits of circumambulation are the great sacred mountains – Kang Rimpoche (Kailash), Amnye Machen, Tsari. The lakes associated with them also provide khorra circuits and are sometimes of greater merit-generating power. Gompas and lhakhangs are also worthy objects of khorra, particularly where a powerful image or lama is seen at the centre of the khorra circuit. Chortens provide obvious objects of khorra practice and attract devotees like bears to honey. Many sacred places, the Lhasa Jokhang, for example, have inner and outer circuits and even a third intermediate circuit. A third mythic circuit is added to the outer and inner circuits at Kang Rimpoche to complete the perfection of the significant metaphysical triad. An image, like the Lhasa Jowo, may take a matter of seconds to walk around; some circuits, like the outer khorra path around Kang Rimpoche, may take days to traverse, or weeks, like the ravine circuit at Tsari.

Since circumambulation is a kriya-yoga – loosely stated, a ritual practice performed with the physical body – the time of practice is important. The periods of first light to dawn and sunset to twilight are most propitious. The number of circumambulations performed is also significant. Three, 13 and 108, the most auspicious numbers in Bon and Buddhist numerology, are best observed. At the time of an eclipse, solar or lunar, or on a particularly favourable day of an auspicious month, the merit gained by circumambulation is multiplied exponentially according to astrological divination.

Regarding the direction of circumambulation, in general Buddhists walk clockwise – with their right shoulder towards the object of devotion – and Bonpos walk anti-clockwise. Buddhists will say that the clockwise direction is identified with 'the white path', the way of virtue, and anti-clockwise with 'the black path', the way of the unrighteous. Indeed, on mountains sacred to both Buddhist and Bonpo, like Kang Rimpoche, and where the Bonpos have been subjugated, they were constrained, historically, to progress in the clockwise mode. But these days the Bonpos can no longer be perceived as 'Black Bon', pagan animal sacrificers, manipulators of the spirit world and inimitable to the path of buddha-dharma, and the New Bon may circumambulate clockwise. Buddhist practitioners of the mother-tantra, on the contrary, should circumambulate anti-clockwise. The designated direction of their progress is the clue to the significance of the differing traditions. A clockwise movement proceeds with the natural and harmonious social energy in the logic of the bodhisattva ethic of the scriptures of the Universal Buddhist Tradition and the father-tantras, while an anti-clockwise procession moves against the natural tide, incorporating both virtue and vice in the ethic of the mother-tantras. The dynamic of the swastika, the solar symbol of good fortune and longevity, follows these same principles. Clockwise, or right-handed, movement indicates light and virtue, while the anti-clockwise, or left-handed, movement, presages the dark and sinister. This symbol was appropriated from the Tibetans by the Nazis as a symbol of solar power.

The efficacy of the practice of circumambulation is not in doubt. Even without the basic support of a meditation discipline, the devotee's mind is calmed and centred and, optimally, a state of heightened awareness is achieved. Circumambulation provides a ritual celebration of this movement and harmony and peace. Through the identification of consciousness with the centre of a circle and the symbolic modifications of its circumference, a mandala is created.

The major khorra circuits on Tibetan pilgrimages tend to have a mountain, a hill or topographical prominence at the centre. The chorten and the lhakhang may be envisioned as ritual forms of the mountain. The mandala that is created may be the basic mandala of the Five Buddhas or the mandala of Namgyelma (Ushnishavijaya), the Mother of the Buddhas, who dwells within the dome of a chorten, or the mandala of the sacred cosmos with Mount Sumeru at its centre. When khorra is coupled with the recitation of a mantra – which is an even more potent technique of pacifying the mind and developing it into a mandala structure – the nature of the mandala will be determined by the deity evoked by the mantra and the mandala will disclose the deity seated at the centre of his palace in his pure-land. If the khorra circuit is in the wilderness, then circumambulation is a potent method of sanctifying and transforming the environment.

On the khorra circuits that pass through a rocky or wilderness environment, around a mountain, a lake, or a large gompa compound, the susceptible pilgrim will find sideshows in rock to distract his attention. Probably the most common is the rocky configuration of the narrow defile of the intermediate state between death and rebirth (*bardo trang*) or the path to hell (*nyelam*). Here the pilgrim must squeeze tightly between rocks or slither through a tunnel, practising for the similarly fearful experience of the after-death state and thus preparing for his death. The sky-burial site on his way offers him the opportunity to sit down, visualize and contemplate his forthcoming death and the bardo experience. Other stops on the khorra circuit are at healing rocks, which by touching or rubbing will cure a bad back, a headache or some congenital malady.

## Recitation of Mantra and Meditation

Pilgrimage can be defined as time given over exclusively to devotions at a power place away from home, but it also includes travel to, from and between power places. At the pilgrimage destination few lay pilgrims will actually sit down and meditate. So the meditation which is the core practice of the pilgrim's devotions is performed while mobile. The principal mode of such meditation is the recitation of mantra.

Khorra, as already mentioned, provides the most valuable time for mantra meditation. However, in contemporary Tibet pilgrims take every advantage of motor transport to convey themselves across the vast distances of the Tibetan plateau, and the roads, constructed mostly by slave labour during the Maoist era, allow easy access to most pilgrim destinations. Motor transport, however, does not inhibit the recitation of mantra and truckloads of pilgrims crossing the open spaces of Western Tibet on the way to Kang Rimpoche, for instance, may all be counting mantra on their rosaries (*tenga*).

Mantra consists of a string of verbal symbols that invoke a particular Buddha. Constant one-pointed recitation provides the concentrated absorption required to enter the visionary realm, where the verbal symbols spontaneously evoke a buddha-deity. The initiation (*wang*) that authorizes the practitioner to practise and that empowers the mantra will have been received by both monks and laymen previously. The form and technique of visualizing the buddha-deity will have been transmitted after initiation. The practice of visualizing the deity while reciting the mantra may form part of the practice of anyone – monk, yogi or layman – able to concentrate to the necessary degree.

The mantra most commonly recited by all Tibetans, particularly on pilgrimage, is the six-syllable mantra of the bodhisattva of compassion, Chenrezik (Avalokiteshvara). This is the well known OM MANI PADMA HUNG. It is the devotional quality of love which it evokes that is probably responsible for the high and compassionate energy that generally accompanies pilgrims on their journeys. The power of this mantra is unlimited. This is Guru Rimpoche's commentary on its effect:

> When [the pilgrim] recites OM MANI PADMA HUNG, by the syllable OM the abyss of rebirth as a god is crossed and the heavens are emptied; by the syllable MA the abyss of rebirth as an anti-god is crossed and the realm of the jealous gods is emptied; by the syllable NI the abyss of rebirth as a human being is crossed and the human realm is emptied; by the syllable PAD the abyss of rebirth as an animal is crossed and the animal realm is emptied; by the syllable MA the abyss of rebirth as a hungry ghost is crossed and the realm of the tortured spirits is emptied; by the syllable HUNG the abyss of

*rebirth as a denizen of hell is crossed and the hells are emptied. After emptying the six realms, the whole of samsara is empty, and there is complete purity. The power that can lead beings into the buddhafield is the heart-essence of The Lord of Great Compassion, which is this six-syllable mantra.*

DOWMAN MS

Devotees of particular religious orders have their own general mantras. For devotees of the Nyingma school, for whom Guru Rimpoche is the all-embracing Buddha, the 12-syllable mantra, OM AH HUNG VAJRA GURU PADMA SIDDHI HUNG, is the mantra of choice. This mantra evokes the blessings of the Great Guru, particularly his indestructible awareness and compassion. Disciples of the Karmapa, belonging to the Karma Kagyu order, may recite the simple formula KARMAPA KHYENO! 'Lama Karmapa is omniscient!' For the Bonpos, the mantra equivalent of Chenrezik's six-syllable mantra is OM MATRI MUYE SALE DU, which evokes the compassionate energy of the teacher Shenrab Miwo. Children may recite the mantra of Jampelyang (Manjushri), the bodhisattva of intelligence, whose mantra – A RA PA CHA NA DHI DHI DHI – improves memory and understanding. OM TARE TU TARE TUREYE SWAHA, the mantra of Drolma (Arya Tara), the female bodhisattva of devotion, is another favourite. For the purification of sin, the mantra of Dorje Sempa (Vajrasattva) is specific – OM VAJRA SATTVA HUNG. Since expiation of sin is a common motivation for pilgrimage, particularly amongst monks and nuns, the long 100-syllable mantra of Dorje Sempa will be recited by some and the visualization of that Buddha will accompany it. For long life and health, the mantra of Tsepakme (Amitayus), the Buddha of Boundless Life, is recited, and for rebirth into Dewachan, the mantra of Wopakme, OM AMIDEWA HRI.

The tantric yogi fully engaged in a tantric practice, the ngakpa or neljorpa, will probably be reciting the mantra of his yidam, the buddha-deity that is his personal protector and the source of his spiritual power and realization. Such mantras are secret and not to be revealed to the non-initiate. The yidams that are most popular are Dukhor (Kalachakra), the Wheel of Time; Demchok (Samvara), Supreme Bliss; Dorje Phurba (Vajrakilaya), the Indestructible

Dagger; Gompo (Mahakala), the Great Black One; and the female buddha-deity Dorje Phakmo (Vajravarahi), the Adamantine Sow.

A mantra should be muttered. It can be sung joyfully and loudly or recited silently, but in order for it to fulfil its purpose as an object of concentration it is best recited in a murmur in which the syllables can be only indistinctly heard and which scarcely articulates the lips. This best facilitates the trance absorption in which the transmutation of thought into a constellation of buddha-qualities can occur. Precise enunciation is a secondary concern. Because Tibeto-Burman speakers are incapable of enunciating the compound consonants common in the mantras derived from Sanskrit, the Tibetan pronunciation is sometimes radically different from the Indian. The mantra should, however, be recited in precisely the manner in which it is transmitted by the lama and if during a long life the pronunciation of an old lama has become idiosyncratic, still it should be taken as the effective utterance. Besides, the disciple Hard-of-Hearing who heard OM MANI PADMA HUNG as 'om moni gimme hung', and who recited that form faithfully throughout his life, received more spiritual benefit than the disciple Exact Copy whose pronunciation was pedantic and whose faith was wanting. The mantras mentioned above are given in their literary form.

In many ways pilgrimage is supportive to the basic practice of mantra recitation and its goal of a unitary bond with the buddha-deity. Away from home, mundane concerns do not distract from concentration to the same degree. The self-avowed intent of one-pointed spiritual practice induces a spiral of increasingly intense application. The pilgrim has like-minded fellow travellers. He interacts with the sacred space through which he travels, or which he finds at his destination, so that simultaneously his visionary imagination imbues that space with sacred significance and his vision is affected by the divine constructs of the sacred space. Prostration, offering and circumambulation provide constant reinforcement of the state conducive to spiritual understanding. The power place heightens his awareness. Magical power objects he encounters suspend the tendency to disbelief. Images of the Buddhas, tomes of scriptures and engraved sacred syllables, chortens and so on reflect the buddha-mindstate that is his internally visualized goal and help realize it.

If meditation is understood as a heightened state of awareness in which the meditator is given intimation of the nature of his buddha-mind and its compassionate emanation, then the pilgrim who leaves himself open to the vibrations of a power place and performs his devotions with faith, particularly the recitation of mantra, may constantly find himself in a meditative state. If meditation is understood as a formal structured practice within a given time frame, then meditation is the preserve of the yogi who sits down in a cave or hermitage at a power place and over a prolonged period dedicates himself to a graduated path of practice. Most Tibetans will understand meditation in the latter sense and attribute any involuntary achievement of insight or heightened awareness to the blessings of the power place or a sacred person in residence there.

The graduated path of meditation in the tantric tradition begins with preliminary practices and continues through three phases. The preliminaries consist of practices of prostration accompanied by a verse of refuge, recitation of the bodhisattva vow, recitation of the 100-syllable mantra of Dorje Sempa with visualization, recitation of a prayer of offering accompanied by a ritual mandala offering of rice, and Guruyoga. Guruyoga, the most significant of these rituals, consists of a complex tantric liturgical meditation accompanied by ritual acts that climaxes in a ritual enactment of initiation into the mandala of the guru-lama. This meditation will certainly constitute part of every yogi's practice in his power-place hermitage. All of these rituals must be repeated 100,000 times, but elements of all of them constitute the devotions that any pilgrim should perform.

The three subsequent phases of meditation are the main practice of all tantric yogis. The first is called the creative phase, in which the mind is conditioned to view reality in terms of male and female deities in a mandala by visualizing the principles and dynamics of understanding in symbolic, usually anthropomorphic, form. The second is the fulfilment process, in which these archetypal images are integrated into the structure of the mind through their dissolution into modes of pure existential awareness. This is achieved through the practice of various yogas that destroy the dualistic vision of ordinary consciousness and create a nondual vision of light and awareness. The yoga of the mystic heat (*tummo*) is one of them. The third phase is perhaps best described as the fundamental

Buddhist meditation of watching the nature of mind. This is a formless meditation and therefore considered most taxing to the untrained practitioner.

Solitary practice of tantric meditation in a secluded hermitage is considered appropriate only for advanced practitioners. Yogis who dedicate years of their life to such meditation are accorded the highest status in religious society. Although monks in the monasteries may also practise tantric meditation, particularly the preliminary exercises, most will be engaged in study and communal ritual observances. Such work is conducive to cultivation of the karma that will allow them to undergo the yogi's intensive meditation retreat. In this way the monasteries should be considered places of apprenticeship for aspiring yogis. The monastic hierarchy, the tulkus, abbots and teachers, most of whom will have spent some time in meditation retreat in the hermitages, are seen as bodhisattvas who have attained the goal of their meditation and returned from their hermitages to the monastic environment in order to help those whose practice is less advanced. Before the Cultural Revolution the majority of men and women outside the monasteries practised devotional exercises that could induce the karma supportive to a rebirth in which ordination in a monastery could be achieved.

## Prayer

Prayer as a ritual act of worship at a power place is certainly the practice of most pilgrims. Tibetans do not, however, formulate prayers of supplication in the personal manner as taught to Christian children – 'Please give me this and that' etc. Their manner of approach is indirect – create the appropriate space and the divine agency will fill it with whatever is required, or, rather, whatever is karmically possible. The manner of creating this space for the Buddhist is first of all the refuge, which is made to the guru-lama and the Three Jewels, and which is also recited with prostration:

| Lamala kyabsuchao! | I take refuge in the lama! |
| Sangyela kyabsuchao! | I take refuge in the Buddha! |
| Chola kyabsuchao! | I take refuge in the teaching! |
| Gendunla kyabsuchao! | I take refuge in the community! |

The most common prayer to Guru Rimpoche is the Seven-Line Prayer:

*HUNG! In the north-west of the land of Orgyen,*
*On the pollen-bed of a lotus flower,*
*Endowed with the miraculous, supreme realization,*
*Padmasambhava, the Lotus-Born, appeared*
*Surrounded by a host of sky dancers;*
*In order that I may emulate you*
*Please come here and bless us.*
*GURU PADMA SIDDHI HUNG!*

Each family lineage and religious order will have its own tradition of prayer.

There are special prayers to be recited at various power places, on special days and for different purposes. The prayer that accompanies the rite of offering is not to be confused with the mantra that is recited by pilgrims walking from site to site, while performing khorra and at every possible other moment of the day.

One special prayer which is a part of every devout Buddhist's practice is the prayer for dedication of merit and it is this prayer that sets the Buddhist (or Bonpo) apart from his materialistic brothers and sisters. It is of crucial importance. This is the prayer for dedication of merit:

*May any merit attained through this practice be dedicated to the*
*enlightenment of all sentient beings.*

'This practice' may be pilgrimage itself or any devotion or meditation practised during the pilgrimage. The merit is the positive balance in the karmic bank that could be exchanged for a mundane boon, or for certainty of success in any financial enterprise. Instead, the pilgrim prays for this merit to be dedicated to the Buddha's enlightenment, for himself and others. No Buddhist devotion or meditation is complete without recitation of this or a similar prayer.

## Vows and Prohibitions

The first vow that the pilgrim takes is to complete the pilgrimage. Only by performing an entire pilgrimage are blessings accrued and objectives – mundane or spiritual – achieved. As well as this vow, many pilgrims will retake the basic Buddhist vows to refrain from killing, stealing, intoxication and sexual misconduct. Some will take the 10 vows of lay ordination to refrain from killing, stealing and sexual misconduct, from lying, gossiping, slander and cursing, and from malicious thoughts, covetousness and opinionatedness. Some will take a special vow of sexual restraint or abstinence from eating meat and/or drinking alcohol.

There is a traditional constraint on hunting and especially fishing during pilgrimage, which although irrelevant in Central Tibet these days, since most of the game has been exterminated, may still be appropriate in Amdo and Kham. This prohibition is most relevant to the nomads, who still depend to some extent on game for their meat. The vow to refrain from hunting and fishing is basic to the arousal of the thought of enlightenment (*bodhichitta*) and the cultivation of the bodhisattva's attitude of compassion towards all living beings. Monks, and particularly nuns, frequently take the prohibition on killing to its logical extreme, taking excessive care to avoid treading upon insects and to preserve the lives of lice extracted from the hair.

There are also constraints on the places for performing bodily functions. In a guide book to Tsari the pilgrim is warned to defecate and urinate only beneath the central khorra path or close to cairns that mark other appropriate locations. 'Apart from at such places, you are not permitted to eliminate – including spitting, farting, or blowing your nose – or perform other unclean actions.' If this prohibition is flouted then there is 'no doubt of your going to hell'. 'Whoever does not heed these orders, even if he succeeds in being reborn in the human realm, will be born deaf, dumb, or leprous. Therefore pay attention to your actions.' Such strictures are not designed in the interests of hygiene, but to preserve the purity and sanctity of the pure-land that is the power place.

## SOURCES OF BLESSING

### Sacred Symbols, Power Objects and Self-Manifest Phenomena

Power places are the destination of pilgrims, but it is the sacred symbols and power objects at the power place, which are virtually inseparable from the place itself, that are the objects of the pilgrim's attention and the immediate source of blessings. Some power places, particularly caves and other natural features of the landscape, have been left bereft of movable artefacts after the holocaust of Chinese invasion and Red Guard depredation. Even here, though, almost certainly the pilgrim will find built-in power objects, such as sculptured reliefs or 'self-manifest phenomena' in the rock. So there will always be some representation of the three kinds of artefacts symbolic of buddha-body, buddha-speech and buddha-mind – images, scriptures and chortens – whose Tibetan name, *tensum*, indicates their function – 'the three objects or supports of worship'.

Images of the Buddha, representing his body, include clay, stone, bronze or wooden statues, sculptured reliefs in stone, paintings on stucco or rock, or on cotton or silk scrolls (thangkas), woven images, images printed on cotton cloth to make prayer-flags or on paper to be secreted in amulets and also self-manifest two or three-dimensional images. The most commonly depicted images are Shakyamuni Buddha or one of the Five Buddhas – Namnang (Vairochana), Mikyopa (Akshobhya), Rinchen Jungne (Ratnasambhava), Wopakme (Amitabha) and Donyodrubpa (Amoghasiddhi); the bodhisattvas Chenrezik (Avalokiteshvara), Jampelyang (Manjushri), Chakna Dorje (Vajrapani), Jampa (Maitreya) and Drolma (Arya Tara); and Guru Rimpoche and the great founding lamas of the religious orders. Each gompa lhakhang will have an image of the principal tantric buddha-deity and the Khandroma Dorje Neljorma (Vajra Yogini) in some form. The guardian Kings of the

Four Directions will be present in murals and the main protectors of the gompa, such as Pelden Lhamo, Nakpochenpo, and so on, will also be evident somewhere.

In the great monasteries, 'scriptures', representing buddha-speech, will mean the canon of Shakyamuni Buddha's sermons (the *Kangyur*) and the canonical commentaries upon them written by the great Indian sages and yogis (the *Tengyur*), all of course in the Tibetan language. Smaller gompas will possess some library of scriptures, perhaps a part of the Kangyur, such as the essential *Prajnaparamita Sutras*, the collected works (*sungbum*) of the gompa's founder, or the key works of the order to which the gompa belongs. Only a few gompas have any scriptures remaining from the pre-1959 period. The Red Guards used the texts to light fires or simply left them exposed to the elements. It is still possible to see piles of jumbled pages in the ruins of a gompa or to find a room in a restored building containing the shuffled remnants of an ancient library.

At cave or rock sites scriptures are represented by sacred syllables and mantras carved in the rock. Sometimes these are of the self-manifest variety. Mani-stones, mantras carved into stones or rocks by devotees to obtain merit, belong to this category. Mani-walls, sometimes hundreds of yards long, consisting of hundreds of tablets inscribed with one or several sutras, represent buddha-speech. But both mani-stones and mani-walls were destroyed during the Cultural Revolution and are often now just piles of fragments. Buddha-speech is also represented by mantras spelt out on the hillsides in letters sometimes yards high.

The third of the 'objects or supports of worship' is the chorten, which represents the buddha-mind. Chortens come in various shapes and sizes, ranging from inches to hundreds of feet. A chorten may be a small bronze image or a painting, a graphic relief in stone, a reliquary within a large lhakhang or a massive monument built of stone and earth. The chortens with in-built treasuries were prime targets for treasure-hunters during the period of persecution and relatively few remain, although crudely built monuments have sprung up at various power places.

Some traditional Asian religious cultures, the Indian in particular, have no greater respect for an old image, book or symbol than a new and recently consecrated one. This is not true of Tibet. Here the power of an object, like the power of a place, is derived from the contact or presence of a saint or yogi. His vision or vibration imbues the object with the power of that buddha-resonance. An image believed to have been made by Jowo Atisha or Milarepa, for example, has the enlightened power of the Buddha within it and its blessings are equivalent to the blessings of the maker. The treasure-objects hidden by Guru Rimpoche have power within them identical to the Great Guru himself. Ancient images, scriptures and chortens are likely, therefore, due to their age, to have been in the presence of great and holy men whose blessings may be obtained from worship of these objects or contact with them.

The same is true of sacred bond-objects. These are the objects that a tantric yogi carries with him with which a bond has been created ritually, through a vow of vision to make no distinction between the symbol and its existential buddha-significance, and through usage. The dorje (vajra) and *drilbu* (*ghanta*), or hand-bell, are the most common bond-objects. They represent – they *are* – the male and female aspects of the basic two-in-one metaphysical reality, compassion and wisdom. They are always present on the yogi's altar, to be employed in virtually every tantric rite. Other bond-objects include the skullbowl (*thopa, kapala*), which is emptiness and may be used by the yogi as a drinking vessel or as a container of symbolic blood or semen in ritual offering, and the phurba (*kila*), the ritual dagger often to be seen stuck in the belt of the ngakpa magician, employed ritually in the subjection of spirits, which is dynamic emptiness. These bond-objects are thought not only to vibrate with the visionary power and awareness of the yogi who employs them, but also to be the buddha-qualities they represent. This category of power object is a potent source of blessing, particularly if the object once belonged to Guru Rimpoche, to a Dalai Lama, or to Drukpa Kunley.

The devotee intent upon attaining the Buddha's enlightenment in this lifetime will tune in to the higher metaphysical reality or vibration of an object, and even if the perceived origin and history of the thing is bogus, his vision will project a buddha-quality and actually endow it with the power that is then reciprocated. A similar function is performed by the fervent devotee who requires a mundane boon, healing or absolution, and the object solicited for its power or blessing then becomes a 'magical object'. The personal effects of saints and yogis are magical objects, and the slippers, robes, staff or begging bowl of a man of power may all be found on power-place altars. The underpants of the late Dudjom Rimpoche were cut up and distributed to his disciples as magical objects.

The same power is attributed to 'self-manifest' or 'spontaneously arisen' (*rangjung*) phenomena. At most of the major power places where Tibetans make pilgrimage – even outside Tibet – there are stone formations that are said to have been spontaneously generated without the benefit of human hand. Sometimes it is a crude relief form of a buddha image in the rock that is so identified or a rough three-dimensional shape that can be seen as the Buddha. Dorjes are also found in this form. Mantric seed-syllables, like A or OM AH HUNG, are also commonly found self-manifest in rock. Most of these phenomena date from the hoary past, like another form of self-manifest object, the fragments of meteoric iron that have fallen from the sky in the rough form of a dorje or other sacred symbol (*tokchak*).

While rangjung manifestations can be considered a physical reflection of spontaneously arisen buddhahood, the imprints in rock left by yogis, most frequently in their meditation caves, demonstrate control over the elements, which is one of the eight great magical powers (*siddhis*) attendant upon the Buddha's enlightenment. The Guru Rimpoche cave at Terdrom is replete with such imprints. Here the pilgrim finds the print of the Great Guru's bottom and back, his headprint and his handprint. His trident (katvanga) and skullbowl have also left their imprints. Handprints and footprints are the most commonly discovered forms of this kind. The Buddha Shakyamuni left his footprints in rock at the four corners of the Kang Rimpoche khorra circuit in order to peg the mountain down and to demonstrate the immutable nature of his enlightened state.

For the devout pilgrim, to find spontaneously arisen phenomena and imprints in the rock at his destination is merely confirmation of the nature and efficacy of the power place, and the power of the yogis who have meditated there. For the more sceptical Western pilgrim it may, at least, produce a suspension of belief. The nature of the pilgrimage will already have produced a relaxation of habitual preconceptions, and the power objects at the power place assist in producing the mindstate that is conducive to forming a bond with the noumenal energy of the place.

## Sacred Substances

There are certain substances that pilgrims acquire at their destination that bestow blessings of various kinds. Some of these are natural materials, water, rock or clay. They may also be alchemical preparations made by a tantric lama under highly controlled ritual conditions. They may be self-manifest substances with magical potency. Some provide relief from disease. Some bestow the spiritual blessings of a lama or a buddha-deity. For the yogi, the sacred substance may be a psychedelic herb.

The grossest of these sacred substances is rock itself, which, impregnated by the power of a sacred mountain, for instance, and taken back to the pilgrim's home, acts like a battery charger, generating the effect of the power place from which it was brought. Or it may be taken home to form the foundation stone or part of the contents of a chorten, which is thus transformed into the mountain of which the stone was a part. On the Amnye Machen khorra path, at Drokdu Nyakha La pass, there is a quarry for such stones. Many power places possess special sources of sacred earth (*sane*), which, again, may be used in the construction of a chorten and also for the manufacture of *tsatsa*. Tsatsa are small clay icons, a few inches high, formed in a bronze matrix and sun dried, showing the form of a Buddha in relief or perhaps a chorten in the round. The clay for the tsatsa is also frequently mixed with the funerary relics of a lama and placed in a chorten or in a purpose-built charnel house. When mixed with the relics of a layman they may be left at a local power place sacred to a particular protector with whom the spirit of the deceased is then connected. It is inappropriate behaviour to remove tsatsa from the place where they have been ritually placed.

Some sacred earth is medicinal, either in the raw form in which it is dug from the ground, or after preparation or compounding by a doctor. On most of the mountain power-place khorra circuits are places (*nesa*) where the pilgrim digs out medicinal earth for a variety of healing purposes.

Water from a sacred spring or lake may also be taken home so that those who could not make the pilgrimage may benefit by a ritual sprinkling, the equivalent of a bathe in its source, or a drop on the end of the tongue, the equivalent of drinking a flask of it at the source. Water taken from a source in a meditation cave, or nearby, that is, from the water source of a realized adept, perhaps magically produced, is especially potent. This is called *drubchu*, the water of realization.

'Sacred substances' may refer more specifically to the preparations made in tantric ritual especially for distribution to devotees. In tantric rites of offering the two primary substances are those that represent the male and female sexual fluids, blood and semen (*rakta* and *dudtsi*), the red and the white. These are represented by a variety of substances, particularly red and white liquids, of which the latter is probably alcohol which may or may not contain traces of menstrual blood and semen. The offering of the female part may be represented as meat. The deity and his retinue are represented in consecrated cones of barley flour and molasses, and, perhaps, alcohol, called *torma*, 'the substance to be scattered or distributed'. Once consecrated and rendered up as offerings all these substances are kept for distribution amongst pilgrims as sources of blessing.

The principal product of alchemical preparation is called 'ambrosial dharma medicine' (*dutsi chomen*). This is a herbal and mineral compound prepared in an elaborate ritual that takes account of the phase of the moon, the declinations of the planets and stars, and the ritual purity of the participants, particularly the purity of the lama who performs the empowerment. The compound may be many days in the making. It begins as a sticky mixture and finally appears as tiny dark coloured pellets. It is usually measured in multiple pounds because it is rarely made and may form a cache that lasts for years. The various tantras prescribe different recipes for this ambrosia, with differing effects. If it is the blessing of a living lama that is being distributed, then bodily fluids of that lama will be the special sacred ingredient. If the lama has passed on to another life then it may contain his powdered relics. Particular herbal ingredients may infuse the compound with the power of the deity of the place from where they were gathered. Herbs taken from Tsari mountain, for instance, may contain the special empowerment of the sky dancers who reside there. These herbs may be medicinal panaceas and may also possess psychedelic properties. Their pharmacological qualities, however, are inseparable from the potency that the herbs absorb in their power-place environment. These qualities are actually identified as sky dancers (khandroma), so that there can be no separation between the active chemical agent and the buddha-presence. Most of these ambrosial substances are produced under the homoeopathic principle of the greater the refinement of the substance, the greater its potency. Certainly, the potency of a substance is not determined by its quantity. A trace element is sufficient. In this way an ambrosia hyped as the relics of the great mystic polymath Longchen Rabjampa, who died more than 600 years ago, offered to a disciple by a contemporary lama, may contain a trace of a batch of the substance that itself contained only a trace, and so on back through scores of batches. Yet this is no less potent a source of blessing than the original relic.

Such magical compounds are effective, first and foremost, in dissolving the veils of emotion and thought-forms in meditation. But they can also create a harmony of vibration in the subtle body and a chemical balance – health – in the physical body. The same herbs that are the source of both medicinal and psychoactive ingredients may be gathered by the yogis, at the power places, for allopathic treatment with allopathic dosage.

The arcane lore governing procedure and preparation of magical compounds will have been orally transmitted by the yogi's lineage. However, even for an initiate of the tantra from which the recipe is derived, it is difficult to gain instruction in some alchemical aspects of yoga. The art in general is called *chulen*, 'the extraction of essences', and various dietary regimes are prescribed for yogis to assist in their meditation. *Chongzhi*, a calciferous mineral, for instance, is employed as a panacea and may comprise an exclusive diet. *Ashvadudh* is a black exudation from rock that increases life-energy and sexual strength. *Lingchen* is a plant that grows in the high meadows on the slopes of Tsari mountain and can induce a state of euphoria and gaiety where levitation and other of the yogi's magical powers are realized. *Ludu dorje* is the most prized herbal psychotropic and also grows on the slopes of Tsari mountain. Spherical pills, *rilbu*, more precious than *chomen*, are compounded from these highly potent substances.

A magical substance that is neither an alchemical compound nor a pure herbal panacea is the self-manifest *ringsel*. These tiny white pearl-like pills fall out of chortens, alone or in countless numbers, and are found lying on the ground around them. They are also discovered in the relics of a yogi who has dissolved into a rainbow body, leaving only a few ringsel behind him, or in the cremation chorten after the body has been consumed. The great quality of a ringsel is that by stashing it in a sacred space it will reproduce spontaneously and then multiply.

## The Sacred Person

If buddha-vision is perfected then everyone met on pilgrimage is perceived as a sacred person. But the tradition promotes specific roles played by specially trained individuals: lamas. The lama is a teacher who through actions of body, speech and mind demonstrates the Buddha's teaching. He may appear as a tulku, a monk, a yogi, a scholar, a wandering ngakpa magician or in a variety of other shapes. For the pilgrim he is the sacred person to be worshipped and he may act as a mirror to the worshipper. When in the devotee's perception he appears as a god, for example, then he is demonstrating a divine apparition; when he is a magician he performs magic, like healing or telling the future; when he is a Buddha he may preach or show some samadhi. In these ways the sacred person gives the Buddha's blessings (*jinlab*) and, therefore, has greater respect and devotion than the Three Jewels. The pilgrim will give prostration, offerings and prayer to the lama at the power place and receive blessings from him.

The most exalted role is that of the tulku. He is a Buddha incarnate. Here, a particularly charmed and talented child is recognized at a very early age as one of a succession of rebirths and in a hothouse climate of monastic education is taught the tantric tradition, so that he knows nothing else and exemplifies the spiritual ideal of tantric Buddhism. At least that is how it frequently happened in the old days, when the cultural tradition was intact, when Tibet was an island society in Central Asia insulated not only from Western cultural influence but also from the Indian and the Chinese spheres, when each gompa was a law unto itself and when daily life unravelled as a long ritual act, so that the tulku's conditioning over 20 or 30 years was given full scope. Perhaps that, too, is an ideal abstraction, but the power of belief is strong, and there is no doubt that the Tibetan people believed, and still believe, in the reality of their buddha-tulkus much as we believe in the stardom of a movie idol, or, come to that, in the inflexibility of steel.

The tulku was the spiritual authority in the gompa and a large gompa would have several tulkus. Because they were also the political authority and the mainstay of the lamaist religion, the tulkus were most harshly treated by the Chinese Communists and formed a disproportionately large proportion of the exiles and of the section of the Tibetan community systematically exterminated. Some remained, but it is uncommon these days to find a tulku resident in a gompa; usually an abbot will preside.

At the cave or hermitage site the lama will probably be present as a yogi. The hermit-meditator is tolerated by the present regime, presumably because he represents no political threat. If he is good enough at his job he will be recognized as a self-created tulku and perhaps begin a line of reincarnations. In the Nyingma tradition of revelation, such a yogi is an emanation of Guru Rimpoche, or put in another way, Guru Rimpoche himself. As such, he has the omniscient awareness and the spiritual powers of Guru Rimpoche and possesses an aura of magical transformation.

The blessings bestowed by the sacred person, whether he is a tulku, a yogi, a monk or a ngakpa magician, do not differ in quality from those obtained from power objects or from the rapport with a buddha-entity in worship. But the sacred person combines the blessing of buddha-body, speech and mind, is easily accessible and has made a vow to serve all sentient beings. Transmission of blessings is one of his primary functions. For this reason the transformed landscape and power objects are secondary to the lama as the focus of pilgrimage. As the primary agent of blessing bestowal he is the spiritual heart of a power place.

The Tibetan word for blessing, *jinlab*, means 'wave of grace', and is experienced as a hit of compassion and benevolence or even a psychedelic high. It infuses the awareness of its recipient 'just as red dye saturates white cloth'. The sacred person's blessing may be transmitted mind to mind, through the medium of a gesture or word, or by the touch of a hand or a power object. It may also be bestowed in a knotted protection cord (*sungdu*) to be worn around the neck to ward off negative influences, or in an amulet in the form of a small square flat bag containing a written mantra, or protective design of some kind, also to be worn around the neck. Any sacred substances bestowed upon the pilgrim by the sacred person are endowed with the extra potency of his blessing.

PART FIVE

# Power Places

Power places are the destinations of pilgrims. 'Power place' translates the Tibetan word *ne*, or *nechen*, which can also be rendered 'sacred' or 'holy place'. The sacred ambience of a place, its energy and the pilgrim's relationship to it should be sufficient to fulfil the pilgrim's wishes. The most momentous power places are the great sacred mountains and the lakes in their proximity, and cover, therefore, large areas, sometimes hundreds of square miles. Within these areas the power centres are the caves, particular peaks and rocks, springs and confluences and sky-burial sites. Sometimes the natural features have been modified by man and the power place has become inseparable from the structure built there – hermitage, gompa, lhakhang, chorten, etc. Regardless of what has been built, every power place gains its significance primarily from its geomantic location. Secondarily, it is consecrated by divine or human activity.

Geomancy is divination of the landscape. The most common form practised in Europe is dowsing, the divination of subterranean water courses. The Chinese have developed the art (or is it a science?) of geomancy, *feng shui*, far beyond any other culture. Literally, it means 'wind water' – 'wind you cannot comprehend and water you cannot grasp'. More specifically it is knowledge of the relationship between topography, water courses, natural *chi* and human modification of the landscape. In practice, feng shui is used to discover a suitable place for building a structure and its ideal alignment. Most new Chinese buildings in Hong Kong are sited according to its principles. However, although Tibet received much of its mystic science and art from China, particularly medicine and astrology, of which geomancy is a part, the developed art of feng shui seems never to have reached Tibet. Tibetan geomancy has to be defined in less sophisticated terms than feng shui: it is more the art of divining the place of perfect harmony of the elements in the landscape, or, in a more modest definition, identifying auspicious geomantic features in the landscape and locating power places. It is performed by yogis with visionary insight into the relationship of mind and landscape.

According to this relationship, where the sky meets the earth at the top of a mountain or hill is a power place. Kang Rimpoche (Kailash), Labchi, Tsari, Nyangchen Thanglha, Bonri, Khawa Karpo and Amnye Machen are some of these most sacred mountains. Every valley has a mountain power place in proximity. Where the earth, sky and water are conjunct at a lake is also a power place. Tso Mapham (Manasarovar), Yamdrok Tso, Lamo Latso, Namtso and Tso Ngon (Kokonor) lakes are such lake power places. Where a major river rises is a power place, like the springs of the four great rivers in the four directions of Kang Rimpoche. Where two rivers meet is a power place, like the confluences of the Yarlung Tsangpo and the Kyichu, and the Yarlung Tsangpo and the Nyangchu, and the river confluence at Labchi. Where fire and water are mixed at a hot spring is a power place, like the hot springs of Terdrom and Tretapuri, and the flames on the water at Chumi Gyatsa (Muktinath). A particular conjunction of space and rock provided by a cave may become a power place. A mountain pass is a power place, providing an altar below a mountain peak.

Certainly there are many places in Tibet that are power places by geomantic definition, but unless they have been consecrated by tradition they lack the association with buddha-mind that endows them with particular sanctity. When both geomantic and human factors are optimized the result will be a great power place, a nechen. Sometimes, however, the geomantic power place will lack any human activity – Tibetan Buddhists, unlike the Taoist Chinese and the Bonpos, do not generally climb mountain peaks. On the contrary, sometimes a place most sacred to a religious order will be devoid of visible geomantic features – the birthplace of a saint or the location of a gompa, for example.

Power places are residences of a buddha-deity, a god or spirit. But identification of such divine abodes implies application of a human mind. So, recognition of power places is the work of a yogi or adept and the identification is confirmed by the sage's continued presence there and his evocation, or propitiation and worship, of the god. The importance of the place is determined by the spiritual achievement of that first sage, for his success will draw other yogis to the place. Success will be seen in terms of the attainment of buddhahood or by spiritual powers demonstrated as magic or miracles.

Perhaps the first great name associated with the place will initiate a lineage of disciples through successive generations who will further sanctify it. Or, if a single lineage does not gain a monopoly of the site, it will become associated with various lineages. Whether of one or multiple lineages, a site becomes hallowed by tradition.

In Buddhist tradition, the most powerful sanctifying activity of a human being was Shakyamuni's enlightenment. It has marked the bodhi tree in Bodhgaya as the centre of the Buddhist world. Located in the middle of the Ganges plains, with no apparent significant geomantic features, Shakyamuni's seat under the tree, called Dorjeden, the Indestructible Throne, is a power place primarily consecrated through human activity. Guru Rimpoche's place of enlightenment at Yanglesho (Pharping) in the Kathmandu Valley is a south-facing rock cave on a ridge. In Tibet, however, the moment of a yogi's enlightenment is not usually recorded as such and it is simply the places of meditation of the innumerable buddha-lamas that are recalled.

Until a power place has been empowered by a buddha-lama, although it may possess auspicious geomantic features it is still part of the profane landscape, perhaps unremarked and unused. If it is a cave, perhaps goat or yak herders have sheltered in it, their animals leaving centuries of accumulated dung along with the charcoal of ancient fires on the floor.

A place is sanctified by a lama or tantric magician. His presence there is alone sufficient to empower it. But if he stays there for a significant length of time, then certainly he will be the subject of legend and this legend will add support to the basic fact of his buddha-awareness impregnating the rock and changing the perceived pattern of energy from a chaotic superficial malignity – or potential malignity – to a point of transcendental awareness at the centre of the mandala. A cave is 'opened' by the yogi whose meditation sanctifies it. A mountain power place is opened by the first adept to circumambulate it. A hidden valley is opened by a treasure-finder who reveals Guru Rimpoche's map and leads his followers into it. The followers of a particular religious order may consider a power place 'open' only if the founder of that order, or one of its masters, opened it.

The conjunction of auspicious geomantic features and the sometime presence of a yogi who has empowered the place produces an ambience immediately accessible to the pilgrim who approaches that power place with devotion. The feelings that are evoked may be described in terms of power, but through Buddhist devotional and meditational practice the yogi transforms the latent energy of the place into transcendental awareness and its compassionate responsiveness. This state of buddha-mind is conducive to the discovery of hidden treasure. Power places are by definition places of hidden treasure, but according to the doctrine of the Nyingma order only those places empowered by Guru Rimpoche or his primary emanations contain caches of accessible treasure. When Guru Rimpoche was travelling throughout Tibet, meditating in the innumerable cave and temple power places, he concealed treasures in each for the fortunate beings of future generations, and these places are called 'treasure power places' (terne).

These treasures (terma) come in three categories: treasures of body, speech and mind. The 'body' treasures are small images and sacred artefacts like sacred daggers (phurbas) and dorjes. The treasures of 'mind' are small chortens. The 'speech' treasures are by far the most numerous and consist of texts that were concealed in various ways. Some were old manuscripts that were hidden in large images and chortens. But most were reduced by Guru Rimpoche and his consort Khandro Yeshe Tsogyel to a mystic formula called the 'dakini script' (khandro dayik) and written down to be hidden within the great elements – earth, water, fire, air and space. Of these the earth treasures (sater) and space or mind treasures (gongter) were most important. The earth treasures were most frequently hidden in the rock of cave power places. The space treasures were concealed in meditation space. Wherever the Great Guru hid a cache of treasure he also concealed separately a 'manifest' which listed the contents of the cache. He also concealed lists of twice revealed treasure, texts that were to be revealed and then reconcealed because the time was unpropitious. Actual keys to the treasuries were also hidden separately. Next the guru would make a wish-granting prayer for those who would discover them, praying that the treasure-finder would be worthy and that the treasure would benefit the fortunate. He then set three seals on the caches and charged the guardians and treasure-finders to keep the treasure secret. Later, he gave prophetic indications as to where the treasures were to be discovered and the identity of the treasure-finders.

The instructions he gave to would-be treasure-finders reveals much about the Nyingma tradition:

*You blessed ones who will discover my treasures in the future, keep this testament in your minds. If you cannot sustain the teaching, misadventure will certainly befall you – so keep it secret. If you reveal the secret teaching before it is time, you will be struck by men's jealousy, envy and abuse – so first let signs of accomplishment appear. If you attain great superiority and fame, and your glory resounds, men will pour down evil upon you – so be prepared with black magical powers.*

*Make your vision as high as the sky; if you have not overcome the limitations of your vision, you will go astray. Your meditation should be as strong as a golden spike in the ground; if your meditation is not stable mere performance of outer ritual forms will not make it so. Your activity should be heroic and confident; pretensions and good intentions will not transform others.*

*The culmination of the path is reached through commitment and compassion; keep your vows pure and treat others with compassion. Until signs of achievement arise in your own meditation practice, do not give spiritual instruction to others; unless others have confidence in your teaching they will give it no respect. Do not expound the teaching and give personal advice at the same time; after having given the disciple instruction he may cut his connection with you, so examine the potential vessel carefully.*

*This teaching on hidden treasure is extremely deep, so practise it with profound discrimination. If you act according to my advice, blessings will spontaneously accrue. You will find Buddha within yourself. All your needs will be provided by other people. You will be respected and served by all. The gods will prepare your food. Your wishes will be fulfilled. You will hold the Buddha's lineage. You will intuitively realize the meaning of the buddha-dharma. You will establish a community and spread the doctrine widely.*

*Otherwise, failing to do as I advise, having gained no experience in the teaching yourself and looking to others for food and wealth, you will disgrace the Buddha, drag the feet of his teaching, and set a*

*bad example in the community, become a sinful master, a counsellor*
*to the damned, and setting yourself on the road to hell you will*
*waste your precious human body. My teaching on hidden treasure is*
*dangerous, so you must know how to sustain it to perfection.*

DOWMAN MS

Treasure-finders have appeared in Tibet regularly and frequently since the eleventh century and the Great Guru prophesied that there would be a treasure-finder in each valley. Each generation should have new revealed texts relevant to their needs and each valley its own Guru Rimpoche surrogate whose very presence would strengthen the tradition that gave him his credentials.

The content of the treasure texts varied a great deal. The Great Guru's biographies were mostly treasure texts. But a majority of them were meditation liturgies for the evocation of buddha-deities and for propitiation of the guardian protectors.

Geomantically significant power places, particularly caves, have been immeasurably enriched by the legends of Guru Rimpoche's periods of meditation there and his concealment of treasure. These places have attracted potential discoverers and a stream of meditators through the centuries who have reinforced the legend and the sanctity of the places.


## MOUNTAINS AND LAKES

### Guides to Power Places

Most of the great mountain power places (*neri*) cover extensive wilderness areas lacking any permanent settlement. Pilgrims travel there from far and wide and their need for valid and detailed information about the place is derived from the texts called 'guides to power places' (*neyiks*). Sometimes these guides were written by the openers of the power places, but more frequently by later initiates of lineages who could add the wealth of minor visionary identifications made by yogis and legends accrued over time to the insights and visionary perceptions of the opener. The importance of these texts is shown in this verse taken from a guide to Tsari:

*If pilgrims abandon the guide to Tsari*
*They are liable to turn into mere sightseers.*
*Without these eulogies to the Tsari pilgrimage circuit*
*They just gossip about the theft of the monastery's yak.*

HUBER 1993

Such guides are excellent indicators of what the pilgrim is seeking and what and how he sees. The way in which a mandala vision of the mountain is created and the elements of that vision are detailed. The importance of the khorra path is evident, since the larger part of each guide is devoted to the descriptions of phenomena encountered on the way. The features that induce a suspension of belief (or disbelief), the self-manifest phenomena and the power objects that effect 'liberation through seeing' are mentioned, together with the phenomena to which are attached legends of miracles performed by great adepts.

The best known mountains in the whole of Tibet are Kang Rimpoche, Labchi and Tsari, the three abodes of the buddha-deity Demchok. They are the most famous hermitage sites not only of the Kagyu yogis but also of all the religious orders. Local mountains may have greater significance for the people living within the territory ruled by that mountain god, and Amnye Machen, Khawa Karpo and Nyenchen Thanglha have national significance, but Kang Rimpoche, Labchi and Tsari are pre-eminent.

## Kang Rimpoche

Shri Kailash or Kang Tise is the most sacred of sacred mountains. It is best known by Tibetans simply as Kang Rimpoche, the Precious Mountain. Located behind the Himalayan divide in Western Tibet, it is far from any population centre and its inaccessibility has always heightened its enigma and increased its magnetism. The pilgrims that once spent months on foot travelling to it from Eastern and Central Tibet can now reach it by truck, but its sanctity is in no way diminished. For the half billion Hindus to the south it is the abode of the Great God Shiva Mahadeva, it is the *axis mundi*, the pivot of the universe, and through pilgrimage to it rebirth in Shiva's paradise is assured. For all Tibetans, Bonpos and Buddhists alike, it is the centre of the cosmos and the boons of pilgrimage are automatically bestowed there.

Many sacred mountains are pyramidal or conical, or show some natural feature that sets them apart. Kang Rimpoche is a dome-shaped mountain protruding well above the surrounding peaks, snowcapped in summer, while its neighbours are starkly grey. Its four faces in the four cardinal directions are easily recognizable by the mark of a swastika on the south face, by an ice fall on the western side, by its sheer north face and the east face visible only for a flash on the khorra path. Its physical magnificence in the Western mind is an overwhelming sensory experience and the inflated prose used to describe it by those few Europeans who visited it when Tibet was closed is now echoed by those who can visit it on a Chinese tour. Tibetan pilgrims are generally insensitive to the physical glory of the landscape, but because the mountain lends itself to a mandala vision, because its symmetry can spontaneously induce that vision, it is particularly adored by yogis. The symmetry of its four faces and the rough circle of its encircling outer khorra path are restated in the location of the sources of the four great rivers that arise in the four directions: in the east the Tsangpo (Brahmaputra) river, known as the Yarlung Tsangpo in Central Tibet; in the south the Karnali, a major tributary of the Ganges; the Sutlej, a major tributary of the Indus, in the west, flowing from Tso Mapham lake; and the Indus itself, rising at the head of the valley on the northern side of the Kang Rimpoche range. The special geomantic feature in the environment is the presence of Tso Mapham lake to the south of the mountain.

As to the divine power of the mountain itself, long before the Buddhists arrived it was the place of the Bon mountain god Gekho. The Bonpos perceived the mountain as a crystal chorten, and the Buddhists elaborated this vision to see the basic Five Buddha mandala signified by the colours of lapis, gold, ruby and emerald, of which the east, south, west and north faces respectively are made. But for the simple pilgrim, the mountain is the king and the lower surrounding peaks his ministers. The southern Buddhists, averse to tantric visualization, see the mountain as the place blessed by Shakyamuni and by his saintly disciple Yenlakjung with a retinue of

500 arhats, who flew there from the south. For the Tibetan who knows the mandala of the Buddhist cosmology, Kang Rimpoche is Mt Sumeru, with a buddha-palace on its summit, the gods in their hierarchical order in the heavens above, the denizens of hell languishing at the root of the mountain, shaped like a dagger that reaches to the bottom of the universe, and the continents with their four rivers spread out in the four directions – China, India, Europe and Siberia.

For the tantric yogi the mountain is the ultimate abode of Demchok (Samvara), the Supreme Bliss. Kang Rimpoche, Labchi, Tsari, Amnye Machen – all of these great sacred mountains are Demchok, but Kang Rimpoche is the first. Externally, the snow peak itself is envisioned as the great buddha-deity Demchok in consummate union with his khandroma consort Dorje Phakmo and the surrounding peaks are their 16 offering goddesses. The three psychic channels of the union of father and mother deities are the slash down the middle of the south face and the two streams that flow on the eastern and western sides. Internally, the mountain is the mandala of Demchok, replete with the 62 goddesses.

The Kang Rimpoche mandala has been consecrated by innumerable Buddhas and yogis over the millennia. First of all, Shakyamuni Buddha himself magically emanated here together with the 500 arhats. His footprints, the 'immutable nails' that bind the mountain to the earth, provide evidence of his presence. These 'nails' are needed because of the mountain's feather-like quality. It is held to have originally come to Tibet from another country for the sake of all sentient beings, but in the age of degeneration, the kaliyuga, there is danger of it flying away. The four nails keep it tied down, while four prayer banners connected by iron chains once kept it from falling into the underworld.

After Shakyamuni, Guru Rimpoche meditated here and hid treasures in the caves where he sat. Later, the great yogi Milarepa came here to meditate, leaving a legacy of legend entwined around the mountain. He engaged a Bon yogi, Naro Bonchung, in magical contest here *(see p.162, p.164)* and the Bonpo's defeat led to the banishment of the Bon order from the mountain. In the thirteenth century the great adept Gotsangpa, Lord of the Eagle's Nest, opened this power place for the Drukpa Kagyu order, and hermits and yogis of his lineage, in numerical terms, have dominated it ever since. Down the centuries some of the greatest names in the Tibetan tradition have made pilgrimage here and meditated within sight of the great snow mountain, like Zhabkar Rimpoche, Little White Foot, who spent three years immured in the nineteenth century.

No other mountain power place has the same density of peaks and rocks identified as palaces, residences or lodges of the Buddhas and bodhisattvas as the Kang Rimpoche mandala, nor so many rock formations envisioned as sacred artefacts and as self-manifest images and power objects. Innumerable cairns and mani-stones and mani-walls also surround the mountain. Five gompas lie on the khorra paths; these were destroyed by the Communists, but all have been rebuilt or restored. There is no space here to identify all these phenomena and all the caves and hermitages that have been sanctified by the innumerable yogis who have meditated near the mountain. Those identified below have been selected, somewhat arbitrarily, as objects with some special significance.

### The Inner Khorra Path

The inner khorra path of Kang Rimpoche takes the pilgrim to the bottom of the south face of the sacred mountain. The degree of purification required to gain the optimal benefit from this close approach is shown by this story. Once a woman from Kham, bending over with a baby tied to her back to drink from the Khandro Tso lake, just below the Drolma La pass, allowed the baby to slip over her head into the icy water and it drowned. Since then the lake has been closed by a covering of ice. The woman began to perform circumambulations around the mountain to expiate her fault and after only 13 circuits she left hand and footprints impressed in the rock and attained rainbow body in the sky dancers' pure-land.

The trail begins, like that of the outer khorra circuit, at Darchen, to the south, and follows the Selung Valley, Grey Valley, to the north, past the rebuilt Selung Gompa. Beyond that is the crystal-like mountain, the palace of Shiva Mahadeva, and to the side a protruding rock called Hanumanju (visible also from the western side of the outer khorra path). Above Selung the trail does a loop around the mountain palace of the arhat Yenlakjung and his 500 arhat attendants, which is envisioned by Hindus as Nandi, the Bull, the vehicle of Shiva Mahadeva. Crossing a pass on the northern side of Yenlakjung, the Serdung Chusum, the 13 Golden Reliquary chortens, are reached. This row of 13 chortens built, and recently rebuilt, on a ledge on the south face of Kang Rimpoche contained the relics of 13 Drikung Kagyu hierarchs, many of whom meditated at Kang Rimpoche between the fourteenth and the nineteenth centuries. Below the Serdung Chusum, to the east of the Palace of Yenlakjung, are two small lakes. These are perceived as skullbowls holding the chief tantric offerings to the buddha-deity Demchok. The first, Rakta Tso, is black (or red) and contains the blood that is the sky dancer offering; and the second, Dutsi Tso, contains the white elixir that is the semen of the Buddhas. These lakes are empowered sky dancer pools. To the east, the peak that appears to have a curtain of white silk screening it is the mountain palace of the divine assembly of Yeshe Gompo, the Protecting Lord of Pure Awareness.

On the return to Darchen, near Selung Gompa, is a path to the east going to Gyangdrak, Ear-Shot, Gompa. This monastery is not a part of the inner khorra circuit and may be included, although it rarely is, on the outer circumambulation by turning west from Dzutrul Phuk and crossing a pass to the Gyangdrak Valley. It is easily accessible from Darchen along the crest of the gorge of the Gyangdrakchu river. The restored Gyangdrak Gompa is the largest of Kang Rimpoche's gompas, a Drikung Kagyu establishment that once housed three more of the Drikung hierarch's reliquary serdungs. It also enshrines the Drikung Kagyu's fierce protecting deity, Apchi Lhamo.

## The Outer Khorra Path

Thirteen circumambulations of the outer khorra path of Kang Rimpoche bring a reward similar to that of circumambulating the inner khorra path and allow entrance to the inner path. For this reason and also because this path does not circle the mountain itself, and is therefore less efficient as a khorra practice defining the mountain as a mandala centre, it is rarely trodden by pilgrims.

The outer circumambulation begins at Darchen on the Barkha plain and proceeds north-west across to the Lhalung Valley. Where the first glimpse of the Kang Rimpoche peak can be caught is Chaktsel Kang, Prostration Ridge. Here, the great adept Gotsangpa, after performing a circumambulation of Tso Mapham lake, wished to make a fire to brew tea, but, looking around for hearth-stones, all he could see was self-manifest buddha-images and sacred syllables in the rocks. So he made prostrations to Kang Rimpoche instead.

At the entrance to the Lhalung Valley is the Darboche, the Great Flag Pole. This 30-foot pole is raised annually on the full moon day of the month celebrating Shakyamuni Buddha's enlightenment, Saga Dawa, usually in May. This essentially pre-Buddhist ritual re-enacts the subjection of the earth and now celebrates the sway of the buddha-deities. To the east, on a ledge against the cliff, is the yogis' sky-burial site, which is the preferred place of corpse disposal for nomads of the area and residents of the gompas. Above this place of death is Naro Bonchung's cave, his place of meditation before he was dispossessed by Milarepa, whose footprint is visible above the cave opening. Below is a spring called Menchu Nesel, whose medicinal waters are a panacea for all diseases. Beyond the great pole of Darboche is Chorten Kangnyi, the Two-Legged Chorten, a gateway chorten, through which it is auspicious to pass. Further up is a footprint of the Buddha, an 'immutable nail', marked by a cairn.

The Lhalung Valley narrows and red sandstone cliffs tower on each side, climbing to peaks that are the palaces of the buddha-deities. On the western side of the valley is the palace of Black Jambhala, the black god of wealth, and in a valley beside it is a Guru Rimpoche cave called Sangngak Chos Phuk, the Cave of the Tantric Teaching, marked by the Great Guru's handprints and footprints, and a spring of the water of realization. Above it is a self-manifest image of Chenrezik.

Above the red cliffs towering up from the Lhachu river valley to the west is a peak called Nyenri, resembling a pitched silk tent, which is the palace of the local mountain god of Kang Rimpoche called Tise Lhatsen or Tsangpa Karpo. On its shoulder is a Milarepa cave called Rechen Phuk, where Milarepa stayed after striding across Kang Rimpoche in his contest with Naro Bonchung. There are many caves and hermitages on its steep slopes. The shrine to the Tise Lhatsen is in the lhakhang of the guardian protectors at Nyenpoi Ridzong, Nyen's Mountain Fortress, a gompa founded by a great adept called Nyen, of ancient but uncertain date. This Drukpa Kagyu monastery, blessed by Gotsangpa, standing at the bottom of the steep eastern side of the mountain, perched on an outcrop, is also called Choku Gompa, because it enshrines the most sacred buddha-image in the Kang Rimpoche mandala – Choku Rimpoche. 'Choku' denotes the buddha-body of infinite space and awareness, here represented in the form of Amitabha. This image of white marble has a historical legend attached. Long ago it appeared spontaneously out of Milk Lake in Lahaul and in the eleventh century it was brought as an offering to the King of Guge by Chenrezik in the guise of a yogi. Centuries passed and Tise Lhatsen, coveting the image, appeared in the form of seven Indian yogis begging alms at the Guge Gompa where it was enshrined. The monks turned them away contemptuously, whereupon the yogis turned into seven wolves and disappeared. Seven days later the image itself vanished, taken by the Kang Rimpoche mountain god. In the seventeenth century the King of Guge sent soldiers to retrieve the image and as it was extremely heavy they tied a rope around its neck and dragged it off. When they stopped for tea and the tea in the pot turned to blood, they fled, leaving the image behind them. An old man found it and it spoke to him, requesting that it be returned to Nyenpoi Ridzong. The old man picked it up and, finding it to be as light as a feather, brought it to the gompa. An old adage indicates the significance of this image: 'Outside, Kang Rimpoche; inside, Choku Rimpoche.'

The gompa possesses two power objects almost as sacred as Choku Rimpoche: a conch and a tea cauldron that belonged to the great Indian yogi and scholar Naropa. The sanctity and power of objects believed to have belonged to Naropa, the Indian master of Milarepa's teacher Marpa Lotsawa, is as great as if they had belonged to Shakyamuni Buddha himself, and the conch brings liberation from the round of rebirth merely by setting eyes upon it. The Cultural Revolution dispersed these objects and it is a miracle that they are again enshrined at Choku. Choku Gompa was the repository of all the images returned by the Chinese after the liberalization in the 1980s.

Returning across the Lhachu river and walking up the trail into the upper Lhalung Valley, there is a stream of five-coloured rainbow light which carries the empowerment of Kang Rimpoche. A great rock dome to the east of the trail is the palace of Gompo Beng, the Indian demon Ravana, transformed into a Buddhist protector, and also his offering of barley dough, his yak and his dog. On the lower edge of the dome is a rock-face with a large boulder protruding that resembles a crystal box. The great adept Nyo Lhanangpa had a vision of the Great Compassionate One here which was absorbed into this box. Beyond is an image of Hanumanju, the Hindu monkey god, Shiva Mahadeva's most solicitous devotee, who kneels facing his master's palace carrying incense as an offering. High on the western side of the valley is a mountain that is the chorten of Namgyelma (Ushnishavijaya) and also seven minor peaks that are the abode of King Ling Gesar's seven brothers.

Beside the trail is a black boulder called the Tamdrin (Hayagriva) Dronkhang, the Horse-Necked Buddha Lodge, adorned with a self-manifest relief of Tamdrin, the buddha-deity who subjects the serpent spirits. Close by is one of the Shakyamuni Buddha's footprints, an 'immutable nail' that binds the mountain to the ground, called Bolnubma, Sunk in Ankle Deep. On the surface of the glacier above, on Kang Rimpoche itself, the gates of crystal which have the appearance of being guarded by the four guardians of the mandala gates can be seen.

Where the khorra trail turns to the east, where both western and northern flanks of Kang Rimpoche are visible and the red sandstone of the Lhalung Valley becomes the grey granite of the Drolmachu tributary valley, is Drira Phuk Gompa, located just to the north in Dronglung, Wild Yak Valley. When the great adept Gotsangpa made a pilgrimage to Kang Rimpoche with the purpose of opening the area as a power place for Drukpa Kagyu meditation, he circumambulated the mountain and a wild female yak appeared as if by magic before him. He followed the yak's trail and from the top of a boulder watched her disappear into a cave above. He climbed up to the cave and found within only the imprint of her horn on the rock into which she had vanished. In his buddha-vision Gotsangpa identified the wild female yak as an emanation of the female Buddha Senge Dongchan, the Lion-Headed Sky Dancer. This messenger showed him the way to the power place and was absorbed into it, leaving the mark of her apparent presence as horn-marks in the rock. Evidence of Gotsangpa's part in the discovery was left in the form of his footprints in the boulder from which he watched the yak disappear into the cave. He sat in prolonged meditation in that cave and was fed by the Lion-Headed Sky Dancer. When he was about to leave it, due to the bitter cold, he pressed his head into the rock and said, 'Anyone who presses his head into this cavity will escape rebirth in the lower realms. This includes birds, rodents and insects.' The valley where he encountered the yak is called Dronglung, Wild Yak Valley, and the cave was called Drira Phuk, Yak-Horn Cave. This cave became a principal power place of meditation for Drukpa Kagyu yogis and Drira Phuk Gompa was built around it. Today only a doll-like image of Gotsangpa adorns the altar. The mountain behind the cave is identified as the abode of the 1,000 Buddhas of our Auspicious Aeon.

From Drira Phuk Gompa, across the Drolma Chu, the sheer north face of Kang Rimpoche dominates. On the surface of the snows clinging to this face can be discerned the forms of Guru Rimpoche riding on a pig and a demoness leading a pig. In the snowdrifts is the palace of the serpent spirit king Tsukna Rinchen, Jewel Topknot, which is named Chumik Ngulbum, 100,000 Silver Springs.

Between Drira Phuk Gompa and Kang Rimpoche are the palaces of Jampelyang and Chenrezik to the east and Chakna Dorje to the west. These are the bodhisattva protectors (Riksum Gompo) of body, speech and mind. Between Chenrezik and Chakna Dorje is a path leading to the place where 'the flesh of Kang Rimpoche', a calcinate deposit and medicinal panacea, is dug from the ground.

From Drira Phuk Gompa the pilgrim climbs to the east up the Drolmachu valley towards the high point of the Drolma La pass. Some way up is Jarok Dronkhang, Crow Lodge. Here Gotsangpa made a torma offering to the spirit-owner of the ground of Lhalung Valley. The entire torma was stolen by a crow, which the yogi identified as a minion of Gompo, the Great Black Lord. He chased it up the valley and just short of the sky-burial site of Silwaitsel, Cool Grove, it vanished into a boulder, leaving its imprint upon it.

Silwaitsel is perhaps the most powerful ritual site on the khorra. It is the famous Indian cremation ground Sitarvana, near Bodhgaya, transposed to Kang Rimpoche. It consists of a simple circle of stones amidst the stony valley bottom of the Drolmachu river. It may occasionally be used for sky burial, but since the main sky-burial site in the Kang Rimpoche area is in the lower Lhalung Valley, in the pilgrimage season the stone circle is covered with articles of clothing, locks of hair, saddle-bags and other personal effects offered to the place and the guardian deity as tokens by which the pilgrim will be remembered when he passes through the narrow defile of the intermediate state between death and rebirth. Offerings of blood, usually induced from the nose, are smeared over the rocks here. In the mythology of the khorra route, the sky-burial site represents the place of death before the spiritual rebirth attained by the intervention of Drolma, the Saviouress, at the top of the pass, and lying down on his back the pilgrim may visualize his own death.

Further along the path are three giant boulders resting one on the other. Naro Bonchung brought the first one there in a contest of magical accomplishment with Milarepa. When he attempted to place the second one on top of the first, Milarepa knocked it off with a fixed gaze. It rolled down to the path, where it can be recognized by the Bon shaman's handprint and Milarepa's footprint upon it. Milarepa then stacked two boulders on top of Naro Bonchung's to make three, representing the three buddha-bodies.

As already related, when Gotsangpa was opening the circumambulatory path of the sacred mountain, towards the top of the Drolma La pass he lost the trail in a field of rocks. He entered the state of awareness called the Sky Dancer's Secret Path and immediately a pack of 21 wolves appeared ahead of him. He recognized the wolves as emanations of the 21 forms of Drolma, the Saviouress, sent to guide him. He followed them to the top of the pass where they magically vanished into the rock. This was the origin of the name of that pass, Drolma La. Wolf paw marks, evident in the rock there, are the imprints of these wolves. The Sky Dancer's Secret Path is physically revealed as a higher, shorter path that leaves the main trail near Silwaitsel, passing to the east of Jampelyang's palace, over the Kandro Sanglam La pass and down to the Lhamchu Valley.

The top of the pass is marked by a large square boulder called Phabong Mebar, the Flaming Rock, upon which a flag pole is inserted in a cairn and from which prayer-flags are strung to surrounding poles. Pilgrims smear butter on the rock as an offering and leave personal effects here. An outcrop to the rear of Flaming Rock is the residence of Drolma into which the wolves vanished. Buddhist and Bonpo mantras are painted onto the rock.

In the mountains to the north of the Drolma La pass are the palaces of Gompo, the Great Black Lord, and the mountain god called Kangwa Zangpo, Totally Good. There is also an enlightenment chorten (Jangchub Chorten) here. Below the Drolma La, within the khorra path, is the Khandro Trumtso, the Sky Dancer's Bathing Pool, evidence of Kang Rimpoche as the sky dancers' pureland. It is also called Thukjechenpo Tso, the Lake of the Great Compassionate Lord. In the past it may have been perennially frozen over, but these summers the ice melts to allow pilgrims to bathe, or at least to take a bottle of the empowered water home. Below, in cliffs to the south of Khandro Trumtso, are the forms of Senge Dongchan, the Lion-Headed Sky Dancer, Chakna Dorje, Dorje-in-Hand, and Tamdrin, the Horse-Necked Lord.

On Melong Teng, Mirror Terrace, three, or perhaps four, footprints of Milarepa are visible where his feet sank into the rock while he was dragging Naro Bonchung around the khorra in the clockwise, Buddhist, direction. Further down in a gully on the right side are eight or nine more of his footprints on the surface of a large slab of rock.

The trail descends steeply from the Drolma La down to the Lhamchu Valley. At the bottom of the descent is a boulder impressed with the footprint of Shakyamuni Buddha, an 'immutable nail' called Drakdokma, Footstep on the Rock. Nearby is a footprint of Guru Rimpoche. Lower down, the Lhamchu Valley turns into the Dzonglung Valley. Here many streams water pastures for the nomads' yak herds.

On the ridge to the east stands the five-peaked mountain palace of the five Tsering Chenga sisters, mountain protectresses entrusted by Milarepa to guard the Kang Rimpoche mandala. Further towards the south, on the eastern side, are mountains impressed with self-manifest images of the protecting buddha-deities Miyowa (Achala), the Immovable One, and Gompo, Mahakala, the Great Black Lord, which were envisioned there by Tsangpa Gyare, the root-guru of the Drukpa Kagyu lineage. On another mountain is an image of Dorje Phakmo, the Adamantine Sow, visualized and imprinted there by the adept Nyo Lhanangpa. Further down, to the east, is the mountain palace of Menlha, the Medicine Buddha, while on the western side is Menlung, Medicine Valley, where medicinal herbs cover the ground and medicinal minerals are gathered from the rocky slopes.

To the south-east of Kang Rimpoche, in the Dzonglung Valley, is the renowned Dzutrul Phuk cave, the Cave of Magical Display, or Cave of Miracles. The gompa that covers the cave provides the chief sanctuary on the mountain's eastern side. Dzutrul Phuk is one of Milarepa's principal meditation caves and he provided the magical display which gives the cave its name in an exchange with the Bon shaman Naro Bonchung. The Buddhist yogi and the shaman were engaged in a race around the mountain, the Buddhist clockwise and the Bonpo counter-clockwise, in their customary modes, and this was the point at which they crossed. At the moment of crossing a cloudburst hit them and seeking shelter they agreed to divide the labour of erecting a sanctuary. Naro Bonchung split stones with his magical powers and Milarepa, to outdo him, employed his power of the fixed gaze to run holes through them. The Bonpo, attempting to emulate him and failing, was left paralytic, his eyes bulging out of their sockets. After Milarepa had finished constructing the walls, a great flat stone raised itself at the master's command to form the roof. Then, making adjustment to the height of the ceiling, Milarepa first raised the stone with his head, leaving an imprint in the rock, then pressed it down from above, his feet imprinting the rock.

An image of Milarepa is the principal sacred symbol on the altar in the cave, showing the great saint in his conventional posture of ease with his right hand behind the ear – some say the better to hear the whispered instruction of the sky dancers, while others maintain he is pressing the psychic nerve behind the ear. The original image was sculpted by his biographer the Divine Madman of Tsang, using some of the master's own blood to mix the clay, but it has vanished. The gompa's chief power object is a stone trident blessed by Milarepa, now broken, located on top of the cave.

There are many meditation caves in the vicinity of Dzutrul Phuk. One small cave is that in which Zhabkar Rimpoche, Little White Foot, lived for three years at the beginning of the nineteenth century. During breaks in his meditation he taught his many disciples through a window in the cave door. For him, the special significance of Kang Rimpoche was the residence there of the Khandro Senge Dongchan, the Lion-Headed Sky Dancer. Nearby is an 'immutable nail' footprint of Shakyamuni Buddha. From Dzutrul Phuk the khorra circuit returns to Darchen through the Trangser Trangmar, the Gold and Red Defile.

## Tso Mapham: Lake Manasarovar

Tso Mapham, the Invincible, also known as Tso Rimpoche, the Precious Lake, fills a basin in the Barkha plain between Kang Rimpoche and the Gurla Mandhata mountain to the south. The lake is 55 miles (88 km) in circumference. In summer, at dawn, it is usually calm and serene. By late morning a breeze has often arisen and its flat surface is broken by crested waves. In the afternoons it is frequently storm-tossed and breakers fall on the lakeshore. In the evening it returns to its placid serenity.

The lake may be envisioned as an eight-petalled lotus or as a mandala square with four doors in the cardinal directions. On its eastern shore those who have eyes can see the Rose-Apple Tree (Jambuvriksha) that is the tree of life of Dzambuling, the southern continent of Buddhist cosmology.

The lake was empowered by Shakyamuni Buddha. He travelled here by magical means with his 500 disciples and the serpent king of the lake caused a lotus of 501 flowers to blossom in the lake. Shakyamuni sat in the centre and his monks sat upon the surrounding flowers while the Lord taught them the buddha-dharma. The serpent king of the lake is a Buddha who took the serpent form to teach the buddha-dharma to the serpent spirits and he still works to increase the rivers, the flowers, fruits, medicinal herbs and forests of the world.

The khorra circuit is 84 miles (134 km) long. Local Tibetans prefer to do the pilgrimage in the winter when they can follow the shoreline. Few pilgrims perform the complete circumambulation these days; some do it by truck in two or tree days. The sandy plain in which Tso Mapham lies is featureless and the absence of rocks means an absence of self-manifest phenomena and abodes of the gods and Buddhas. The only distractions from the pilgrim's focus on the lake itself are the gompas that surround it. There are eight gompa sites situated approximately in the four cardinal and four intermediate directions which provide seats for the lamas, protection for hermits and shelter for pilgrims.

On the eastern side of the lake is Seralung Gompa, Thornbush Valley Gompa. This is not only the eastern bathing door, it is also the entrance to the mandala of Tso Mapham. Built originally in a sheltered spot on the lakeshore in the eighteenth century and recently rebuilt close to the old site, it was a Drikung Kagyu establishment. About a mile to the south of Seralung are three hills that are the abodes of the three bodhisattva protectors of body, speech and mind, Chenrezik, Jampelyang and Chakna Dorje, and down on the lakeshore near here is the place called Jema Nanga, a narrow strip of violet sand, from which sand of the five colours of the mandala may be culled. A taste of this sand is one of the lake's most prized blessings.

In the south-east, where the Richung river flows into the lake, are the ruins of Nyego, Pleased Head, Gompa. Jowo Atisha stayed here for several days in the twelfth century on the way from Bengal to Guge. It was a Sakya foundation. In the south is Trugolho Gompa, a Geluk establishment built directly on the lakeshore. Its name means 'southern bathing door' and it is the most portentous place to bathe in the lake. This is the last stretch to freeze over in autumn and the first to thaw in the spring.

Behind Trugo Gompa is the mountain Gurla Mandhata, with five sister peaks, the abode of the mountain goddess Menmo Namgyel. It is also the abode of Lhamo Yangchan, the Sweet-Voiced Maiden, the bodhisattva Sarasvati. This power-place mountain is as yet unopened, awaiting a Buddha or yogi to envision its divine nature and features.

To the west is Gosul or Gotsuk Gompa, situated on a prominence above the lake. The focal power place here is the cave wherein Gotsangpa stayed and because it was Gotsangpa who established the Drukpa Kagyu tradition at Kang Rimpoche the cave was called Gotsuk, the Beginning. Later, in the nineteenth century, a gompa was built over the cave. The cave in which Jowo Atisha meditated is located on the lakeshore.

In the north-west is Jiu, Small-Bird, Gompa, built atop a rocky outcropping where the Gangachu river leaves Tso Mapham. The monastery is built in the style of the Glorious Copper-Coloured Mountain Pure-Land, for Guru Rimpoche meditated here in a small cave below the assembly hall. Drukpa Kagyu monks now attend it. It is the western bathing door.

On the northern side of the lake is Serkyib Gompa, Bird Shelter of the Golden Bluff, situated in a sheltered valley with meditation caves in the cliff behind. Shakyamuni Buddha prophesied that this place would be the cave site where he and his 500 monks would stay while paying homage to Tso Mapham. The northern bathing door, Langpona, Elephant Trunk, Gompa, stands well back from the lake on a hill shaped like an elephant, while the Langchen Phuk, Elephant Cave, is located near the lakeshore.

To the north-east, located on Bonri hill itself rather than on the lake, is Bonri Gompa. After Naro Bonchung had been defeated by Milarepa in the contest for supremacy at Kang Rimpoche, he begged Milarepa for a place from which he could pay homage to the great snow mountain. Milarepa threw some snow into the air and when it landed on this hill he gave the place to Naro Bonchung and the Bonpos. The Bonri Gompa, however, is a Geluk establishment founded by a yogi from the Sera Gompa in Lhasa. It has yet to be restored.

A river called the Gangachu links Tso Mapham to Lanka Tso lake in a zigzag channel. Its water level fluctuates from season to season and year to year, according to the favour of the serpent king. Lanka Tso is a demon lake, a black lake of poison in the shape of a hide-couch made of human skin. It is the abode of the mountain god Bengchen (Ravana) who is a great guardian protector of the buddha-dharma.

## Labchi: The Yogi's Paradise

On the well-watered southern aspect of the Himalayas, in the region to the west of Mount Everest, between Gaurishankar and Jowo Bamare peaks, a gorge ascends to a river confluence where the Labchi mountain rises over rich flowery pastures and forested valleys, the enshrouding cloud and mist lending it an illusory pureland aura:

*The rock mountains are like elegant peaks of diamond,*
*The chain of snow peaks are laid out like pearls,*
*The beautiful forests are arrayed like handsome flowing robes:*
*Surely the Mighty Lord with his powerful retinue is sporting at this spot!*
*The flat ground is covered with attractive green turf,*
*Clothing it like a mantle, ornamented and wreathed by flowing streams,*
*And the falling water emits the sound of lutes and bells:*
*Seeing this adornment of unprecedented beauties,*
*At first we doubt the evidence of our eyes, and think,*
*Is this place heaven, the immortal abode?*
*Is it an illusion created by magicians?*
*Or is this the experience of a lucid dream?*

HUBER 1989

Here the Himalayan divide has been cut through by the rivers that meet at the confluence and flow south into Nepal. The rugged rock power-place mountain has been left standing high behind the confluence with successive peaks rising behind it. This ridge is part of the Labchi Kangyi Rawa, the Labchi Range, stretching north to the Tingri plains, to Nyalam valley in the west and to Rongshar and Chuwar in the east. The rocky face of the Labchi mountain, which is actually within the political borders of Nepal, gazes down the Kangchu Valley towards the heart of Nepal.

In the mythic geography of Labchi, this central power place consists of the rocky mountain peak itself and the rough triangular apron that drapes from its upper heights to the confluence point of the Kangchu and the Takialingchu rivers. The mountain is the male phallic peak and the triangular plain the symbol of the female Buddha. The sacred caves that are the glory of Labchi are located within this triangle. This is the heart of the place and also the heart of Godavari, for Labchi is identified as the major power place that is one of the 24 great abodes of Demchok, the buddha-deity who vanquished Shiva Mahadeva and established this place as a primary point of access to the Demchok mandala. The full extent of the Labchi-Godavari pure-land embraces the Himalayas and the valleys and plains behind it from the Kyirong Valley in the west to the Rongshar Valley in the east, and this area approximates the field of activity of the buddha-yogi who opened and consecrated Labchi mandala as one of the premier places of meditation and pilgrimage in Tibet. This was Jetsun Milarepa, whose brilliance illuminates the most obscure corners of Labchi.

The mythic history of Labchi begins during an early period in the kaliyuga, the aeon of degradation and strife. At this time, Ugra Bhairava, a terrific form of Shiva Mahadeva, the Great God, gained ascendancy in the heartland of India. His demonic minions of the three worlds appropriated the lingams at the 24 power places and, lost in a perverted vision, became obsessed with lascivious love and angry conflict. Since Mahadeva was their refuge, the Great God came to reside in the lingams himself. Then, after the passing of time, the Buddha Dorje Chang (Vajradhara) and his consort sought to benefit sentient beings by the conquest of Mahadeva, and in an extremely violent emanation of compassion called Heruka, he trampled him underfoot in a wrathful dance. Heruka took up residence on Kang Rimpoche, the erstwhile palace of Shiva, and assumed the retinue of the 62 deities of the Demchok mandala.

The Labchi mountain, the phallic peak that had been the residence of Mahadeva, already known by the name Godavari, was the centre of the personal domain of a pair of virulent odour-eating sky-gods (driza, *gandharvas*), who had poisoned the place. When Heruka vanquished Mahadeva, Dorje Chang and his consort in union likewise overcame these sky-demons. Their conquest was an internal transformation of the demons, and the form and accoutrements of the ky-gods remained unchanged. After Dorje Chang's victory Labchi was established as the abode of Demchok, who thus resided in the lingam-peak with his retinue of 62 deities. In the internalization of the 24 power places of pilgrimage, Labchi was located in the left ear of the subtle body of the yogi, but this, perhaps, fails to do justice to the renown and power of this place, for it is also the throat chakra of Demchok, the centre of his manifestation as speech, vibration and vision, while Kang Rimpoche is his head chakra and the manifestation of the illusory wheel of sensory emanation, and Tsari his heart chakra and the centre of the wheel of mind and pure awareness.

In this way Labchi was established as the mandala of Demchok and a most auspicious place for the practice of tantric meditation. But until the Indian founder of the Mahamudra tantric lineage, the master Saraha, visited Labchi and recognized the actuality of Demchok's existence there, it was the playground of flesh-eating sky-dancer couples. Various Indian masters visited Labchi after its opening and meditated there, the great Tibetan kings pacified the area, Guru Rimpoche came and bound the flesh-eating sky dancers by oath, and Labchi became a place where ordinary human beings could benefit from the residence of Demchok.

In the eleventh century, the sublime yogi Milarepa opened Labchi completely, subduing the local gods and demons. Consecrating it by his enlightened presence and meditation, he provided a legend that inspired and protected the people of the area and attracted pilgrims from all over Tibet. Milarepa was born into a peasant family in Mangyul, the region to the north of the Langthang Himal (and the Kathmandu Valley). He lost his father at an early age, saw his uncle steal his patrimony and watched his mother decline in servitude and social ostracism, his sister suffering along with her. These early experiences filled him with a deep and lasting bitterness and a virulent hatred towards those who had caused the ruin of his family. He sought vengeance through black magic, which he mastered and subsequently inflicted upon his persecutors. But the murder of his uncle left him ridden with guilt and remorse and the next phase of his life was dedicated to the purification of his karma. He became the disciple of one of the great masters of his age, Marpa Lotsawa, who had received the transmission of the Demchok tantra from the renowned Indian master Naropa. Marpa, the relentless taskmaster, charged the peasant youth with the practice of building and then destroying and rebuilding, over and over again, a stone tower of nine storeys, until not only had he been purged of his sins but his ego had been utterly demolished. At this point Marpa initiated him into the Demchok mandala and the preparation had been so comprehensive and profound that only a minimal experience of meditation gave him realization of buddha-vision. His master then urged him to mature his meditation in the caves of the central Himalayas:

*Take refuge in the solitude of the barren mountains, the snows or forests...In the wilderness cave you have an open market where you can barter samsara for nirvana...In the crystal [mountain] palace of the gods you will be witness to your own victory.*

LHALUNGPA 1977:94,97,98

Labchi was one of the chief places to which Marpa directed his brilliant disciple. But first Milarepa went to the Kyirong Valley where he spent 12 years in the cave at Drakar Taso, White Rock Horse Tooth, in fully developing his meditation and achieving buddharealization and the magical powers attendant upon it. Thereafter, although secluding himself for long periods in retreat, he dedicated himself to working for all sentient beings: binding gods and demons, teaching his disciples, sanctifying places of meditation and so on, and one of his first acts was to open Labchi.

## The Opening of Labchi

Milarepa approached Labchi from Tashigang, the western door of the power place, which is located on the Kathmandu–Lhasa highway. On the Zullekang La pass, named after one of the wild woman demonesses of the area whom the master took as a consort in meditation practice, he encountered the first opposition to his agenda. Gods and demons provoked thunder and lightning and the mountains moved to squash him, damming the river on the other side and creating a lake. Milarepa stuck his staff into the dam and drained the lake. Today that empty glacial lake is called Mudzing.

Below the path, the gods and demons sent waves of boulders down upon the master, but the sky dancers created a safe snake-like path between them called the Khandro Sanglam, the Sky Dancer's Secret Path, and the waves of rock can still be seen frozen in the landscape. At the bottom of this path, with a samadhi of fixed gaze Milarepa vanquished the gods and demons.

Nearby, he meditated on what is now called Jamgang, the Ridge of Loving Kindness, before descending to Chuzang, Auspicious Stream Valley, where he was assailed by Ganesha, the elephant-headed god who is the Lord of Obstacles, both creating and removing them, and who guarded pre-Buddhist Labchi. Ganesha had transformed himself into a Newar-priest demon and, surrounded by a vast demonic retinue, threw down mountains and a hail of weapons upon the master. Recognizing the illusory nature of this magical display, Milarepa bound Ganesha by oath and thereafter he not only protected the tradition at Labchi but also became the generous patron of the master and his lineal successors.

At Namphukma, Sky Cave, at Ramding, the Labchi sky dancers brought offerings and left their footprints in the rock. But further down, at Lagu Lungu, Nine Passes, Nine Valleys, is the miraculous stone on which the master kneaded his penis, erected in anger when demons assailed him with hallucinations of many large female sexual organs, and where with a fixed concentrated gaze he dissolved them. Just before entering the central place of Labchi, he was greeted by Ganesha, who requested instruction in the Buddhist tradition and having received it dissolved into a boulder that is now enshrined in the small protectors' lhakhang just above Labchi village. Then Milarepa found the Dudul Phukmoche cave, meditated there for a year and consecrated the site.

## The Mountain and the Chojung

There is no lake associated with Labchi. Its central power places are the phallic mountain and the vulvic plain below. The Labchi mountain is the palace of glorious Demchok and his mandala of 62 goddesses:

> On the outside it has the appearance of a lifeless mountain soaring into the sky in lofty splendour. But inside, in the centre of a heavenly mansion constructed of self-luminous cognition are the illusory emanations of the 62 deity mandala of the Lord Demchok.
>
> HUBER 1989

The triangular plain at its base is the *chojung* of Dorje Phakmo, Demchok's consort. Chojung (*dharmodaya*) means 'the source of all things' and as a triangular symbol represents the female sexual organs, including the womb. The chojung of Dorje Phakmo is the source of the great all-inclusive cosmic illusion conceived in buddha-vision. The representation of it in the landscape at the base of the Labchi mountain is seen as threefold: triangles of the elements earth, water and space. The subsidiary power places of Labchi are located here. So although the mountain can be circumambulated by passing through Nyalam, Tingri and Rongshar on an immense swollen circuit, there is no great khorra circuit at

Labchi. The power places are visited – and circumambulated – arbitrarily within the triangle.

The geomantic perspective at Labchi from the vantage point of the yogi at one of the cave sites thus provides a half-moon mandala, his back against the mandala centre and his vision proscribed by the wall of a semi-circle of surrounding snow peaks broken by the gorge that allows the Kangchu river an outlet. The mass of the Jomo Tseringma (Gaurishankar) mountain dominates to the south-east. Within this outer wall lie the mountain palaces of the bodhisattva protectors of body, speech and mind: the Great Compassionate Lord Chenrezik in Karpo Bumye to the south-east; the Master of the Secret Tantra Chakna Dorje in Nakpo Bumye to the south; and the bodhisattva of intelligence, Jampelyang, in Serpo Bumye to the south-west.

The place of greatest power in the chojung is Dudul Phukmoche, the Great Demon-Binding Cave, where Milarepa consecrated Labchi through his meditation. It is located towards the point of the triangle under a giant boulder and fronted by a lhakhang. At the back of the lhakhang a tunnel, known as the sexual organ of Dorje Phakmo (Vajravarahi), leads into the original meditation cave. The identification of the tunnel as Dorje Phakmo's vagina is part of a wider vision that sees her head at Drubphuk Rechen cave, her belly at Sengkhyam Phuk and a rock in front of Dudul Phukmoche as her knee. These identifications may be considered a low-level, local, attempt to make sense out of the lamas' esoteric mystic vision that identifies Dorje Phakmo as the chojung triangle in the landscape beneath the cliff. The simple pilgrim wants an anthropomorphic Dorje Phakmo. This would appear to be a harmless, not to say faith-inducing, parallel of the higher process of transformation of the landscape through buddha-vision, but in the Labchi guidebook it is seen by the writer to be a pernicious degradation of the tradition, 'foolish talk that should not be believed'. Perhaps this view is motivated by an insistence upon retaining non-dual buddha-vision as the only means by which such identifications can be made. Indeed, the writer expresses the opinion that the central Labchi power place is not meant for ordinary people – local devotees and lay pilgrims – because it is the field of activity of the Buddhas. This, I think, does not imply that ordinary people should not go there, but that they should not attempt any comment on the visionary realm of nondual perception.

The sanctity and power of caves like Dudul Phukmoche are measured by the perceived degree of enlightenment of the inhabitants down the centuries. Jetsun Milarepa had attained the Buddha's accomplishment of awareness and magical powers before his sojourn here, so not only the cave but also the entire mountain was permeated, and transformed, by his vibration, and meditation is quickened and blessings more easily obtainable here. Legends report that once he was snowed in for six months and during that period subsisted on a single pot of barley flour. Again, when he was old he had the inclination to walk on the mountain Nakpo Bumye to the south, and he induced it to incline its peak to the cave to pick him up and then return to its upright posture. Later Milarepa flew back down to the cave. For a period he shared the space with his spiritual heart-son Rechungpa, whose reputation as a sceptic and something of a maverick in the lineage served merely to enhance his real attainment. After Rechungpa the cave was used by a succession of Kagyu yogis, mainly of the Drikung and Drukpa Kagyu orders, all of whom became renowned adepts. The divine madman Tsangnyon meditated here in the fifteenth century and perhaps composed his famous biography of Milarepa in this very cave. Zhabkar Rimpoche, a Nyingma yogi, meditated here at the beginning of the nineteenth century.

To the west of the Dudul Phukmoche is a large boulder, shaped like a garuda's egg, on which can be seen the mantra OM MANI PADMA HUNG. When two factions of Milarepa's disciples, from Nyalam and Rongshar, quarrelled over his corpse at Chuwar in Rongshar, the body was miraculously replicated and brought here to be cremated on this rock, an event accompanied by rainbows, a shower of flowers, and perfume and music in the air. The mantra on the rock was self-manifest at that time.

High above the Dudul Phukmoche is the cave lhakhang of Drubphuk Rechen, in which, before the construction of the Chora Gepheling Gompa, the devotees of Demchok were wont to assemble on the moon's tenth day. This cave, particular to Rechungpa, Milarepa's heart-son, has the footprint of the master imprinted on its roof. In his ardour to greet his disciple, who was returning from an Indian pilgrimage, Milarepa flew to Drakmar Chonglung in Rongshar and upon his return he impressed this footprint. The divine madman Tsangnyon painted it gold. The principal icons on the altar within are a victory chorten, the reliquary of a local yogi made good called Labchiwa and some 20 sandalwood sculptures of principal figures in the Kagyu lineage.

On the western side is Bepa Gong, the Upper Secret Cave, which is also known as Bepa Kunsel, the Secret All-Illuminating Cave, where Milarepa absorbed the 62 deities of the Demchok mandala into his being and where a Nyingma treasure-finder dissolved his body into a rainbow upon the completion of his Dzokchen practice.

At the top of the chojung apron, at the base of a cliff that towers up to the sacred heights of the Labchi mountain, is Wosel Zewa Phuk, Clear Light Jewel Cave, which was inhabited by Milarepa for a long retreat. A three-room chapel has been built in front of a hollow in the cliff. Nearby the cave, to the east, is the footprint Milarepa impressed there when he flew to Chuwar. To the west is a spring, his water of realization.

Dudul Phukmoche, Drubphuk Rechen, Bepa Kunsel and Wosel Zewa Phuk are the four chief caves of Labchi. But there are others of similar sanctity consecrated by the master's meditation or that of his successors in the lineage. The Sengkhyam caves, for example, are spaces under overhangs in rocky outcropping above Dudul Phukmoche. On the western side are Western Rechen, Labchiwa Phuk, Taktsang Phuk, Tiger Lair Cave, Bepa Wok, Lower Secret Cave, and Yuthok Phuk, the Cave of Yuthokpa, the founder of Tibetan medicine, all of which were empowered and sanctified by great adepts. Finally, by the confluence, is Lungten Phuk, Injunction Cave, so called because a Drikung Kagyu hierarch described this place to an aspiring yogi as 'the red-heart of a man in the mouth of a poisonous snake running downwards', enjoining him to stay there in meditation retreat. Labchi is a traditional power place of serious meditators intent on buddhahood, and the caves and adepts are like castles and kings – the first is redundant without the other.

Until the nineteenth century Labchi was the preserve of yogis who resided in caves or their adjunct lhakhangs. After that, however, the decline of the Drikung Kagyu left it without a strong monastic base in Central Tibet and the stream of yogis dried up.

The monks who lived in Drubphuk Rechen and elsewhere had become 'loose with their sexual organs' and monastic discipline had de-cayed. In 1819 the inimitable Zhabkar Rimpoche, Little White Foot, came to Labchi on pilgrimage and meditation retreat, and while he was there he restored the caves and the discipline of their inhabitants and founded a monastery – the Chora Gepheling Gompa. It is situated on the edge of a ridge that points west at the confluence. Within the courtyard (*chora*), in the monsoon-prevalent Himalayan style, is the square lhakhang structure with a slightly inclined roof surmounted by a small central turret. This lhakhang, down the centuries, has become the repository of the buddha-images and power objects of Labchi, particularly since 1962 when the boundary of Nepal and Tibet was altered to bring the heart of Labchi into Nepal. Through this extremely auspicious circumstance Labchi was not subjected to the ravages of the Red Guards and the structures at the site are all original. A few of the images and power objects have even been saved from sale to art dealers and from the plunder of art thieves, and are now to be seen in Chora Gepheling.

Amongst the images on the altar, at the centre is a gilded bronze image of Milarepa, life size, the personal vision of the divine madman Tsangnyon; an old sculpture of Drikung Kyabgon, the founder of the Drikung Kagyu lineage; a fine clay image of Ganesha, the protector of Labchi, made out of medicinal clay; several large bronze images of Dorje Chang, the adibuddha who emanates the Demchok mandala; life-size gilded images of Gampopa, Milarepa's disciple, and also Tsangnyon.

To the south of the monastery, atop a hill where rhododendrons and medicinal plants grow, is a chorten called Thongdrol Chenpo, 'the chorten that brings liberation by the sight of it'. Zhabkar Rimpoche built this monument.

## Tsari: The Crystal Mountain of Supreme Bliss

The Immaculate Crystal Mountain of Tsari provides the definitive Tibetan pilgrimage. It is the palace of the buddha-deity Demchok, Supreme Bliss, and his mandala of deities. And it is also a principal abode of the sky dancers, amongst whom Khandroma Dorje Phakmo is supreme. More than Kang Rimpoche and Labchi, it is the tantric power place *par excellence*, a testing place for yogis where the sky dancers dwell. It is a place of breathtaking beauty, the snow mountain rising out of verdant pastures and forests, while in the valleys below is thick jungle:

> White and brilliant, the colour of crystal,
> The central mountain is a king on his throne
> Surrounded by lesser peaks as ministers.
> Multicoloured flowers blanket the whole place.
> Blossoms and fruit bedeck the trees.
> Its meadows are like golden trays,
> Carrying their blue lakes like mandalas of turquoise;
> Its rivers unfold like white silken scarfs.
>
> RICARD 1994:248

Nevertheless, jungle makes it inaccessible and dangerous, and pilgrims put their lives on the line in the ravines.

The mountain lies at the south-eastern end of the Great Himalayan range. It is one of the last peaks before the Yarlung Tsangpo (Brahmaputra) river cuts through the range in the world's deepest gorge. The mountain is surrounded by the tributaries of the Subansiri river which drain into the Brahmaputra in Arunachal Pradesh to the south. It is located in the old Tibetan region of Loyul but the area was split politically by the McMahon line, the boundary between India and Tibet. Its identification as Charitra or Devikota includes it amongst the important sub-continent mountain power places.

Paramount, Dakpa Shelri, the Immaculate Crystal Mountain, is a great chorten made of crystal. It is a self-manifest chorten that is the buddha-mind. Specifically, it is perceived as an auspicious chorten of many doors (*tashi gomang chorten*) and its dome contains the divine mandala, the wheel of sublime bliss and perfect cognition that is Demchok's mind:

> At its apex dwell the lamas and the buddha-deities,
> At its middle dwell the Buddhas of the three times
> At its base dwell the protectors and guardians.

*Round about it dwell the male and female sky dancers;*
*And its environs comprise a heavenly palace.*

HUBER 1993

The foundation of the Demchok mandala lies in the underworld, the domain of the serpent spirits, in the form of crossed dorjes with a central point projecting vertically to the top of the mountain of jewels and gold. The foundation is also envisioned as a swastika revolving clockwise. In the central peak of Dakpa Shelri, the centre of the mandala, is the root-lama emanating as Demchok and Phakmo dancing in union upon the corpse of Bhairava and the breasts of Kali:

*The Hero Heruka whose feet are coated*
*By the red blood which pours from the slain Bhairava,*
*And the sky dancer who tears down the veils to awareness,*
*These form the Immaculate Crystal Mountain that vanquishes demons.*

HUBER 1993

The topographical features that are the keys to this mandala are the four summits in the four directions which are the palaces of the four male and female buddha-deities in union. The four doors into the mandala are marked by four passes, four ravines, four rivers with water of four different colours, four stone thrones, four caves and four lakes. The entire mandala is surrounded by a wall of dorjes. The four doors are at Chikchar in the north, the Parpa Rong ravine in the east, the Jowo Them La pass in the south and Domtsang Rong ravine in the west. These were the doors entered by the yogis who opened the mandala and here they encountered the guardian protectors of the mandala: the Khandromas Dorje Yudronma and Senge Dongchan and the Lord of Death, Shinje Marpo.

The four sacred lakes of Tsari are located around the upper part of the mountain. Kala Dungtso, Conch Shell Lake, Photrang Kyokmotso, Ladle Lake Palace and Photrang Yumtso, Turquoise Lake Palace, are the chief lakes but there are many more small lakes above the central khorra path. These lakes are 'like windows in the hard rock and earth walls of the great palace through which one can see or enter into the chambers of the divine residence' or they are mirrors reflecting the divine reality. They are also life-spirit lakes (*latso*) whose waters contain the life-force of the deities and protectors of the mountain. The waters of these lakes absolve the sins of pilgrims who bathe in them.

The vision of Tsari as the abode of Demchok and Dorje Phakmo in union is the principal vision of the mountain, but some yogis concentrate solely upon the female aspect of Demchok's mandala, upon the mountain as the abode of Dorje Phakmo and the sky dancers. In this vision the four central peaks are called the Four Pure Mountain Abodes of the Sky Dancers, which comprise the buddhafield of Dorje Phakmo called Dhumatala. The sky dancers and their male counterparts, because their nature is space, are visualized externally as residing in the sky around the mountain peaks. When they are embodied, particularly when they lack the eye of wisdom and rejoice in flesh and blood, and when they are guardian protectresses, they live around the base of the mountain mandala. So the great Indian adept Lawapa, meditating at the Dorje Phuk cave in the lee of a Pure Mountain Abode, received ultimate realization and magical powers from a sky dancer and went to the Pure Abode upon his death. Magical powers are the special provenance of the sky dancers, which makes Tsari the special destination of yogis of the mother-tantra practice.

The name Tsari is derived from 'Charitra', which was one of the eight great tantric cremation grounds of the sub-continent, usually located in Orissa, India. The root of the word 'Charitra' means 'action' and the activity implied here is the directed practice of the yogi on the path of the mother-tantra, which is best performed in a cremation ground. Tsari is also identified as Devikota, one of the 24 great power places of the sub-continent. In the schema of these 24 places, divided into the three mandalas relating to the sky, the earth and the underworld and transformed into the body, speech and mind of Demchok, Devikota belongs to the mandala of mind. It is, therefore, a special abode of the sky dancers, whose nature is space, and Charitra is the field of activity of the tantric yogi whose best allies are the sky dancers – messengers from the visionary realm, muses showing the location of hidden treasure, sources of initiation, the genii of psychotropic herbs and, as embodied beings, consorts in the practice of tantric yoga. Zhabkar Rimpoche, Little White Foot, says:

*In the centre, on the Immaculate Crystal Mountain,*
*Dwell two thousand eight hundred deities.*
*In each of the surrounding hills, rocks and lakes*
*Are countless heroes and sky dancers.*
*And the men and women who live here*
*Are all of the race of heroes and sky dancers.*

RICARD 1994:248

Didactic etymologies of 'Tsari' also make it 'Herb Mountain' and 'Mountain of the Psychic Channel', both relating to the activity of yogis *vis à vis* the sky dancers.

## Testing Ground of the Great Adepts

The caves and hermitages of Kang Rimpoche, hidden amongst the rock and shale mountains, are cold and bare. At Labchi the meditation environment is a paradise. Tsari, surrounded by jungle, its approaches infested with cannibal tribes, wild animals and poisonous insects, is accessible only by endangering life and limb. Certainly in the early centuries of its inauguration, which anyway was later than the opening of Kang Rimpoche and Labchi, it was the haunt only of truly dauntless yogis and serious tantric practitioners, and was rarely visited by monks or laymen. It was the power place of great Indian adepts practising the alchemical yoga of *rasayana* and exercising the sexual yogas of the mother-tantras together with the sky dancers of the region and even with the protectresses of the mountains. When Je Gampopa was sending off yogis from Central Tibet to open up Tsari for the Kagyu orders he warned them:

> *It is a place where the offerings of meat and alcohol to the Khandro-ma Dorje Phakmo (Vajravarahi) is appropriate, where all the magical powers are realized as desired by those with the requisite karma and fortune, and where those without fortune are destroyed by the worldly sky dancers who rejoice in flesh and blood. The entry path is frequented by tigers and leopards, savage bears, wild men and poisonous insects.*

HUBER 1993

When Je Tsongkhapa, the great monastic reformer, came to Tsari on pilgrimage, as a fully ordained gelong monk he refused to have anything to do with alcohol and even when suffering considerable pain in his feet he refused the alcohol that was offered him. As a result he 'felt pain like bamboo splinters piercing his feet'. Only after he had ingested some consecrated substances did the pain leave him. Tsongkhapa is painted as a rather dull dog compared to the Kagyu yogis, but such a portrait is unfair to this buddha-figure. The tale is told as if monks were not suited to pilgrimage at Tsari and that it were best if they stayed away from this quintessentially tantric place. But any monk who did the Tsari khorra was automatically a yogi.

The Indian adept Lawapa had come to Tsari centuries before with his disciple Bhusuku, who was destined to become a master the equal of Lawapa, but at that time he lacked the one-taste awareness sought by the tantric masters.

A Nyingma lama relates the following salutary story with a warning on the futility of approaching the throne of Demchok without the appropriate attitude. The Indian Buddhist sadhus had entered Tsari through the eastern door and climbed from Chikchar to the Dorje Phuk cave high up on the mountain. Here Lawapa perceived 21 virgins dancing in a circle in the valley below and ordered Bhusuku to go and fetch the one in the middle. But leading her back to his master, Bhusuku's concentrated vision wavered, the virgin vanished and he found himself standing with a radish in his hand. Lawapa instructed him to prepare radish soup for them both, but believing the soup was the flesh of the virgin, Bhusuku was unable to follow his teacher in drinking it. Instead he threw it out to a dog. Lawapa and the dog floated to the peak of the Khandro mountain, into the pure-land of the sky dancers, and stayed there, until Bhusuku, feeling abandoned, prayed to his master to return. Lawapa then appeared before him in an aura of rainbow light and simply peeled off his skin to reveal the mandala of Demchok's 62 deities within his body. The radish is Bhusuku's desire, which is transformed in tantra, particularly the Demchok tantra, into pure awareness.

For the Kagyu orders, who were to dominate the caves and hermitages of Tsari down the centuries, Dakpo Lhaje Gampopa, in fulfilment of Marpa the Translator's prophecy that Jetsun Milarepa's disciples would open Tsari, sent his disciple Kyepo Yeshe Dorje to open up the place. At his first attempt Yeshe Dorje failed miserably. A local guardian sky dancer told him to go home and try again next year. He was to come back with a rainhat, rainboots and a staff, and, abandoning the pretences of monkhood, to try approaching with song and dance. On his second attempt Yeshe Dorje reached Photrang Yumtso lake and some local sky dancers gave him a dose of *lingchen*, a local psychotropic herb, and he attained magical powers.

The rough and ready activity of Tsangpa Gyare, the founder of the Drukpa Kagyu order, seems more appropriate to entry of Dorje Phakmo's mandala. It was he who destroyed an illusion of enticing vulvas by penetrating them and who took the very fierce protectress Dorje Yudronma, who was the original mountain goddess of Tsari, as his consort in the guise of a yak herder. When confronted with a serpent spirit in the form of a giant frog, he jumped on its back and trampled it. Doinying Phuk, Stone Heart Cave, was his meditation cave.

Guru Rimpoche, who entered the mandala by way of the southern door, over the Jowo Them La pass from Jar, meditated here for seven years, seven months and seven days in the Zilchan Sangphuk, the Brilliant Secret Cave, where he hid many treasure texts. A little later the Dzokchen teacher Vimalamitra came to Tsari by magical means and taught the gods and demons. But Kagyu mythology relates how difficult the opening of Tsari was for the serious yogis who attempted it. The principals were Yeshe Dorje, Tsangpa Gyare, Nyo Lhanangpa and Gotsangpa. The names of these last two are familiar from the legends relating to the opening of Kang Rimpoche, and as at Kang Rimpoche and Labchi, the Drukpa and Drikung Kagyu lineages were to dominate the caves and hermitages of Tsari down the centuries. Je Tsongkhapa's fifteenth-century pilgrimage linked the Geluk order, which he founded, to Tsari. During the last centuries, the Lhasa government supported the great 12-year pilgrimages to the place by providing military escorts and paying off the fierce Lopa tribals.

## The Three Khorra Circuits

Tsari is circumambulated on three levels. Yogis traverse the peak path (*tsekor*), which encircles the four sacred peaks, touches the caves sanctified by tantric meditation and takes two to four days. Laymen and monks traverse the middle path (*zhungkor*), which crosses seven passes over the ridges that radiate from the peaks and is still the easiest route, taking up to a week. The ravine circuit (*rongkor*), the long arduous passage through the deep valleys that flank the massif on three sides, takes two weeks and is the course of the great pilgrimage every 12 years. Whichever circuit the pilgrim takes is fraught with difficulty and the Kagyu pilgrim recites this prayer:

> *Glorious Tsaritra, Pure Power Place of the Sky Dancers,*
> *Masters of the Kagyu lineage, Buddha-deities*
> *Sky Dancers, Dharma Protectors: we pray to you.*
> *Purify sins and obscurations through your blessings;*
> *Pacify adversaries and dispel dangers;*
> *Bestow upon us supreme realization and magical powers.*
>
> HUBER 1993

The peak path, the Tsari tsekor, which is only open during the summer period, begins and ends at Chikchar, the northern gate into the Tsari mandala, in the Tsari Valley. Chikchar, 'the place of immediate realization', is one of Tsari's chief power places. It is the residence of Shinje, the Lord of Death, a local guardian and one of the doorkeepers of the Demchok mandala, bound in the form of an eight year old by Tsangpa Gyare. Here is the temple of Dorje Phakmo built by Padma Karpo in 1570. It was here that Tsangpa Gyare, as already mentioned, found the path blocked by non-humans appearing as a multitude of vulvas. His penis arising in anger, he penetrated them each in turn and they were transmuted into rock. The impressions of vulva and penis are clearly visible today (*see also Dotsen below*).

The valley above this major staging-point on all three khorra circuits was the location of the hermitages of the Drukpa Kagyu meditation community, whose advanced tantric meditation was *tummo*, the mystic heat. An annual winter ritual prescribed that the lightly dressed yogis remain for a night in the snows of the upper part of the valley. Zhabkar Rimpoche, Little White Foot, stayed in the Yangon hermitage here for a year and a month.

From Chikchar the path ascends to Drolma La pass, skirting the Lawa Phuk, Lawapa's cave, where the great adept first meditated with his disciple Bhusuku before they climbed up to Dorje Phuk. From Drolma La it descends to Mipak Rong, Human Skin Ravine, ascends to the Shakam La, Dry Flesh Pass, drops down to the Jampa Rong, Loving Kindness Ravine, and continues up to Takma La, Tigress Pass. Here the peak path diverges from the main path to cut across high to the south of the four sacred peaks. Dorje Phuk, where Lawapa consumed the virgin in the form of a radish, and other caves suitable for Mahamudra practice, are located in the area to the north of it. Then, joining the main path again, it passes through Khandro Tsokhang, the Assembly Place of the Sky Dancers, descends into the Taktsang Rong, Tiger Lair Ravine, and ascends to the Shangu La pass. It then turns to the north-east beneath the north face of Dakpo Shelri. This is the essence of Tsari and the high point of the khorra ritual. Here, immediately below the summit of Shelri, is Kala Dungtso, Conch Shell Lake, which proffers Demchok's white sexual fluid (white *bodhichitta*) frothing on its surface and caves for Mahamudra meditation practice. As for the peaks themselves, to yogis practising the phases of tantric meditation, Dakpo Shelri is the union of perfect insight and skilful means, Demchok and Dorje Phakmo in union, while the Dorje Ri and Sherab Ri peaks represent the separate male and female aspects. Proximity to one of these three is prescribed for the yogi according to the relevant phase of his meditation – creative, fulfilment or their union.

On the other side of Dakpo Shelri is the Photrang Kyokmotso lake, Ladle Lake Palace, also called Sindhura Gyamtso, the Ocean of Sindhura, because red lead powder is suspended in its waters, giving it a red tint and making it the elixir that is Dorje Phakmo's red sexual fluid (red *bodhichitta*). Tsangpa Gyare meditated in a cave here called Mikra Phuk, Eye-Shade Cave, because Dorje Phakmo gave him eye-shades woven from her own hair. The springs bubbling up from under the mountains nearby provide especially potent water of purification and even the sacred urine (*sangchab*) of Dorje Phakmo. There are prohibitions forbidding the collection of the red and the white elixirs until 13 central khorras have been performed or a three-year tantric retreat completed.

The path back to Chikchar crosses the Kyobchen La pass and skirts the Trakshe Latso, the life-spirit lake of a protecting deity. On the descent from Kyobchen La is found the psychotropic plant *ludu dorje*. This rare herb (*codonopsis convolvulaceae* or *ovata*), called the 'supreme herb', is collected here and prepared in a decoction to be taken by yogis intent upon attaining magical powers or as medicinal panacea:

> *This balm of medicinal elixir,*
> *Served by the Sky Dancer of Pure Awareness,*
> *Consumed with pure tantric commitment*
> *Removes the tendency to bad rebirth.*
>
> HUBER 1993

It is not known to what extent the potency of this herb is dependent upon the sky dancer, the yogi's faith and the ritual procedure, rather than upon an active pharmacological ingredient.

The central khorra path begins in the Tsari Valley at Dotsen (or Bod Dotsenchan). This was the way that the remarkable yogi Kyepo Yeshe Dorje entered and opened the main circumambulatory path. The opening of the path is ritually repeated each year at the time of the full moon of the third month. The significance of Dotsen is provided by the residences of the guardian protectors located there. *Dotsen* means 'Tibetan sex rocks' and the place is considered by some to be the power centre of the entire Tsari mandala. Rocks in the form of phallus and vulva (lingam and yoni) are found here, and sacred water flows from the vulva, 'which looks like thighs pressed together'. These rocks are exceedingly famous. They represent the lingam and yoni of Mahadeva and Uma, who were vanquished by Demchok, and, furthermore, the vulvic rock is the residence of the Lion-Headed Sky Dancer and Protectress Khandro Senge Dongchan. For childless women it is a place to gain fertility – from the blessings of the stone, the water or a yogi-sadhu who may wait here in the night to bestow his physical blessings.

The central khorra path leads to Chikchar and then up to the Drolma La pass. Here female pilgrims must turn back, for they are prohibited from celebrating the entire khorra. They return to Dotsen and then proceed counter-clockwise, the mother-tantra direction, to Domtsang on the western side. To explain this sexist discrimination on a tantric mountain, a major abode of the sky dancers, there is only an asinine story concerning Drolma, the saviouress, who lay across the pass in order to judge the moral quality of men and women. The first man to encounter her walked around her, the first woman stepped over her. The lack of sensitivity in this representative of the female sex resulted in the exclusion of all women from the southern, more potent side of the khorra circuit. But the mountain identified as Dorje Phakmo, as its female protectresses Dorje Yudronma and Senge Dongchan, is surely big enough to encompass and purify any moral or ritual impurity in any person or gender, so the reason for this exclusion remains obscure.

From Drolma La the path continues to Takma La and then to the south on a long high route to Photrang Yumtso, the Magnificent Turquoise Lake Palace, at the southern extreme of the khorra circuit. This is the chief of all the Tsari lakes, the source of all magical powers, and contains the entire mandala palace of Demchok: to see it is to enter the mandala. It was sanctified by the Drukpa Kagyu yogi Kyepo Yeshe Dorje who realized the entire 62-deity mandala of Demchok here. He also ingested the psychotropic herb lingchen and through the mediation of the sky dancer, whose nature is identical to the herb, attained magical powers, beginning with levitation. He celebrated his euphoric experience with dance and song, and left a memorial of it by thrusting his staff into a rock. Photrang Yumtso lake is the major recipient of offerings around the khorra circuit. Jewellery and coins are thrown into its waters.

The route returns to the Tsari Valley by way of Tagyuk La pass, Galloping Horse pass; the Khandro Tsokhang, Assembly Place of the Sky Dancers; Taktsang Rong, the Tiger Lair Ravine, the location of flesh-eating sky dancers; the Shangu La pass, very close to the western side of Dakpa Shelri peak; Domtsang Rong, Den of the Bear Ravine, the limit of the women's khorra path on the western side, which is in a forest of fir trees. The path climbs up to the Khargyuk La pass and down to Yulme in the Yulme Valley, which was previously a Drikung hermitage site. Then it runs finally over the Ribpa La pass and down to Chozam in the Tsari Valley.

The ravine circuit, the Tsari rongkor, consists of a two-week, 94-mile (150-km) trek through the ravines that effectively encircle the Tsari mountains. The great 12-year pilgrimage, celebrated during the winter of each monkey year (1992, 2004), was probably the most popular pilgrimage in the whole of Tibet during the nineteenth and the first half of the twentieth centuries, attracting tens of thousands of all kinds of people from the whole Tibetan ethnic area. Resumption of the old tradition commenced in 1992. Yet the Tsari rongkor is the most dangerous, demanding and death-defying pilgrimage. The floors of the ravines to the south are covered with impenetrable jungle, which is inhabited by hostile tribals still outside a devotional mandala; the climate is atrocious, the area possessing one of the highest rainfalls in the world; insects and animals make life very uncomfortable; open wounds and bites tend to immediate infection; and all supplies for the two-week expedition must be carried on the pilgrim's back. Zhabkar Rimpoche, Little White Foot, who performed the pilgrimage in 1812, watched pilgrims dying of illness and starvation, while the strong carried the ailing on their backs. Scores would die during every great 12-year event. Even after the pilgrims reached the place where they started, some would die from exhaustion and dehydration. While pilgrims do not seek death on the rongkor, they consciously put themselves in the way of it, for there is perhaps no better method of contemplating the proximity of death and gaining the spiritual advantage from the purification that is automatically induced.

The circuit begins further down the Tsari Valley than Chikchar, beyond the place called Bodzok Sumdo, the Confluence where Tibet Ends, at an open space near Lo Mikhyimdun village. This is the frontier with Arunachal Pradesh, in India, in what the Tibetans call Loyul, the Land of the Lopas, where 'Lopa' denotes a savage, a barbarian, a tribal – an outsider as far as the buddha-dharma is concerned. The route follows the ravines of the Tsari river to the southeast, turns to the west up the gorge of the Jayul river (Subansiri river), then north-west up the channel of either the Yulme or the Jar river until a pass is traversed back into the Tsari river system. There are no settlements on this route until the Sangngak Choling Gompa is reached in Jayul, to the west of Tsari district. This is the principal monastery in the Tsari region, a Drukpa Kagyu gompa built by

Padma Karpo and restored in 1986. The pilgrimage concludes on return to the Tsari Valley.

## Amnye Machen: The Robber-Bandits' Shrine

Amnye Machen is the sacred mountain of all the people of Amdo. It is the most important mountain power place in Tibet after Kang Rimpoche, Labchi and Tsari, and can be considered the Kang Rimpoche of Eastern Tibet. The focal massif of three main peaks stands towards the western end of the range, itself called Amnye Machen, that rises out of the Amdo plains. Some 125 miles (200 km) long on an east–west axis, the range lies to the east of the twin lakes Kyering Tso and Ngoring Tso, within the giant dog's-hind-leg curve of the Machu river, which is the name of the Yellow River in Tibet.

Amnye Machen, the mountain god, is sovereign of all the lords of the earth (sadak) of Amdo. He is also the warrior god (dralha) of the whole of Amdo, the enemy of all assailants of the land, the people and the buddha-dharma. *Machen* refers to the territory that he rules; *Amnye* means 'ancestor': Amnye Machen is 'the Ancestor of the Amdo people'. Sometimes Machen is understood as 'magnificent peacock' and so Amnye Machen becomes 'the Great Peacock Ancestor'. He is also Machen Pomra, where Machen is the region and Pomra the mountain, and he is Magyel, the King of Ma. The Bonpos call him Manyen Pomra, probably the oldest of his names, and so identify him as a nyen god, the greatest and wildest of the mountain gods. As such he is envisioned at the centre of a mandala of the 360 Tibetan mountain gods, with Nyenchen Thanglha, the principal Central Tibetan nyen mountain god, being only an emanation of Machen in the northern direction of the mandala. The great mountain Amnye Machen is the presiding god of the region, but for the yogis it is, first and foremost, the abode of the tantric buddha-deity Demchok, Supreme Bliss.

For non-Amdowa Tibetans who would do pilgrimage to Amnye Machen, its remoteness in the far east of Tibet heightens its mystery and increases its renown. Central Tibetans have little idea of its location, although lamas will know that its mountain god is one of the great protectors of Tibet and the buddha-dharma. In the past it has been rendered inaccessible not only by its outlying location but also by the ferocity of the nomad tribes whose sheep and yak herds graze the pastures to the east and south of it, and who also dominate the region to the north. These warrior tribes are the Goloks, who have the reputation as the most predatory and savage people in the entire Tibetan ethnic region. Historically they were the bulwark against Muslim encroachment from the north-east and against Mongolian and Chinese military incursion. In the late nineteenth and first half of the twentieth centuries, they guarded the borders against Western explorers, killing, wounding or scaring off those who penetrated their domain. The Chinese Communists preferred to leave them alone, protecting as best they could the single arterial road in the far north of the Goloks' sphere of influence. The tribes were finally pacified by neglect rather than conquest.

The Goloks' fierce independence and recognition of no external authority gave them the reputation not only as warriors but also as bandits. So Amnye Machen is known as 'the robber-bandit shrine'. The Goloks would certainly exact heavy tribute in goods from the caravans moving across Amdo from Xining and Lanchou to Central Tibet, and the traders perceived this as banditry, particularly when their reluctance to contribute to the material well-being of the Goloks resulted in their death or mutilation! Bands of interloping pilgrims, *en route* to Amnye Machen without credentials or blood-link or luck, were also fair game to marauding Golok horsemen. Even yogis secluded in mountain caves were not immune to their depredations. Zhabkar Rimpoche, Little White Foot, was robbed during his retreat near the Amnye Machen khorra path, although after convincing the Golok robber that he was stealing from a yogi of power he turned robbery into an opportunity for generosity, giving the man part of his food cache along with his blessing.

The predatory nature of the Goloks reflects the ferocity of the mountain god Amnye Machen untamed. This god is not only savage but also intractable. When Guru Rimpoche subjected all the mountain gods of Tibet and then summoned them to Samye Chokhor as protectors of the buddha-dharma,

*The great mountain god Machen Pomra refused to come. So the master caught him in the heart with his hook-gesture and dragged*

*him there. In the guise of a shaman priest, wearing a wolfskin cloak and waving a monkey-skin head, with one foot placed in Amdo and one foot in Hepori, he fell with a thud into the master's presence.*

*'I am a giant fang,' he told the master. 'But, little monk, I could not resist your insistent command. What are your orders?'*

*'Accept these offerings and fulfil the king's wishes,' the master replied.*

*'I shall do as you say,' said Machen Pomra. 'But I am exceedingly greedy and I like precious things. I am not satisfied with this offering of dough balls made of flour and water. Give me material objects!'*

*The master took five kinds of precious stone, and grinding them to dust set them on a plate, blessed them and offered them to Machen Pomra. At this the great mountain god placed himself at the master's command and entered a commitment to serve the buddha-dharma.*

DOWMAN MS

Upon this final subjection of Amnye Machen by Guru Rimpoche, the mountain god reached the tenth and final level of the bodhisattva path where Chenrezik dwells. In this way, not only were his innate ferocious warrior qualities placed at the disposal of the buddha-dharma, but also his motivation became as pure as the bodhisattva of compassion. His iconography shows him attired in armour and carrying weapons, but with a handsome white body with the marks of a hero, riding a flying horse. By Je Tsongkhapa's time Amnye Machen was well enslaved and the founder of the Gelukpa order made him protector of the Geluk tradition at Ganden Namgyeling.

The central Amnye Machen massif consists of eight main peaks of varying heights. The chief three of these are the pyramidal Chenrezik in the south; the domed Amnye Machen, the lowest of the three, in the middle; and Dradul Lungshok, the highest, in the north. For the Bonpos and the lay buddhist, the central peak is the palace of Machen. Surrounding peaks are the residences of his consort, Gungmen Lhari, which may be rendered as Tigress-Demoness, a wild woman (menmo) who carries a pot of nectar and a mirror and who rides a stag; his nine sons, who like their father are dressed in armour and carry weapons and ride horses; and his nine daughters, who ride cuckoos. But for the yogi practitioner of the mother-tantra, the Amnye Machen peak is a mandala of Demchok (Samvara) surrounded by his offering goddesses, with male and female sky dancers in the sky above. The Demchok mandala is delineated on the ground by the Amnye Machen peak in the centre, the surrounding peaks, and the doors in the four directions. In this mandala Machen himself, as a mere guardian-protector, is relegated to a subsidiary position in the west. It is difficult, however, to be precise regarding identifications on the ground.

Also associated with the Amnye Machen massif is King Gesar of Ling, the archetypal Tibetan warrior-hero and guardian-protector of the Buddhist teaching, also known as Sengchen Gyelpo, the Great Lion-King. He once liberated Tibet from enemy hordes and awaits his call to provide similar service again. His legend is known by all Tibetan people, but, particularly, his name is sung by the bards of Eastern Tibet, where Ling is located. His sword stands concealed in the centre of the Amnye Machen peak.

Pilgrimage to Amnye Machen has always been constrained by its inaccessibility and the wild nature of the landscape. Since the relaxation of religious suppression in the 1980s it has been almost exclusively Goloks who have returned there as pilgrims. However, the last horse year of a 12-year cycle, marking the most auspicious year for Amnye Machen pilgrimage, fell in 1990, and in that year, in the ninth lunar month, hundreds of pilgrims circumambulated the mountain. The khorra path is about 112 miles (180 km) long. A few pilgrims circumambulated performing full-length prostrations, which took about 40 days; most walked in groups, driving their pack-yaks in front of them, finishing in seven days; many rode horses, completing the khorra in three days. This last mode, rather than illustrating a cavalier attitude to the doctrine that riding generates only a fraction of the merit gained by walking or prostrating around a power place, indicates the Goloks' inseparability from the horse's saddle, in which they virtually live from cradle to sky burial. It is said that rather than walk the few yards between his tent and his neighbour's the Golok will stay at home. Many of these pilgrims carried rifles; again, rather than indicating a contempt for the proscription against hunting that lies on all pilgrimage, this indicates the Golok's attachment to his weapon, which accompanies him wherever he goes.

A flat elliptical circuit, the khorra path lies at an average altitude of 14,000 feet (4,300m), sometimes close to the massif and sometimes distant from it. It is reached in the north-east from Zhozan Kunghe, an hour's walk from Chuwarna; in the south-east from Tawo Kongma, the Golok capital, three hours' ride from Tselnak Khamdo; and in the north-west from Tawo Zholma (Xiadawu), three hours' march to Nuwo Dradul Wangchuk. In the north-west, near Nuwo Dradul Wangchuk is Guru Gompa, the only gompa on the khorra path, which is a Nyingma gompa associated with Dodrub Chode. The Amnye Machen mandala is depicted there in murals. The gompa is to be visited at the end of the khorra.

The northern gate to the mandala is Nuwo Dradul Wangchuk, 'the Younger Brother Enemy Subduing Lord', which is a great rock. This is the abode of the younger brother of Amnye Machen. Zhabkar's handprint is impressed here.

Travelling to the north-east, at the top of the Chungon, Blue Water Valley, is the Drokdu Nyakha La pass, a place where stones (*nedo*) are gathered to be taken home and enshrined on an altar or in a chorten. At the bottom of the pass is a place (nesa) where earth is dug out and dried for later medicinal usage. The path follows the Yekhokchu river down to its confluence with the Yonkhokchu at Chuwarna, Confluence Point. But before reaching Chuwarna, above the Yekhok Valley on the northern side, is the palace of glorious Yeshe Gompo, the Lord of Wisdom. The palace is envisioned as a charnel ground grove. Its wrathful protector stands at its centre in the middle of the blazing fire of primordial wisdom, surrounded by a retinue of guardian protectors. He performs service to Demchok for the sake of all sentient beings.

At Chuwarna is a large restored chorten, the Chorten Karpo, in a walled compound. This is the eastern gate to the mandala. From here the path turns to the south up the Yonkhok Valley, which is sparsely wooded. Then at Gotson, Weapons, a flat area by the trail, on a large rock, is the handprint of Gesar's elder brother Gyatsa Shelkar, White Moon-Face. Gotson is the armoury of Machen Pomra, of the Goloks and of Gesar. It is located in the mountain above this place. Further, a peak above Gotson is filled with the wild women who form part of Machen Pomra's retinue. Charming to look upon, they are naked, their bodies red, dancing, swaying their hips to the left. Above Gotson, to the south, is the mountain residence of the Tsering Chenga, the Five Long-Life Goddesses, called Abur Barlung, where, under a vast tent of flowers in a square chamber of gold, the five goddesses, their principal Tashi Tseringma in the centre, perform the rite of the tantric feast with their retinue of sky dancers. Behind Gotson is the heart-shaped mountain abode of Machen's consort Dorje Drak Gyelma, who is one of the female guardians of the passes into Tibet (*tenma*).

At the eastern extreme of the khorra path is Tselnak Khamdo, named after the red and black earth found here, along with two great cairns. Then to the south-west the path crosses pasturelands to Ludung Shukpa, the Serpent Spirit's Juniper Tree. Here are the giant tree, two caves and Drolma's spring, and also masts with prayer-flags strung between. Further to the west is the highest point on the khorra path, Tamchok Kongpa, the Heights of the Sovereign Horse, a tall mast used for prayer-flag offerings. Here also lie a pile of horses' skulls, hair of their manes and reins offered to increase the luck of the pilgrims' horses. This is the southern gate to the mandala. Below the pass is a plain called Ngangwai Shokteng, On Geese's Wings, dominated by the snow peak called Nyerwa Drongyi Shelkar.

Across the plain is a small lake, a mirror-lake, that may be the spirit-lake of Amnye Machen. Behind it is a rocky escarpment with numerous outcroppings called Mowatowa, Diviner, Exorcist. At the bottom of this scarp are the broken walls of a hermitage that was occupied by the renowned Amdowa yogi Zhabkar, Little White Foot, who meditated here for a few months in 1809 and sanctified the place. He came with two attendants who 'built a small stone hut, just my size, under a rock overhang in a sunny spot', before leaving him there for the season. The hermitage overlooked two lakes when Zhabkar stayed here. The great yogi composed many songs during that summer, several about the wild life in the area, particularly the herds of wild asses (*kyang*). He mentions Amnye Machen only as the residence of Machen, the protector on the tenth bodhisattva level. One day he climbed one of the peaks and lost himself in the experience of the space. He described his samadhi like this:

*Like the sun shining in a clear autumn sky, the luminous emptiness that is the true nature of mind was laid bare. In a state without centre, without limits, empty like space, all phenomena – forms and sounds – were present in spontaneity, vivid as the sun, moon, planets, and stars. Mind and phenomena blended completely in a single taste.*

*Friend and enemy – no difference; gold and stone – no difference; this life and the next – no difference. Having seen this for myself, I was ready to sit among the glorious sky-like yogis.*

RICARD 1994:175

Mowatowa is the place of the bodhisattva vision. Above Mowatowa itself is the mountain abode of Chenrezik, the bodhisattva of compassion, 'his body the colour of snow-covered mountains caressed by a thousand suns', according to the guidebook. On his left is the residence of Chakna Dorje, the master of the tantras, his body the colour of lapis lazuli, surrounded by a vast host of bodhisattvas. On the right of Chenrezik is the abode of Jampelyang, the bodhisattva of intelligence. Nearby, at the edge of a glacier is the residence of Drolma, the female bodhisattva of devotion. 'These abodes of the bodhisattvas look like heaps of earth and stone, but they are actually the pure-lands of the bodhisattvas, such as the Potala.'

Further west, having climbed off the plain, is Jema Drudel 'grains of strewn sand-barley', a place of sand dunes. Here is an entrance to the palace of the great protector of the Buddhist tradition Machen Pomra who is essentially the Great Compassionate One, Thukjechenpo (Mahakarunika):

*He has a body white in colour, similar to a snowy mountain, with a reddish tint. He has one face and two hands. In his right hand he holds an arrow that fulfils all wishes, made of a hollow reed and adorned with coloured silks, and in his left hand he holds the wish-fulfilling gem to his heart. He wears silks and jewel ornaments, a brocade vest, a coat of mail and a golden helmet. He is mounted on the sovereign white horse with a turquoise mane, seated in the posture of royal ease on a golden saddle decorated with precious ornaments.*

BUFFETRILLE MS

A short distance beyond is a river and upstream is a spring called Drolma Drubchu, the Spring of Drolma's Accomplishment. Progressing a little further, the pilgrim reaches Goku Chenmo. A *goku* is a giant appliqué thangka, and here the variegated colours of the rock-face above the site give the appearance of a gigantic thangka. This is a mast site, the masts again linked by prayer-flags, and there is a cave in the rock-face. Behind the goku, perhaps through the cave, is the western gate into the palace of Machen and within the gate are saintly hosts of monks who liberate fortunate beings through their melodious chanting of the Buddha's teaching.

Beyond Gokuchenmo is the Gethuk La pass and near the pass is a rock with an oblong stone resembling a handle projecting from it. This handle was used by Ling Gesar to tie his horse as he rested on the pass. Below the pass, in the valley of Gethuk Nang, is a place called Shinje Gyama Dang Melong, the Scales and Mirror of the Lord of Death, where the pilgrim may foresee his death and judgement by Shinje, the Lord of Death, as he crawls through a narrow tunnel evoking the after-death experience, and, arriving at its end, hangs by his feet to reach a protruding rock below. Having survived this ordeal, the pilgrim picks up a boulder and carries it in circumambulation of a mani-wall, perhaps evoking the hellish rebirth that awaits him at the end of the bardo. This is the final power place on the khorra path, which ends at the Guru Gompa in the north-west.

## Bonri: The Great Bon Mountain

At Kongpo Bonri we enter the mythic paradise of the Bon order. Bonri is the most important Bon power place in greater Tibet. Central Tibet is virtually devoid of Bonpo sites – the Bon have never recovered their strength there after being expelled by King Trisong Detsen in the eighth century. In the region of Bonri, however, they still flourish and their sacred mountain stands as a living monument to their tradition.

The old province of Kongpo, lying to the south-east of Lhasa, to the east of old Dakpo province and north of the Yarlung Tsangpo river, forms an intermediate geographical region between Central Tibet and the wet jungles further to the south-east around Tsari on one hand, and the forested valleys and uplands of Kham on the other. It is a forested region once known for its fine horses. From the perspective of both the Central Tibetans and the Khampas, the Kongpo people are considered too closely related to the Lopas, the tribals of the eastern Himalayas, to be quite pukka. The people of Kongpo eat frogs and snakes, they say, nephews and uncles fight and kill each other, brothers and sisters copulate, and beware of death by poison while travelling through the region! Whether they meet their death by poison or other means, the flesh of travellers is usually eaten by the Kongpo people and it is a lucky trader or pilgrim who escapes this fate. It is not surprising, then, that the old shamanic religion of Bon is represented here at Bonri, on the eastern side of the geomantically auspicious confluence of the Nyangchu river flowing from the north into the great Yarlung Tsangpo flowing from west to east.

The gompas of Bonri, however, do not practise the old pre-Buddhist shamanism. They belong to the reformed New Bon order and apart from anti-clockwise circumambulation the casual Western pilgrim will not discern any major distinction between the Bon tradition here and Buddhist practices at Kang Rimpoche or Tsari. The activity on the khorra circuit appears identical; but here the pilgrim is muttering Bon mantras and prayers, the names of the yogis and the deities invoked are unfamiliar, and the images in the temples and on the prayer-flags are of strange, Bon, provenance. And whereas in the Buddhist guidebooks the yogi-pilgrim to Kang Rimpoche, Labchi and Tsari is exhorted to visualize the mountain as a mandala, the Bon guidebooks concentrate more on the mythic events that absorbed Shenrab Miwo, the Bon buddha-exemplar and prophet, when he visited this place.

First and foremost, though, the mountain is envisioned as the mind of Shenrab Miwo. The great founder of the Bon order had flown from Takzik, his homeland in the Persian sphere, to subdue the demonic powers of Tibet and convert the people (see p.59). The chief of Tibetan demons was Khyabpa Lagring, who had stolen seven horses from Shenrab Miwo and taken refuge in Kongpo. Khyabpa created a black mountain to block the Yarlung Tsangpo valley, but the master merely flicked that mountain away and emanated Bonri, a larger mountain, out of his mind:

*From his heart there emanated a ray of purple-brown light, the
length of an arrow, which penetrated the billion realms and produced a mountain like a heap of blazing jewels...and it appeared as
Tsomchok Khagying [the Supreme Lord Noble-Sky] standing in
union with his consort, having three faces, six arms and two legs...*

RAMBLE MS

The mountain is thus inseparable from Shenrab's mind – an immaculate illusion.

Much later, in the legendary period of Tibetan history, Nyatri
Tsenpo, the first Tibetan king, descended from the sky on his sky-
rope to the top of Bonri and the first king not to return to the sky on
his sky-rope, Drigum Tsenpo, was interred here. Guru Rimpoche
came to Bonri and consecrated the place through his meditation,
leaving hidden treasures and also his footprints impressed in stone.
The mountain was opened for meditation and to pilgrimage for
Bonpos only in the fourteenth century, by a yogi called Ripa
Drukse from Amdo, where the Bonpos had never been persecuted.
This yogi, as the opener of a mountain power place at Bonri, has the
same status as Gotsangpa has at Kang Rimpoche. He meditated for
three years on Bonri, during which time he bound the local protectors to the Bon tradition. Then the goddess Sipai Gyelmo appeared
to him as a tiger and introduced him to the power places of the
mountain and their mythology. Ripa Drukse built a monastery on
Bonri and left innumerable imprints in rock as evidence of his spiritual realization.

The five caves on the sides of the mountain and the five lakes
hidden within the mountain delineate the place as a mandala with
the buddha-deity Tsomchok Khagying at its centre. The five cave
power places were hallowed by Shenrab Miwo himself and by the
meditation of scholars, adepts and by Bon priests. Each cave has a
specific cycle of meditation associated with it, each has treasure
texts concealed within it, and each has body prints of the saints and
yogis who meditated there.

Three peaks protrude from the Bonri massif: Lhari to the
south-west, Muri in the middle and Shenri to the eastern end of
the ridge. The concept of three peaks, extraneous to the vision of
Bonri as a mandala, introduces the threefold reality of Shenrab

Miwo – his buddha-body, speech and mind. Although it is considered spiritually brash for Tibetans to climb these peaks, there are paths to the top of each of them, perhaps because they are easily accessible and because the Bonpos are more inclined than the Buddhists to emulate the Taoist Chinese. Lhari, the Divine Peak, is best known as the place of Nyatri Tsenpo's descent on his sky-rope. The full name of the peak is Lhari Gyangtho. Close to its high point is Nyatri Tsenpo's footprint, in the form of an unusual raised, positive, mould. This peak is also the residence of Ama Yongma, territorial protectress of the village of Liding, which lies below.

## The Bonri Khorra Circuit

The Bonri khorra path can be accessed from the highway on the south bank of the Yarlung Tsangpo by boat, probably a coracle, from Chabnak to Miri. On the northern side of the mountain is the town of Nyingtri, Nyingtri Xian, on the main Lhasa–Chamdo highway, which intersects the khorra path and is where most pilgrims will begin their circumambulation. The khorra route is about 38 miles (60 km) in length and takes about two days to complete. Both Buddhist and Bonpo perform the khorra in an anti-clockwise movement because legend has it that in a Bonpo adept's contest of speed of circumambulation with a Karmapa, the Karmapa was stopped in his conventional clockwise progression by a tiger. Since then Buddhists have done it the Bonpo way. This khorra circuit is replete with minor power places and only the most significant in the Bonpo mind are mentioned here.

On the western side of Nyingtri is a compound that protects the most sacred of Bon trees, the Kushuk Demdruk, which has the same status for the Bonpos as Tso Mapham's mythical Rose-Apple Tree has for the Buddhists. It is the original tree of life, a protecting tree, and a source of longevity and magical power.

The khorra path begins above the town and the first main power place is the rebuilt and functioning Sigyel Gompa, founded by Ripa Drukse, near the village of Kharsamo. The Taktse Yungdrungling Gompa, the Place of the Tiger-Top Swastika, an Amdowa establishment, lies on the route to the village of Pangna.

Further on is the village of Miyul Kyithing and between the foot of Bonri and the Nyangchu river is a cemetery called Mijik Tri, Fearless Throne Cemetery. This is the sinister chief of 108 places of corpse disposal around the mountain. The large earthen mound here is the legendary site of burial of King Drigum Tsenpo, who due to his proscription of the Bon religion was the first Tibetan king to be denied ascent into heaven on the sky-rope.

Close to the confluence of the Nyangchu and the Yarlung Tsangpo rivers is the village of Drena and in this area are the most significant sites on Bonri. Just before Drena is the spring called Tashi Chumik Dadrang, the Auspicious Arrow-Hole Spring. In the final act of the play of magical powers between the white and the black forces embodied by Shenrab Miwo and Khyabpa, the Kongpo demon promised the Bon master that he would embrace the Bon tradition if the master could penetrate seven shields with a single arrow. Shenrab performed this feat and from this spot, the place that the arrow was withdrawn, this spring erupted. Drena is so called because pounds (*dres*) of turquoise and gold were offered here to Shenrab after his victory over the demon. It was also here that the seven horses that Khyabpa had stolen were returned to the master and washed in springs close to the village.

On the southern side of the mountain is the village of Yung-drungdzin, Bearer of the Swastika, where an eighth-century pillar commemorates Nyatri Tsenpo, Drigum Tsenpo and the Kongpo king's rights of dominion. Past the ferry post is the Do Jowo Lhakhang, Stone Buddha Lhakhang, part of a Nyingma gompa that enshrines a self-manifest stone image of the Buddha, a substitute in Kongpo for the Lhasa Jowo. This lhakhang has been rebuilt.

From Miri village the path leads to Drakar Zhabje, White Rock Footprint, where on a large flat white stone is the footprint of Shenrab Miwo, commemorating the master's victory over the demon Khyabpa, impressed as immutable testimony to the magical power that accompanied the master's realization.

From this spot there is a gradual ascent to Bonri La pass and this stretch of the circuit through enchanted forest contains innumerable places of power. First there is Shenrab Shuktri, Shenrab's Meditation Throne. Then at Thangshing Durtro, Fir Tree Cemetery, there is a spirit-tree (*lashing*) where babies' tiny coffins are strung from the branches to ensure that the spirits of these karmically unformed beings have no obstacles in the bardo state between death and rebirth. Further up the path, offerings of ladder-like notched sticks have been lodged against the rocks so that spirits of the dead can climb from the bardo into a heaven, like the ancient kings who at their deaths ascended the sky-rope from earth back to heaven. Above, on the main path, is the eastern cave site Takla Drubphuk, the Cave of Takla, one of the principal meditation caves on the mountain. Two thirds of the way to the pass is Bardo Trang, 'the narrow defile of the intermediate state', a narrow gap between two rocks through which the pilgrim crawls to facilitate his later passage through the bardo. Higher, there is Dikpa Phabsa, a rock on which the pilgrim sits to set down his sins and to rise bereft of them.

Just before the pass is a large rock from which the daughter of a renowned treasure-finder of the last generation, Sangngak Lingpa, extracted a treasure text in 1986 in an elaborate public ritual. Here she demonstrated that the magical Bonri mountain, impregnated with the vibrations of Bon's greatest adepts and replete with treasures concealed by Shenrab Miwo, had been undefiled by the Communist holocaust and still contained initiatory messages for Bon devotees seeking liberation from the round of rebirth.

On the descent, on the northern side of the mountain, the main stop is at Dikdo Taksa, the spot for leaving sin stones, stones into which mental traces of the pilgrim's transgressions are transferred and left behind. From here the path descends into the town of Nyingtri.


## THE CAVE: WOMB OF THE BUDDHAS

An hour before dawn the yogi's consciousness rises from deep sleep into the realm of dream and his meditative day begins. Dream yoga allows him detached contemplation of the uninhibited flow of illusionary dream image. A few moments later his eyes open and he snaps up from his semi-supine posture in his wooden box lined with a yak-hair mattress and, pulling his woollen chuba around him and taking full meditation posture, he energizes his bodymind with nine deep breaths, flushing the dead air from the bottom of his lungs and breathing in the pristine *prana* of the thin mountain air. Then relaxing, in slow motion, he begins the practice of the liturgical ritual of his yidam buddha-deity, using only the dorje and bell that stand beside a small pile of handwritten manuscripts and a wooden tea bowl on the shelf at the end of the box-bed.

The wall across the cave entrance is broken by a door and a small window. Upon the altar at the back is a recently made rough painted plaster image of Guru Rimpoche 3 feet (1m) high, clothed in the robes of the ngakpa, a grimy katak scarf around its neck. A small most precious cast bronze image of the yogi's yidam stands beside it – a gift from the headman of his village who had recovered it from a cache buried at the time of the Red Guards' destruction of their local gompa. An intricately modelled torma, an abstract symbol of the yidam made of roasted barley flour and molasses, stands beside it. Seven upturned bronze bowls lie in a row one upon the other in the front. A brocade icon of Shakyamuni Buddha hangs from a nail on the wall, a product of a Shanghai factory that produced millions of the icon for Buddhist consumption. Next to it is a tattered paper icon of Chenrezik printed in India. At the side of the cave is a crude hearth made of three round stones, a kettle sitting upon them over seemingly dead ashes. A butter-tea churn stands by the hearth. A small cotton sack of tsampa, a packet of low-grade tea, a plastic bag containing yak butter and a small cotton bag of salt comprise the stores stashed under the altar.

The yogi appears to be dozing during a break in the recitation of his liturgy. Dawn has long since broken outside and the rays of the sun stream through the window and strike the image of Guru Rimpoche on the altar. The yogi stirs and utters a piercing yell before completing his meditation liturgy. He rouses himself from his box and steps outside into the sun. Behind him is the rock-face, rising to a peak in which the cave is located. The permanent snowline at 16,000 feet (4,880m) is visible above. In front of him, to the south, rock-studded terraces of grass and flowers, with the occasional scrub-juniper bush, fall away slowly into space. Some hundreds of yards to both east and west the terraces end in precipices that drop to rivers meeting at a point way in front of him out of sight. After the confluence, a silver snaking river can be seen disappearing down a chasm through a low ridge where the high snow-peaked ridges to the east and west seem to converge.

The yogi moves to the side of the cave where a short hollowed branch conducts a slowly dripping flow of water from a crack in the rock into a pristine pool beneath. He performs his ablutions and collects water in the kettle. Stirring the ash, he finds a glow that he blows into life through a rough tube of tin. He feeds the fire with the last winter's leavings of dead scrub-juniper leaves and roots. The kettle boils, he adds tea, then pours the decoction into the churn and adds a spoonful of butter and a pinch of salt before churning the mixture. His breakfast consists of a bowl of barley flour mixed with tea.

The cave is called Dorje Drubphuk, the Indestructible Meditation Cave. Although it was probably first inhabited by Bon shamans, Guru Rimpoche himself is said to have visited it in the eighth century and meditated here, the vibration of his meditation impregnating the rock. The Great Guru subjected the local demons and spirits, at once freeing the inhabitants of the villages below from fear and binding the energy that may be used positively in the yogi's meditation. Where Guru Rimpoche once sat in meditation, succeeding yogis' practice is free from obstacles. Further, the Great Guru hid treasure texts in the cave. For all these reasons there has been a long succession of yogis meditating here during the intervening 12 centuries. This unbroken stream ended when the Red Guards climbed up to this eyrie in 1967, broke down the wall, despoiled the altar and took away the gilded image, along with the incumbent yogi, who was then imprisoned down in the valley. But twice during those 1,200 years, yogis had discovered the key to the secret of the treasures hidden here and produced revelations that were practised by their lineal disciples for several generations before they were replaced by revelations more relevant to the time.

Dorje Drubphuk could be any one of numerous caves in the valleys of Tibet. Even small valleys boast a Guru Rimpoche cave. Essentially, for the yogi who lives there in the Buddha's visionary realm, such a cave is a place that supports meditation practice, a place conducive to the attainment of realization and spiritual power. For the layman and devotee coming from a profane milieu it is a window into the visionary realm. For beings whose karma ties them to a belief in external reality it is a hole in the enveloping fabric of material existence wherein the vast space of the Buddhas can be glimpsed. It is gate into the mandala circle of the Buddhas. It affords an opportunity in time and space to connect with the resources of our spiritual substratum. It provides an avenue to the sources of divine energy and awareness.

A good cave location gives onto vast space. Emerging from Dorje Drubphuk and looking straight ahead, the yogi sees only the sky. The importance of a wide spatial vista for the yogi's meditation cannot be exaggerated. The sense of living in a vast space of brightness, clarity and light provides a sense of freedom and enormous potential in the mind. Meditating with open eyes upon the sky clears the mind. But more than that, sensory awareness of external space is transferred to an awareness of internal space, so that the sky is not only a metaphor for mind but becomes the reality of mind. Tilopa, the root-guru of the Kagyu order, expresses this importance in a song of Mahamudra precepts:

> Gazing intently into the empty sky, vision ceases;
> Likewise, when mind gazes into mind itself,
> The train of discursive and conceptual thought ends
> And supreme enlightenment is gained.
>
> The mind's original nature is like space;
> It pervades and embraces all things under the sun.
>
> Pure space has neither colour nor shape
> And it cannot be stained either black or white;
> So, also, mind's essence is beyond both colour and shape
> And it cannot be sullied by black or white deeds.
>
> The mind, like pure space, utterly transcends the world of thought...
>
> DOWMAN N.D.:2

In Buddhist metaphysics, this space is emptiness (*tongpanyi shunyata*), and identification of consciousness with emptiness is the necessary condition for generating the mandala that represents the awareness, the dynamic and the qualities of the Buddhas. The Dorje

Drubphuk yogi's sense of sitting at the centre of his mandala is supported by the topographical vista that he perceives by lowering his eyes from the sky to the mountains. The ridges on either side form a semi-circle, while the peak behind him, which contains the cave, seemingly forms the centre of a circle of which the mountain ridge is a part.

For the yogi inhabitant of the cave intent upon attaining the power and realization of the Buddhas in this lifetime, the Dorje Drubphuk power place offers the ideal location for retreat. For the local devotee, the power place has a different function. First, the yogi and the power place are one, and, struggling up the mountain to the cave, thought of the yogi is uppermost in his mind. The yogi is the lama, and the karma that has brought him to that place has set him apart. His life-style, his tantric initiations and his meditation practice have endowed him with the aura of the buddhahood that he knows he has yet to achieve. The yogi propitiates the gods, demons and spirits of the place and has power over them. Maybe the yogi himself is a god or spirit, for he has a reputation for magical manipulation, shape-shifting and flying in the sky. So the devotee brings the yogi an offering, probably of food, tsampa if he is a farmer from the valleys, and butter, milk, cheese, curd or buttermilk if he is a nomad from the high pastures. The offering will earn him merit, and if the yogi is benign perhaps he will give him the boon that he seeks, ward off evil influences and allow him the forbearance of the local gods. If the yogi is potentially malevolent, at worst his offering will persuade him to reserve his malignancy for others. The devotee is making an exchange with the yogi – offerings in return for blessings.

Through constant exposure and familiarity, the yogi and the local devotee become accustomed to the powerful spiritual influence of the cave power place. The pilgrim who approaches it for the first time, having travelled long and hard to arrive at his destination, with his anticipation increased by the legends of the cave and self-fulfilling expectation of the rewards of blessing, is most receptive to its effect. Approaching the sanctity of the cave with devotion and faith, there is awe and amazement. Entering into sacred space changes his body's metabolic rate and his awareness is heightened. His sensory perception becomes more acute: colours are brighter, shapes are better defined and focused, hearing is keener, sound is sharper, and smell, taste and touch are more intense. Perhaps the pilgrim sees apparitions and hears echoes. His body may feel weightless, as if floating, his movement seemingly in slow motion. Thoughts may be drifting in and out of his consciousness, free of any attachment. Perhaps a feeling of high clear ecstasy arises where the sense of time is suspended. This is a time of vision potential. With entrance into the mythic realm, messages and symbolic indications affecting his life-path can arise.

## The Great Guru Rimpoche Caves

The sacred mountain power places provide a macrocosm of sacred space; the caves and hermitages are the microcosmic power centres within the greater mountain mandalas. Guru Rimpoche caves are found at the major mountain sites, but also in most of the important valleys in Tibet. They are the caves of antiquity where contemplatives and yogis have retired from the world to develop the power of the mind. Many of these power places were undoubtedly consecrated by the shamanic tradition long before the advent of Buddhism. But with Buddhism, with its emphasis on solitary retreat and meditation, the caves of Tibet became highly sought after real estate.

The Nyingma tradition was first to give canonical recognition to meditation caves by identifying them as sites consecrated by Guru Rimpoche. Later, the Kagyu order gave special attention to the caves blessed by Milarepa. The Sakyapas and Gelukpas also have their cave power places, but these more studious monastic orders did not attach so much importance to them.

The popular legendary biographies of Guru Rimpoche relate how, after he had fulfilled King Trisong Detsen's ambition of building the great Samye Chokhor monastery, he travelled all over Tibet to sit in meditation in all of the power-place caves. At least, if they were not power places before his visit they were when he rose from his meditation seat and departed. The places and the time spent in each are listed in the old texts. In other minor texts mention is made of the hundreds of local sites where the Great Guru sat: 'All these solitary, isolated places were blessed as places of meditation.' His blessings of these places consisted of binding the local spirits, making the caves secure and giving them protection, and also impregnating the rock with his meditative awareness. This last function is an automatic effect of the Buddha's awareness. While sitting in samadhi in a cave, the Great Guru's mind encompasses the surrounding rock and it is said that the power of that awareness is impregnated into the rock. This removes obstacles to meditative achievement for his successors, for once a karmic process has been achieved it becomes increasingly easy to duplicate by imitators. So after Guru Rimpoche had gone through his meditative repertoire in the caves of Tibet, his successors achieved the same end with ever-decreasing effort. Such was the Great Guru's blessing.

The story of Guru Rimpoche's peregrinations throughout the whole of Tibet are undoubtedly apocryphal. He may have meditated in any of the caves of Central and southern Tibet, but it is highly unlikely that he travelled to Kham, for instance. When it is said that Guru Rimpoche meditated in a cave in Kham, it should be understood that one of his emanations did so. Upon his passing, the Great Guru became one with a basic strata of mind out of which subsequent incarnations, tulkus, were emanated. These tulkus, or incarnate Buddhas, were of the same spiritual mould as his original historical form, possessing the same qualities and karmas. So a tulku of the Great Guru meditating in a cave power place would have the same effect as the Great Guru himself. His consort, Yeshe Tsogyel, and others of the 25 historical disciples and their tulkus had the same influence.

The Guru Rimpoche caves are grouped according to their importance. There are 21 important caves called tiger lair (*taktsang*) caves, for example. The principal group is called the Five Power Places of Solitary Meditation. Each possesses some quality or geomantic feature that makes it an extraordinary attraction. These five are related to the Great Guru's body, speech, mind, quality and activity, that in turn are associated with his five chakras – the head, throat, heart, navel and base chakras.

### Yangdzong in Drak

Drak Yangdzong, the Uttermost Citadel, is the power place of the Great Guru's body. Drak is a district on the northern side of the

Yarlung Tsangpo, accessible by ferry from Chitesho. It is renowned as the birthplace of Jomo Yeshe Tsogyel, Guru Rimpoche's main Tibetan consort, and her life-spirit lake is located on the trail that takes the pilgrim up the Drak Valley. Drak Yangdzong is located high on the western side of the valley where outcropping of the limestone ridge creates a wide amphitheatre. The caves can barely be detected part way up the high sheer white scarp on the south-facing side. This cliff is called Shinje Rolpai Photrang, the Citadel of the Dancing Lord of Death. Climbing the cliff face on bridges of timbers secured with wire, passing the ruins of several retreat huts, the pilgrim reaches the entrance to the Great Guru's cave. Within is a large space, about 100 feet (30m) high and as broad and deep. A lhakhang constructed within long ago has been preserved, along with several hermits' cells. The grotto has all the facilities of a small retreat centre and is now used as such again.

To the left of this grotto is a path leading to the upper cave system. A ladder allows the pilgrim to slither up through a difficult narrow tunnel, a veritable birth canal, that opens into the wall of a large womb-like cavern. Invisible on the far side of the cavern is a ledge with a small opening at waist height that gives access to a small circular cave, the embryo attached to the wall of the womb. This cave, a shrine within, is the heart of Drak Yangdzong. Tiny pearls of crystalline rock are found amongst the limestone powdered in a hole in the rock; this is the ringsel prized by pilgrims for its medicinal and protective qualities. Such small secondary caves deep within a mountain grotto sacred to Guru Rimpoche are often called the Khandroma's Secret Cave, which may be likened to the cosmic seed of emptiness that is the heart of the sky-dancing khandroma.

The lower cave is the meditation cave where Guru Rimpoche himself meditated and hid the treasure texts relating to Dorje Phurba, the Indestructible Dagger. After his sojourn here the cave was used by his close disciple Sangye Yeshe, who through skill with the magical ritual dagger (phurba) was able to summon spirits and liberate them from their suffering, and also to pierce rock. After that a school of meditation was established here and the 55 yogis of Yangdzong took their place in the annals of Nyingma meditation success. Down the centuries innumerable yogis have emulated them.

## Chimphu near Samye Chokhor

Chimphu, the site of the most renowned caves in Tibet, is located at the head of a valley that runs north some 8 miles (12 km) from Samye Chokhor. Where the valley opens up and climbs steeply to form a broad south-facing natural amphitheatre divided in two by a stream, there are innumerable inhabited caves and hermitages that form the power place of the Great Guru's speech. This was his preferred place of meditation while the Samye monastery was being built. After its completion he initiated his 25 close disciples here and most of the caves are named after those adepts who consecrated them. Chimphu became Samye's retreat centre and most of the great names of the Nyingma order are associated with this place. The caves and hermitages were all damaged by the Cultural Revolution, but today Chimphu is again flourishing.

On the western side of the gully and one quarter of the distance up the amphitheatre is a conical crag about 50 feet (15m) high protruding from the valley side. This is known as Zangdok Pelri, the Copper-Coloured Mountain Pure-Land of Guru Rimpoche. The crag consists of a pile of glacial debris covering a rocky outcrop, and the spaces between the boulders cleared of earth and small rocks form excellent caves, with a walled-in overhang perhaps forming a detached kitchen. Other hermitages are built into rock overhangs. Zangdok Pelri is one of the most remarkable and sacred geomantic features of Chimphu. Upper and lower khorra circuits encircle it. The chief caves in the crag include the Metok Phuk Cave, Flower Cave, where Jikme Lingpa received the three visitations of Longchenpa that gave him full understanding of the Heart-Drop of the Vast Expanse, and the upper and lower Nyang Tingngedzin caves, where Nyang and King Trisong Detsen meditated and where Dzokchen treasure texts were discovered by Longchenpa.

The chief cave sanctuary of Guru Rimpoche and the mystical centre of Chimphu is Drakmar Keutsang, the Red-Rock Treasury, located above Zangdok Pelri. A new lhakhang has been built over it and also over Bairo Phuk cave. Both these caves are now devoid of their visual meditation supports. In Drakmar Keutsang Guru Rimpoche gave his principal disciples their initiations and meditation instruction. New images of the Great Guru flanked by his consorts

Mandarava and Yeshe Tsogyel dominate the altar. In front of the cave, in the middle of the floor of the assembly hall, is the rock on which Princess Padma Tsel, daughter of King Trisong Detsen, who had died prematurely, was brought back to life by the Great Guru.

The Bairo Phuk, the cave of Bairotsana, is reached through about 12 feet (4m) of tunnel that opens out into a small chamber barely long enough for a man to stretch out.

Higher in the amphitheatre are several other important caves where the Great Guru, Yeshe Tsogyel and her Nepali consort Atsara Sale meditated, while at the top of the ridge is Gurkar Tsephuk, the White-Tent Peak Cave of Guru Rimpoche. To the east of the gully are many more hermitages, but the main power place on that side is the reliquary chorten of Longchenpa, who died there. Longchenpa was the greatest of the treasure-finders who revealed treasures from the large caches that the Great Guru concealed in the Chimphu caves. The history of the place is the story of the adepts who discovered them.

### Kharchu in Lhodrak

Kharchu is the name of a gompa in Lhodrak in southern Tibet. It stands at the end of a ridge and snow peaks frame the skyline in every direction. Within this mandala is the hill called Chakphurchan Ri, the Mountain of the Great Iron Dagger, and within Chakphurchan Ri is a great cavern in which Guru Rimpoche meditated for an apocryphal seven years. This is the solitary place of the Great Guru's mind. Here the mountain is actually identified with him and the cavern with his belly. Within the cavern is a three-storey wooden hermitage which gives access to subsidiary caves on each level. The highest leads to a passage that takes the pilgrim to the secret cave of the Iron Dagger. Although this cavern was first consecrated by Guru Rimpoche, the founder of the Drukpa Kagyu order, Tsangpa Gyare, also meditated here and it is sacred to his lineage.

### Sheldrak in the Yarlung Valley

Guru Rimpoche's Crystal Cave, the solitary place of meditation that represents his qualities, is located in the pyramidal peak of the

Sheldrak mountain on the western side of the lower Yarlung Valley. When the sun has passed beyond the western ridge of the valley, the cave site winks like a white eye from the darkened scarp at the top of the mountain. Sheldrak is the epitome of the 'eagle's nest' hermitage and commands the entire Yarlung Valley. The amphitheatre ridge provides the sense of a mandala while offering protection to a site at a height that normally would receive the full force of the elements. After Guru Rimpoche meditated here, subjected the local gods and spirits, and hid treasures, Sheldrak became as renowned as Chimphu and Drak Yerpa. The 30 adepts of Sheldrak achieved realization here.

The chief cave is a walled-in overhang about 10 feet (3m) deep, an ideal meditation cave, with an expansive view across the Yarlung Valley. Rangjung images are discernible on the cave wall. The power objects that originally sanctified the cave have vanished, although the talking bronze image of Guru Rimpoche that was the principal support to meditation can now be seen at Trandruk Gompa.

Below the cave is a flight of steps leading down the rock-face to the rebuilt Guru Tsengye Lhakhang, the temple of the Great Guru's Eight Forms, and 150 feet (50m) below to the south-west is a valley where a retreat centre stood and the spring that provided water for the hermits. The Great Guru's consort, Yeshe Tsogyel, had her own favourite cave, the Secret Tsogyel Cave, around the ridge to the south. The place where the most significant of the Great Guru's treasures were concealed was the Padma Shelphuk, the Lotus Crystal Cave, around the amphitheatre to the north-east. Here the fourteenth-century treasure-finder Orgyen Lingpa discovered texts inside the statue of Rahu that guarded the door to the cave. His most popular revelation was the *Padma Kathang*, our chief source of legend of the Great Guru's life.

## Nering Senge Dzong in Monkha

The extraordinary power place of Nering Senge Dzong is in the Monkha district of Bhutan, east of Bumthang, north of Kurto and three days north of Lhundrub Dzong, close to the Tibetan border. This is the power place of the Great Guru's activity. The main cave of Senge Dzong has a small temple built in front of it, containing images of Guru Rimpoche and Yeshe Tsogyel. Nearby is a gompa with a lhakhang where the principal power object is a reliquary containing ancient artefacts, sacred daggers and images, probably from the time of Guru Rimpoche. Some 1,500 feet (500m) above Senge Dzong, above the tree-line in a high basin, is a small lake and above the lake is a ledge fronting a retreat cave. Around from this ledge is a milk-lake.

Guru Rimpoche and Yeshe Tsogyel are associated with both the lower and the upper caves of Senge Dzong. Guru Rimpoche appeared here in the form of Dorje Drolo, Adamantine Fat Belly, a wrathful emanation. Senge Dzong and Taktsang were the places where he revealed the *Dorje Phurba tantra*. Yeshe Tsogyel practised her austerities here and achieved her enlightenment.

## The Milarepa Caves: In the Footsteps of the Master

While the Guru Rimpoche caves are found throughout Tibet, the Milarepa caves are located only in the swathe of Himalayan territory where the great yogi wandered – from Rongshar to Kyirong with an extension to Kang Rimpoche. These caves have formed the primary hermitages of yogis of the Kagyu order. All the caves mentioned here have been identified and their existence confirmed since the Communist holocaust.

Jetsun Milarepa was born and spent his early, unhappy, life in Gungthang, a high desolate area of the plateau drained by the Kyirong (Trishuli) river. His address: the house Four Columns and Eight Beams near the field Fertile Triangle, in the small village of Kya Ngatsa, in the upper Tsalung Valley, in the old kingdom of Gungthang, in the upper basin of the Kyirong river, to the west of Pelku Tso lake, in the region of Mangyul, in the province of Tsang. Only a chorten marks the place today. Kya Ngatsa is now called Tsalung.

In Drowolung in Lhodrak, not far from the Bhutan border, Milarepa met his teacher, Marpa Lotsawa, who set him to work building and rebuilding a nine-storey tower called the Serkhar Guthok in order to purify his karma. After he was initiated and received meditation instruction, he meditated in the Taknya Lungten Phuk, Nape of the Neck Prophecy Cave, a half-day's walk from

Drowolung to the south, where he remained shut away for a year with a butter lamp on his head to keep his spine straight.

Later, returning from Lhodrak to Mangyul to settle his mother's bones and to look for his sister, Milarepa stayed in the Tsalung Kangtsuk Phuk, the cave 'standing on my own two feet', so called because he finally resolved upon a life of renunciation there and gave his family field, his last worldly possession, to his craven aunt. From Kya Ngatsa he went to the cave called Drakar Taso Umadzong, the Middle Way Citadel Horse Tooth White Rock, where he was to spend 12 years maturing his mind in the ascetic extreme of privation and self-abnegation that later marked his reputation. The hermitages and meditation cave of Drakar Taso, not so far from Kya Ngatsa, are perched on a high sheer cliff reached by a precipitous path. The meditation cave in the rock-face is reached by ladders from the hermitage buildings. Here Milarepa attained the Buddha's enlightenment and also magical powers, such as the ability to fly. He was seen flying to the cave called Khyung Dribma Phuk, Cave of the Eagle's Shadow.

According to Marpa's instruction, from Drakar Taso Milarepa moved to the easternmost point of his wanderings, to Rongshar, then known as Drin, to the north of Gaurishankar mountain. Here he stayed in Kyi Phuk, Happy Cave, where his sister came to meet him. In Chuwar, the centre of the Rongshar Valley, he stayed in the Khyung Gong Phuk, Eagle Egg Cave. A house has now been built in front of it and close by are the ruins of the Gephel Photrang Gompa. Up the Menlung Valley to the south-east is Dom Phuk, Bear Cave, where the master transformed himself into a bear. To the west of Drinthang is the secluded meditation sanctuary of Drakmar Chonglung, the Red Rock of Chonglung Valley, which was very significant in the master's life. Here he bound Ganesha, the Hindu elephant-headed god *(see p.171)*.

In the area of Drakmar Chonglung Milarepa blessed the Khyung Dzong, Eagle Castle, Potho Namkha Dzong, a simple stone hut, and Kyiphuk Nyima Dzong, Happy Cave Sun Citadel. At Khyung Dzong the Five Long Life Sisters, sky dancers, appeared to him at the head of an army of demons that filled the sky. One appeared as a fierce demoness with skeleton-like appearance; one as a jackal-faced demoness with orifices pouring blood; one as a fierce demoness like

The return of the Seventeenth Karmapa toTsurphu Gompa.
*Ward Holmes*

The oracle-lake, Lhamo Latso, the life-spirit of Tibet, from the Dalai Lama's throne. *Keith Dowman*

Samye Chokhor: Tibet's first monastery, eighth century. *Keith Dowman*

The rebuilt Serdung Lhakhang amongst the ruins of Ganden Namgyeling Gompa. *Keith Dowman*

The twelfth-century clay sculpture of bodhisattvas at Iwang. *Stone Routes*

Je Tsongkhapa's tooth mould at Kumbum Gompa.
*Stone Routes*

The giant silk appliqué scroll at Tsurphu Gompa showing
Shakyamuni Buddha. *Keith Dowman*

The great Jampa (Maitreya) image at Tashi Lhunpo.
*Meryl Dowman*

Yama, the god of death, playing sun and moon cymbals; one as a black woman throwing planets and stars on the ground, shouting, 'Strike! Kill!' and the last as a beautiful smiling seductress. Unable to disturb his samadhi, they acknowledged him as master. Later, as five beautiful women, they brought him offerings of longevity, a clear mirror, food and prosperity, a treasury of jewels, and cattle. Again they came, offering incense, flowers, food and drink, and the master initiated them into the Drolma and Kurukulle mandalas and gave them tantric precepts. Later, the chief of the five, Tashi Tseringma, became sick due to the unhygienic practices of a Rongshar household and Milarepa ministered to her in a silk tent on the high slopes of her mountain abode. He healed her and she became his consort in meditation practice.

From Rongshar Milarepa went to Labchi, but it appears that he took the long way around in order to enter from the main, western, gate to the Labchi mandala at Tashigang in Nyalam county. His cave at Tashigang is called Dropa Phuk, Belly Cave, since it is located in a belly-shaped rock, and he returned to it several times. From Dropa Phuk he entered the Labchi mandala and, binding demons as he went, opened the mountain power place for meditation and hallowed the four great caves there *(see p.173).*

Returning to his Mangyul homeland, Milarepa stayed at the Lingpa Drakmar Dzong, the Red Rock Citadel of Lingpa, located near the village of Longda, where he bound the demoness of the cave. Then he proceeded to Riwo Pelbar mountain in the Kyirong Valley where he stayed in the Rakma Jangchub Dzong, the Citadel of Enlightenment in the Rakma Valley, which is located on the western slopes of Riwo Pelbar, high on the valley side overlooking the gorge of the Rakmachu river. On his second stay in this cave he taught a shepherd boy named Sangye Khyab Repa. After this he stayed in Kyangphen Namkha Dzong, Banner of the Sky Citadel, located north of Rakma near the Kyangphen Gompa where the Kyirong river gorge widens into a plain.

Thereafter the master travelled to Yolmo, north-east of the Kathmandu Valley. His principal cave residence here was Takphuk Senge Dzong, Tiger Cave Lion Citadel, to the south of Tarkyi Gaon by the river, a small cave under a boulder, now enclosed. Perhaps on this foray into Nepal Milarepa stayed in the cave at the Gurta mountain, in Mon Nyishang, also known as Manang Bhot, high on the south-facing side of this Nepali valley on the northern side of the Annapurna massif. The story runs that he was meditating here when a deer appeared and dropped exhausted at his feet. The deer was followed by a hunting dog that lay down contented. Finally, a hunter arrived and was converted by Milarepa. Under the name Kyirepa Gompo Dorje this hunter was to spread the fame of the master in Nepal. The footprints of a deer are clearly marked in a rock by the cave. Some people identify Nyeshang Gurta with a cave within the Kathmandu Valley on the slopes to the east of Bhaktapur where Milarepa received an invitation from the Bhaktapur king to reside in the luxury of his palace, an offer he disdainfully rejected.

Returning to Gungthang, he first stayed in the Kuthangi Phukron Phuk, the Kuthang Pigeon Cave, on the northern side of the Sum Valley, on the western flank of Ganesh Himal. Here he sang 'The Song of the Pigeons' and taught gods who had taken the form of pigeons. After this perhaps he stayed in the secret cave in the Kyimolung hidden valley.

Then, crossing back into the Kyirong Valley, he travelled up to Dzongkha, the seat of government. Here he stayed in two villages, Rala and Rongphu, in the Zawok Phuk, Brocade Cave, in Rala, and the Wosel Phuk, the Cave of Clear Light, in Rongphu. In Rala he first met Rechungpa, who was to become his chief disciple. Rechungpa had contracted leprosy and walled up the master in this cave while he went to India for a cure.

From Dzongkha Milarepa went to Drakya Dorje Dzong, the Adamantine Citadel at Grey Rock, located to the north-east of Drakar Taso, halfway to the Pelku Tso lake and south of Tsalung mountain, near Drakya village and gompa. The cave is on the northern side of the river, built in its precipitous cliffs. Milarepa returned to this place several times.

After visiting Rakma, Labchi and Tsang, the master went to Kang Rimpoche and stayed in the Dzutrul Phuk, the renowned Cave of Magical Display or Cave of Miracles. Here he stayed in meditation, which was distracted by Naro Bonchung, the Bon yogi, whom he engaged in magical contest *(see p.164)*. Also at this time he stayed in the Rechen Phuk on the Nyenri peak after striding over Kang Rimpoche in his contest with Naro Bonchung.

Again in Gungthang he stayed in the Dragkya Dorje Dzong with Rechungpa and was served by the sky dancers. Then on the eastern shore of Pelku Tso lake, he was shown the Bephuk Mamo Dzong, the Secret Cave at the Mamo Goddess Citadel, by a shepherd who became his disciple, Tsiwo Repa. Then, also by the Pelku Tso lake, at the bottom of a high cliff near the present Laphuk Gompa, he stayed in the Laphuk Padma Dzong, Wild Radish Cave Lotus Citadel, and here he healed a dying Bonpo and converted his family. The wild radish is a plant employed in alchemical practice. In the Pelku Tso lake area Milarepa also stayed at Betse Doyon Dzong, the Sensory Pleasure Citadel at Betse, and at Lango Ludu Dzong, Citadel of Elephant Gate Serpent Spirit Assembly.

Finally, the master returned to Rongshar to die. In Drinthang, a village below Chuwar, is the cave where he was poisoned by the scholar Tsakpuwa, who was incredulous of his spiritual achievement and then murderously jealous. The place of his passing is in the Menlung Valley south-east of Chuwar in the Driche Phuk, Dri Tongue Cave, so called because of a protruding rock that appears like the tongue of the dri, a hybrid yak. The cave has two levels, the lower, secret, cave being Milarepa's meditation chamber and the place where he died. It contains a rock which the master brought from Labchi and which is impressed with his handprint.

## HIDDEN VALLEYS

In the mythic tradition of Guru Rimpoche, before the Great Guru left Tibet for the Glorious Copper-Coloured Mountain, he travelled throughout the entire Tibetan ethnic region consecrating places of meditation, hiding treasures and also locating hidden valleys (*beyuls*). Amongst the vast number of treasure texts (termas) he left behind him as part of his legacy to the Tibetan people were guides to these hidden valleys. They have been revealed down the centuries by treasure-finders, emanations of the Great Guru with the requisite karma.

The principal discoverer of these guides and the chief propagator of the tradition of the hidden valleys was Rikdzin Godem, who discovered hidden valley guides amongst the large cache of revealed texts called the Northern Treasure (*jangter*). Rikdzin Godem was born in the province of Tsang in the fourteenth century and founded one of the two great lineages of revealed treasure that was later to be established at the Dorje Drak Gompa, not far from the confluence of the Kyichu and the Yarlung Tsangpo rivers.

Essentially, the guides to the hidden valleys identified their locations and described the gates in the four directions through which they could be entered. They detailed the time when it would be propitious to enter and the omens that would occur. They also described the topography of the valleys, the power places that would be found there and the magical nature of life therein.

The valleys were located throughout Tibet, but the bulk of them were to be found in the high mountains that surround the country, in the Kunlun range that separates Tibet from the Takla Makhan desert to the north, and particularly in the Himalayas to the south where population was sparse and unpopulated valleys were topographically credible. On the southern side of the Himalayas deep gorges can open up into inaccessible but inhabitable valleys, unexplored even by the local people.

To the north of Kalimpong, a major staging-post for Indo–Tibetan trade before 1959, near the village of Laba, is the gorge of the Neora river, in which lies a hidden valley that has no reference, as far as we know, in the treasure texts. The walls of this valley defied a British expedition in the 1920s and an Indian army expedition just 20 years ago.

Of the Eight Great Hidden Valleys listed by Takzham Nuden Dorje in the Northern Treasure tradition, three are in the Himalayas: Dremojong in Sikkim, Padma Ko in Powo and Budum Lung in Bhutan. The three great hidden valleys mentioned in the *Padma Kathang*, the most authoritative of the books of the Great Guru's legends, are Dremojong, Khenbalung and Lungsum Jong. At least five hidden valleys are located in the Nepali Himalayas: Dunglo Jonpa north of Mount Daulagiri; Kyimolung or Kuthang in Nubri, on the northern side of Mount Manaslu; Pemthang in Yolmo, north of Kathmandu; Khenbalung on the eastern side of Mount Everest in the upper Arun Valley; and Padmagang to the south-west of Mount Kangchen Jungnga. It is as if every distinct region in the Himalayas has its own hidden valley.

The time of revelation and opening of each hidden valley for habitation is fixed and cannot be altered. Dunglo Jonpa, for instance, cannot be opened until the year 2172. The hidden valleys are safe refuges for the faithful in times of extreme insecurity, such as invasion or persecution of the buddha-dharma. A treasure-finder who can read and interpret the guide, follow its directions and lead his disciples successfully into the hidden valley is the primary requisite. If the time is unpropitious, or the conditions lacking, then the attempt to penetrate the valley will fail. Several stories of recent failed attempts are current in the Himalayas. In the 1960s, Tulshok Lingpa, a Sikkimese lama, attempted to lead a party to Pemagang, high on the south-west side of Kangchen Jungnga, but although he was able to read the guidebook and the conditions were apparently auspicious, an avalanche overwhelmed the party, killing several of them, and the rest turned back. In 1956, Kanjur Rimpoche, an eminent buddha-lama and treasure-finder from Riwoche in Kham, fleeing from the Chinese persecution, attempted to lead his party of refugees into the inner sanctum of Padma Ko. He alone could penetrate the cave passage into the inner sanctuary, so that he returned and led his disciples on into India. Oleshe, the late Sherpa hermit and artist from Jumbesi, attempted to enter Khenbalung, but, as he related it, a *yeti* barred the way and deterred him from entering the hidden valley.

The chief purpose of the treasure-finder who leads his disciples into a hidden valley is to provide sanctuary from the bleak conditions of the kaliyuga, the 'iron age' of degradation and despair, or, more specifically, from foreign invasion. Meditation is the primary pursuit of the treasure-finder and his retinue. A guidebook to Khenbalung promises:

> *Just by being in Khenbalung, compassion and benevolence will increase naturally, and greater wisdom and knowledge will come. It is better to meditate one year in this place than a thousand years elsewhere, better to do one month's retreat here than a year's retreat outside.*

BERNBAUM 1980:64

In 1975 Sangye Dorje, Chatrul Rimpoche, opened a hidden valley called Phemthang to the north of Targye Gaon in Helembu. Sangye Dorje is a renowned meditation instructor and his purpose of opening this hidden valley was solely to provide a sanctuary for his disciples to do meditation retreat.

The hidden valleys are described as mandalas. The surrounding peaks define the mandala's circumference and its centre is an adamantine rock, an indestructible spot. At Padma Ko this spot was described by Kanjur Rimpoche as being on an island in the river that divides the valley into two.

Kyimolung, Happy Valley, in Nubri, is an excellent example of the valley mandala. The centre of an encircling mountain ring is a three-floor pagoda temple in the style of the Glorious Copper-Coloured Mountain. The peaks on the valley rim are the residences of protecting mountain gods who keep unwanted visitors out and the blessed inhabitants in – the latter being accomplished by an elixir of forgetfulness. Physical inaccessibility is the best method of keeping intruders out.

The principal power places of the hidden valleys are caves, blessed by Guru Rimpoche and probably containing treasures that he concealed there. The hidden valley itself is a buddhafield in which the landscape is transformed and where the natural progress of the seasons produces an abundant harvest without human effort or engagement:

> *Dunglo Jonpa is a valley of 500 villages, and gathers a harvest without planting; all its waters are like beer and milk, its white earth like tsampa and its wood like meat.*

> RAMBLE 1995:107

The Himalayan people who live in proximity to the hidden valleys, and who are rarely educated in the mystical lore of higher tantric Buddhism, are more mundane in their expectations of a hidden valley, but they too are catered for. By drinking from the springs of Khenbalung:

> *All women will become beautiful; they will bear beautiful children and have an unbroken line of descendants. In addition, the water*

*will cure all their illnesses. If men drink it, they will become as
strong as the warriors of [the legendary hero-king] Ling Gesar and
as swift and skilful as birds.*

RAMBLE 1995:63

The water of the springs will make women sexually passionate, give
the men renewed vitality, and bestow eternal youth and longevity
upon whoever drinks from them.

The literary tradition of the hidden valleys mixes geographical
and mythic elements in a tantalizing potpourri. Geography provides the base material, and buddha-vision, employing mythic terminology, transforms the natural landscape into a pure-land; but
contemporary experience of the hidden valleys which were opened
hundreds of years ago seems to be at variance with the guidebooks'
utopian descriptions. Many of the discrepancies can be removed by
applying the conceptual anodynes of the tradition. There are outer,
inner and secret aspects of the hidden valleys. The geographical
locations, providing secluded and idyllic environments for meditation, particularly the gates of the mandala, constitute the outer
aspect. Through empowerment and meditation and the transformative effect of buddha-vision, the perfect reality of the inner hidden
valley is entered. The secret hidden valley is the space of buddha-
nature, full awareness of which transforms whatever is in the sensory fields into a buddhafield.

Geographically, Khenbalung can be identified with the upper
valley of the Phumchu (Arun) river, where it cuts across the Nepal–
Tibet border. This valley was opened by Rikdzin Godem in the
fourteenth century and rituals reopening the doors were performed
annually until very recently when the lineage died out. The gates of
the hidden valley mandalas are frequently major power places
themselves. Devotional pilgrimage to Chorten Nyima, the northern
gate into Dremojong, can in itself provide the empowerment and
buddha-vision necessary to enter the hidden valley to the south.
The northern gate to Khenbalung is the powerful mountain power
place of Tsibri. The importance of meditation as the open sesame of
the gates to hidden valleys is indicated by the location of a door into
Khenbalung – in a blank rock-face at the back of a dark cave way
down the Arun Valley.

# The Hidden Land of Padma Ko

Padma Ko is the most renowned of Tibet's hidden valleys. Stretching from Lower Kongpo and Pome in the north into Arunachal Pradesh in India to the south, it encompasses both sides of the Yarlung Tsangpo gorge, before and after the great river has turned south to cut its giant chasm through the Himalayas to exit into Assam. From the borders of Dzayul in the east to Lhoyul in the west, it embraces vast tracts of valleys and hills. Access for pilgrims is gained into western Padma Ko over Dashung La pass, and into eastern Padma Ko from the South Tibet highway running through the Pochu Valley and then over the Pomi range into the heart of Padma Ko across the Su La, the Gawalung La or the Dashing La passes. The Bhaka Gompa of Bhaka Tulku Padma Tendzin, below the Su La, is one starting-point. The size of Padma Ko does not make it more accessible. The deep gorge and valley of the Yarlung Tsangpo splits it in two and every crossing of the river is fraught with danger. The jungles at the bottom of the valleys, particularly to the south, are virtually impenetrable. For 100 years they frustrated British explorers intent upon proving that the Tibetan Yarlung Tsangpo and the Indian Brahmaputra were the same river. The area is sparsely populated with Monpa in the north and erstwhile head-hunting Mishmi and Abor tribes to the south. Tigers, bears, leopards and a large variety of venomous snakes inhabit the jungles at the bottom of the valleys. The humidity is pernicious and infection rampant.

The inaccessibility and dangers of this hidden land serve only to enhance its mystery and spiritual fertility. Its enigmatic legends only heighten its allure. Its natural environment is especially hostile and unforgiving, yet Padma Ko is described in the guidebooks revealed by the treasure-finders as a pure-land paradise of Buddhas and bodhisattvas existing in an environment perfect in every respect. Buddha-vision appears to operate here in an extreme transformative mode, as if a realm of hell is being spontaneously transmuted into a buddhafield.

The principal configuration of the landscape that supports this transformation is the body of Dorje Phakmo, the Adamantine Sow, which lies supine across the entire region. The energy centres (chakras) of her subtle body and her body parts are located at the physical features of the landscape. The Yarlung Tsangpo is her central channel, and at her heart centre, the heart of the hidden land, is a crystal mountain and a lake. The actual identification the topographical features that relate to her body is a perplexing exercise, however, due to the variety of different indications given in the treasure texts and the lack of consensus amongst pilgrims who have used the guides. This serves only to heighten the sense of enigma and acts as a spur into the mythic realm of Padma Ko.

One tradition identifies the mountain Gyala Pelri, to the north of the great bend of the Yarlung Tsangpo, as Dorje Phakmo's head and her crown chakra of great bliss; the throat chakra at 'the junction with the lowlands' is the valley area at the confluence of the Pochu and the Yarlung Tsangpo rivers where Gompo Ne is located; her heart chakra at the Lotus Crystal Mountain, Padma Shelri, the gathering place of the sky dancers, which may be identified with Kundu Dorsem Photrang, and the life-force lake at its foot, her heart-essence; her right breast at the mountain Namchak Barwa, the Blazing Mountain of Meteoric Iron, within the bend of the Tsangpo on its western side; her left breast Zumchen Phakmo Dong, Radiantly Smiling Sow-Face Mountain, somewhere to the north-east; her navel chakra at 'the great junction', which is sometimes identified with Rinchen Pung Gompa close to Kundu and above Metok Xian; her secret place, the karma chakra, further south in the jungles, at a rock precipice called Choying Gyeltsen, Victory Banner of Infinite Space, from which falls a stream of the nectar of rakta, the sky dancers' sexual fluids, and this location, yet to be precisely identified, is probably on the other side of the Indian border.

In the vision of the hidden land of Padma Ko as a vast lotus, Padma Shelri, the Lotus Crystal Mountain, is described as the heart of Padma Ko and this is sometimes identified with the heart of Dorje Phakmo at Kundu Dorsem Photrang. Thus Padma Shelri is the principal pilgrimage destination in Padma Ko and its main mountain power place. The peak is called the Kundu Dorsem Photrang, the Palace of the All-Embracing Dorje Sempa (Vajrasattva), and Dorje Sempa, the buddha-lama, encompasses all the peaceful deities in a mandala within the Shelri peak. Since this mountain is Dorje Phakmo's heart it is the gathering place of all the sky dancers. The lake in the lee of the mountain's northern side contains the life-force of the Khandroma. The chief gompa close to the mountain in the north-west is Rinchen Pung. The mountain stands at the centre of a 1,000-petalled lotus (the Lotus Form that is Padma Ko) defined by the valleys that fall away from it, and by their subsidiary valleys, by power place rocks (dzongs), by caves, rivers, lakes and cemeteries.

Padma Ko was not opened until the seventeenth century. Guru Rimpoche had visited the hidden valley and later concealed treasure texts elsewhere that prophesied its opening at a time of war, famine and dire conditions in Tibet. But the revelations that describe the place tell of a fabulous hidden land accessed through a door in a rock-face hiding a long tunnel that opens upon an emanation buddhafield, a magical valley of milk and honey, wild rice and medicinal trees and plants, where disease is unknown and old men become young again. Climbing out of this valley to a high pass in a rocky mountain of emerald and pearl, the faithful devotee of Guru Rimpoche enters the palace of infinite simplicity, where a rain of flowers falls constantly through a sky laced with rainbows upon beings with rainbow bodies, where wishes immediately come true and offering goddesses call for attention. This is Dewachan, the pure-land of Amitabha *(see pp.35–8)*. If Padma Ko cannot be reached in this lifetime the pure-land can be attained in the next life providing that pure faith supports the prayer.

Pilgrimage to Padma Ko is dominated by the Nyingma order and the place is sacred to Guru Rimpoche, although Kagyu yogis from Daklha Gampo were also active in its opening. The treasure-finders were the authoritative openers, so it is not surprising that the sacred sites on the khorra paths around the Padma Shelri mountain relate to Guru Rimpoche and the Nyingma tradition. There are three circumambulatory paths: the peak path around Dorsem Photrang, the middle path around Padma Shelri, and the long and tortuous ravine path around the entire area. In terms of merit accrued, one circuit of the peak path is equal to 13 circles of the middle path, and one circuit of the ravine circuit is equal to 13 circuits of the peak path. These three paths touch many lakes, life-spirit lakes of the buddha-deities and protectors of the Nyingma tradition. The caves in the vicinity of Latso, also called Kundu Lake, were especially blessed by Guru Rimpoche because he overcame the devil-spirits here and they still contain the treasures that he concealed.

The sustained interest of treasure-finders in Padma Ko, which began in the seventeenth century, has continued into the twentieth century, despite disaster and the occasional death of a master. Dudjom Lingpa, the previous incarnation of the late master Dudjom Rimpoche, died during his attempt to enter a gate of Padma Ko in 1903. Dudjom Rimpoche himself was born in Padma Ko, at Terkung, on the eastern side of the Tsangpo. As already mentioned, Kanjur Rimpoche attempted to lead his refugee party from Riwoche into the hidden valley in 1956, but only he could enter the inner valley. Many Tibetans fleeing their homelands from Chinese oppression had similar aspirations. We do not know how many succeeded.

## GOMPAS AND LHAKHANGS

The cave, a hole in a mountain, in its high secluded position, charged with the vibration of buddha-lamas, provides a sense of ultimate security, a womb-like safety. In the religious culture where buddhahood is the ultimate goal and solitary meditation is perceived as the best means of achieving it, the cave in a practical sense is the womb of buddhahood, of spiritual regeneration, and the place of rebirth. It provides the original inspiration for both Buddhist and Hindu temple and shrine design, which mimic a cave lodged in an ideal mountain peak. The cave is also the inner sanctum of Hindu temples, where the god resides. Its Sanskrit name, *garbha-griha*, means 'womb-house'. Whether of shikhara or pagoda design, a temple sweeps upwards from a massive square base to its pinnacle-peak, its roof, with upturned corner-tips, representing ascending mountain crags. It is designed to provide the qualities that the yogi finds in the cave: a quiet centre, emptiness and transcendence.

Early Tibetan temple architecture has the inner sanctuary, containing buddha-images, sacred symbols and power objects, within a massive square windowless stone structure surrounded by a circumambulatory passage, as at the Samye Utse. This lhakhang imitates a cave and in similar Buddhist temple structures in Pagan-period Burma, the *sanctum sanctorum* was actually called the cave (*gu*). It also forms the centre of a mandala structure. The monastic assembly hall was built in front of the lhakhang and subsidiary chapels were appended to it. The walls are slanted inwards and the winged roof-tips still evoke ascending mountain crags.

There were no gompas in Tibet when Guru Rimpoche arrived. But the lhakhangs that had been built by King Trisong Detsen's forbears were already vital power places consecrated by tradition and worship. Without exception these temples had been built in the valleys and they were sited with reference to different geomantic principles than the cave power places. It is tempting to minimize the part that geomancy played in the location of these temples because most of them lack any evident geomantic features. The Lhasa Jokhang, however, pre-eminent amongst them, was sited by King Songtsen Gampo and his Chinese wife, Wencheng Kongjo, according to Chinese geomantic principles. Wencheng Kongjo had brought texts on geomancy from China and probably Chinese geomancers too. The legendary texts explain in a non-technical manner Wencheng's geomantic concerns and her divinatory conclusions *(see p.20)*. If geomancy was applied to the siting of the Jokhang then it is possible that the same principles were applied to the siting of all the missionary temples.

The missionary temples are all important power places, consecrated by human activity, worship and meditation. Their foundation at the beginning of the Buddhist tradition, their association with the great Buddhist kings and, not least, Guru Rimpoche's visits, meditation and concealing of treasures at these sites makes them major power places. The same sanctification by human activity applies to the places to which myth and legend is attached. The Yambu Lhakhang, the oldest building in Tibet, for example, was consecrated by the residence of the semi-divine King Nyatri Tsenpo after his descent by sky-cord from the heavens.

Samye Chokhor and the Lhasa Jokhang are equally important amongst the gompa power places of Central Tibet and the Trandruk Gompa in the Yarlung Valley completes a triad. During King Trisong Detsen's reign these three became the valley gompa supports for three important cave sites. The Jokhang was linked with Drak Yerpa, Samye with Chimphu and Trandruk with Sheldrak. Samye Chokhor was designed in imitation of the cosmological mandala *(see. pp.47–9)*, with the central Utse Riksum surrounded by four major lhakhangs, eight satellite lhakhangs in the cardinal directions and four chortens in the intermediate directions. It is a power place of hidden treasure with caches in the Utse Riksum, in all 12 lhakhangs, in the Sun and Moon Lhakhangs, in the four chortens and in the gates in the encircling walls. There was no important structure in the Samye compound that was not consecrated as a power place by Guru Rimpoche.

The antiquity of these power places located in the cradle of Tibetan civilization and their association with Guru Rimpoche give them particular significance for all Tibetans. But the majority of latter-day pilgrims in Central Tibet lack a developed sense of linear time and history. The Tibetan calender is based on the Jupitarian cycle of 60 years, the first of which began in 1012. The succession of cycles since then is counted, but it is an arcane concern of astrologers rather than the knowledge of the common people, so that the progression of time in the Tibetan mind is cyclic rather than linear. Western scholars' obsession with history is not shared by traditional Tibetan scholars and the number of Tibetan histories written through the centuries can be counted on two hands. For these reasons the ancient power places of the Nyingma order have no more practical significance than the power places associated with the great lamas who founded religious orders during the second dissemination of Buddhism from the eleventh century onwards. Apart from geomantic features, it is a sense of personal lineage informed by legend that makes a particular power place of greater significance than any other for the individual pilgrim.

The founders of the later schools of Buddhism were, like Guru Rimpoche, yogis who sat in caves to achieve their realization and power and by so doing identified and sanctified a power place. In the eleventh century, for example, Milarepa wandered and meditated in the Himalayas from Labchi to Kang Rimpoche *(see pp.211–15)*. He delighted in solitude and shunned human society like the plague for part of his life, so some of his caves are located in high, virtually inaccessible eyries in the mountains. Later, when he required the proximity of human habitation, he lived in caves closer to the villages. Many of the high mountain valleys in this sparely populated area, on both sides of the Himalayan divide, boast a

Milarepa cave in the same way as Central Tibetan valleys have a Guru Rimpoche cave. Here, though, a single valley may have both, or a single cave may be associated by different traditions with either Guru Rimpoche or Milarepa.

Milarepa's disciple Je Gampopa, a great scholar and meditation master, moved the tradition of the whispered teaching (*kagyu*) to Central Tibet, where a momentous religious renaissance was in progress. Je Gampopa himself and his disciples Dusum Khyenpa, Taklung Tangpa, Drikung Kyabpa, Tsangpa Gyare, Drogon Dorje Gyelpo and Lama Zhang all established themselves in Central Tibetan cave power places and achieved the meditative accomplishment of Milarepa. Their realization acted as a magnet for both the devotion of disciples and the patronage of wealthy landowners, and either in their lifetimes or the lifetimes of their followers large monastic establishments were founded with their caves as the focal points of power within the gompa compounds. In time each of these gompas became the centre of wealth and political power and the seat of a reincarnation of the founder, a potentate of immense spiritual and temporal prestige. The power of the original cave sites, each endowed with extraordinary geomantic features, was magnified by subsequent human activity until the gompa itself, along with its living Buddha on the monastic throne, was identified as the power place.

At present Tsurphu Gompa, with its Karmapa again in residence after a lapse of 36 years, is the greatest of these Kagyu power places. The cave site where the Karmapas meditated is an eyrie located above the gompa. The meditation place of Drikung Khyabpa is within the temple compound of Drikung Thil, a still thriving gompa with a vital tradition of meditation. Many other gompas are in the process of restoration, including the great Ralung Gompa in Tsang, the home power place of the Drukpa Kagyu order, built over Tsangpa Gyare's hermitage. Daklha Gampo, the gompa built over the site of Je Gampopa's hermitage, is also being rebuilt. Taklung Gompa, after various political vicissitudes, is also being restored. The gompa temple of Densathil, built over the hermitage of Drogon Dorje Gyelpo, where he meditated in a spectacular geomantically-appointed site in a juniper forest, long ago lost its primacy but retained its attraction for pilgrims of the Phakdru Kagyu lineage.

Once the cave power places of the yogi-founders of the Kagyu lineages became the sites of great gompas, the geomantic features that had once led yogis to choose them for meditation were overlaid by monastic structures. The gompa temple, as mentioned earlier, was essentially an architectural reconstruction of the cave and the seat of power in the cave was transferred to the ritual seat of power in the gompa. This was the lama's throne (*kuden*). The lama was an incarnation, tulku, of the enlightened yogi who had originally consecrated the cave. The gompa power place was consecrated by the meditation and ritual activity of the lama and the monks. This change occurred during the growth of monasticism which paralleled the increase of monastic ritual activity as distinct from ascetic meditation. Meditation in the caves and hermitages continued to be the underlying source of spiritual vitality of the gompa, however, and the gompa provided a reservoir of candidates for meditation retreat.

The home gompas of the Kagyu order best illustrate the change of focus from cave to gompa. But even while Milarepa was still meditating in his caves, monasteries were being built in Central Tibet by the disciples of Jowo Atisha in the Kadam order. These gompas were places of study and monastic discipline and it was the refined vibration of generations of studious monks and nuns who consecrated them as power places.

Later Je Tsongkhapa reconsecrated by his presence and meditation many gompas that had been built by the Kadampas, notably Reteng Gompa, which became one of the most powerful Geluk power places. The greatest Geluk power-place gompa is undoubtedly the gompa of Ganden, which was built around Je Tsongkhapa's cave hermitage. Likewise, the home gompa of the Sakya order, consecrated by the five founding lamas of the order, and also Ngor Gompa, established by Ngorchen Kunga Zangpo, are power places of extraordinary potency.

Another presence that consecrates gompas as power places is that of the protectors of the Buddha's teaching and the tradition. Every gompa has a gomkhang that is the special abode of the protectors of the dharma and of that gompa. But there are special protectors that act as oracles through the medium of a specially trained lama.

For example the dharma-protector Pehar, whose original abode was Samye Chokhor, was moved, under the aegis of the Great Fifth Dalai Lama, to Nechung Chok, near Lhasa. Here Pehar became the State Oracle, the most important of Tibet's oracles. It is his presence at Nechung that gives that gompa its special magnetism for pilgrims and makes it an extraordinary power place.

## CHORTENS AND CAIRNS

A chorten (stupa or *chaitya*) is a monument of brick and stone of any size consisting of the piled design features of plinth, dome, box and spire. It is a power place marker and, like the lhakhang, further consecrates the place. But, also, if the site of a chorten lacks any evident geomantically auspicious features, then through its design and content and the constant worship of it, it creates a power place. Proximity to a chorten is an auspicious geomantic feature of a cave or hermitage site. The chorten is a spiritual battery that charges its devotees merely by its presence. It is as close to an image of buddha-mind as the creative Buddhist imagination has produced. Shakyamuni's relics were encased in chortens and, ever since, wherever Buddhism has travelled, chortens have been a primary focus of devotion.

Before the Cultural Revolution chortens of stone were a common feature of the Tibetan landscape. In the valleys each village would boast at least one. Sometimes there were protecting chortens at the entrance and exit of the village's major path. Wherever there was need for special protection around the village a chorten would be built.

Along the path in the wilderness a chorten may mark a power place, where, perhaps, a yogi meditated or a miracle was performed long ago. Perhaps a demon, subdued there, is encased in the plinth. More often, though, chortens were built as reliquaries, enshrining the bones of a great or holy man.

Chortens are rarely located high on ridges against the skyline, although they are sometimes built on passes to replace a cairn. Only a few old chortens survived the Cultural Revolution, but many have been rebuilt in the last decade and the chorten is again a familiar shape in the landscape.

The great chortens of Tibet are called kumbums, '1,000 buddha-image chortens'. They have lhakhangs appended at every level so that the chorten is transformed into a multi-levelled temple containing innumerable sculpted and painted images of the Buddha. They are a development of the many-doored chorten (see below) and are found in the province of Tsang and the Yarlung Tsangpo valley. Only five were ever built and only one has survived the Red Guards unscathed. That is the magnificent Gyantse Kumbum. Those at Riwoche and Jonang have been restored. The Drampa Gyang kumbum and Dranang Jampaling Kumbum are still in states of devastation.

The kumbum's terraces of lhakhangs appended to the plinth exaggerate the size of its base and dramatize the dome and spire protruding from that mass. The dome, as with most ancient Tibetan chortens, has the shape of a flattened cylinder, the 13-fold spire of discs holding the symbol of the sun and moon at its top. Like the stupas of Sri Lanka and ancient India, the Tibetan chorten appears as a rivet on the face of the earth, anchoring it down, whereas in the stupas of Burma and Thailand the movement of energy leads up from the base to the pinnacle and beyond into the heavens.

The earliest Tibetan reliquary chorten is a small stone chorten, built in the Indian style, in the Drolma Lhakhang, at Nyethang, near Lhasa. It enshrines relics of Jowo Atisha. But the chorten as a reliquary is best seen in the Potala and the great Geluk gompas. In their cavernous interiors, golden jewel-encrusted chortens, called *kudungs* or *serdungs*, several yards in height, enshrine the relics, frequently the mummified bodies, of lines of tulkus. The Potala houses the reliquary chortens of many of the previous Dalai Lamas. Most recently, the late Panchen Lama was mummified and enshrined in a very large kudung in a purpose-built temple at Tashi Lhunpo. These chortens are built in one of eight designs that constitute the Eight Tathagata chortens (*Deshinshekpa chortengye*). All possess the base plinth called the Lion Throne, a dome, the flattened box on its top, the spire of 13 discs, and an umbrella surmounted by the sun and moon. All have a vase-shaped dome except the nirvana chorten, which is bell-shaped. The other seven are identified by the design of the steps between the Lion Throne and the dome. The steps may be undecorated, in lotus form, gated with many doors, simple gated, with staircase, octagonal or circular. Neither the enlightenment chorten nor the nirvana chorten have shrine-niche or window. Each is associated with one of the principal events of Shakyamuni Buddha's life and has a special name:

*The enlightenment chorten (jangchub chorten)*, a memorial to Shakyamuni's enlightenment under the bodhi-tree in Bodhgaya, is the most common chorten, recognizable by its four simple steps, and absence of shrine-niche and window.

*The piled lotus chorten (pepung chorten or sugata chorten)* symbolizes Shakyamuni's birth at Lumbini. It has four or more steps in lotus design.

*The turning of the wheel chorten (chokhor chorten)*, also known as the auspicious many-doored chorten *(tashi gomang chorten)*, is associated with Shakyamuni's first sermon in Sarnath. Its steps are gated, each section at each level showing several niche-doors. This is the style of the Tibetan kumbums.

*The miracle chorten (chotrul chorten)*, a memorial to Shakyamuni's performance of miracles at Shravasti, is similar to the many-doored chorten except it has no niches in the steps.

*The descent from Tushita Heaven chorten (lhabab chorten)* is similar to the miracle chorten, but Shakyamuni's descent from the Tushita heaven into Mayadevi's womb at Kapilavastu is indicated by the staircase running down the steps in the middle of each gate.

*The reconciliation chorten (yendum chorten)* is a memorial to Shakyamuni's reconciliation of the monastic community at Rajagriha. It has octagonal steps of equal length.

*The victory chorten (namgyel chorten)* is a memorial to Shakyamuni's prolongation of life at Vaisali. It has three circular steps.

*The nirvana chorten (nyangde chorten)* symbolizes Shakyamuni's passing away into nirvana at Kushinagara. It is identifiable by the absence of steps, its bell-shaped dome on the 10-virtue base, and the absence of shrine-alcove and window.

On the ground in Tibet, the differences in style are not always apparent, but there is a generic chorten form that lends itself to the mythic imagination. Every devotee knows that the chorten is a tangible representation of buddha-mind, and initiates may identify it is as the Buddha as in his aspect of infinite space, awareness and light (*choku*). Otherwise the chorten's symbolism is interpreted by the visionary in various ways. If the chorten represents the Buddha, then its base plinth is the Buddha's seat; the stepped plinth his legs in lotus posture; the dome his torso, centred in his solar plexus; the flattened box his head, from which his eyes sometimes peer forth; and the axis or mast (*tsokshing*) that penetrates the entire monument is his spine and the central channel of tantric yoga that reaches from the lowest chakra to the 1,000-petalled lotus on the crown of his head. The spire is the protuberance in his head (*ushnisha*), his transcendent mind, the 13 discs indicating the 10 stages of bodhisattva realization and the three dimensions of his metaphysical reality.

If the chorten is a cosmic symbol, then the plinth represents the turtle, the supporting foundation of all things. The dome is the cosmic egg and the womb of time and space, and also the vase of fertility, for within it lies the potentiality of all things. The dome is also the cosmic breast, nurturing all creation. It is an image of the female principle, while running through it is the axis or mast, the male principle. This wooden axis is also the tree of life, the spreading Tree of Enlightenment, and the *axis mundi*.

If the chorten represents the five great elements – earth, water, fire, air and space – then the square plinth is earth, the circular dome is water, the conical spire is fire, and the surmounting half-moon and flaming seed of the sun are air and space respectively. A devotee versed in the tantras, internalizing the symbolic value of the elements and their shapes, will identify the square earth as the idealized internal passion of pride, yellow in colour; the element water, circular, as the pure nature of ignorance and sloth, blue in colour; the element fire, conical, as the pure passion of desire, red in colour; the element air, half-moon, as the immaculate passion of jealousy, green in colour; and the element space, the flaming seed, as the purified passion of anger, white in colour. For him the mast of the chorten is the central channel with the five chakras relating to the five purified passions and the dynamic of the chorten is an upward movement integrating the five aspects which are consummate in the space of buddha-mind in the flaming seed at the top.

Anyone who has observed the construction of a chorten will have the vision of it as a three-dimensional mandala indelibly reinforced. The square base plinth is divided into nine chambers, which are filled with relics, power objects, gem-stones, grain and the like. The circular central chamber is the mortice for the tenon-mast. The dome is the residence of the buddha-deity which may be represented by an image, sometimes visible through a shrine window. The deity is commonly the Buddha Mikyopa, or the bodhisattva Chenrezik or two-armed Drolma, or it may be Namgyelma, the multi-armed Drolma, who here takes the role of mother of all the Buddhas. The flattened box on top of the dome surmounts the central chamber. Relics are also sometimes enshrined here. Viewed from above, the 13 concentric discs produce the effect of a spiral whose centre is the flaming seed.

The contents of a chorten, ritually enshrined, increase its power, and they also make of it a cache of treasure. The chortens of Guru Rimpoche's day were power places that provided ideal hiding places for his treasures. The four chortens that stand in the intermediate directions of the Samye Utse are chief amongst them and they concealed major caches. Manuscripts were the treasure-finders' first harvest of treasures from the earliest chortens and down the centuries chortens have given up very important texts, like the *Chojung* of Longchenpa, found in the twentieth century by Kanjur Rimpoche, besides images and power objects. These representations of the buddha-body, speech and mind, gems, gold and silver make the chorten a treasure chest and a teaching model for devotees. Like any treasury of material wealth it acts as a magnet to people enthralled by wealth. When the constraints of tradition and belief have been released during times of war, when greed has overwhelmed fear of divine retribution, the chortens have been plundered by treasure-seekers. They were particularly alluring to the Red Guards.

During the period of Sakya ascendancy, hundreds, if not thousands, of small bronze chortens were cast in the style of miniature reliquaries and found their way into gompas all over Tibet. Now, in the bazaar, they are known as 'kadam stupas'. The quantity – much greater than any other cast icon ever made in Tibet – indicates the universal devotion to the chorten and their fine quality indicates the degree of attachment to their symbolic significance. The Drolma Lhakhang houses several kadam stupas.

Cairns (*lhatse*) are primitive chortens and mark power places in the wilderness. On the top of every pass, at the point where ascent becomes descent, the traveller will find a cairn. Maybe a chorten once stood there. These high points are the closest to the residence of the mountain gods that most men reach. They are places of communion with the sky gods and the cairns and chortens that mark them can be considered altars.

A fraction of the large amount of merit that is accumulated by building a chorten can be gained by adding a stone to a cairn or perhaps a traveller will build a three-stone pile himself. Anyhow, he will utter a prayer and end it with *'Lha sollo! Lha sollo! Lha gyello! Lha gyello! Kei! Ho Hoo!'* 'Victory to the god!' As at any power place the traveller may also attach a prayer-flag, singly or in a string, to the mast that protrudes from the centre of the cairn. The symbols and prayers printed on prayer-flags purify the wind and please the gods.

## SKY-BURIAL SITES

The major sky-burial sites (*durtros*) of Tibet are important power places. The greatest of them are located on a mountain, or near a cave or gompa power place, although their very nature is sufficient to sanctify a place. The common belief that liberation from the round of rebirth, or certainly a better rebirth, can be obtained by disposing of the corpse at one of the great sky-burial sites induces relatives to transport it from far away. This is a dubious belief from the standpoint of both orthodox and tantric Buddhism, since the karma that determines the nature of rebirth is set by the time of death, but, perhaps like most after-death rituals, the journey to a major power place and the ritual acts performed there benefit the living more than the dead. The local town and village sky-burial sites are usually located well outside settlements, although the principal Lhasa site, the Phawang durtro behind Sera Gompa, is now close to the northern Lhasa suburbs.

High lamas were once mummified or cremated, and victims of plague and epidemics may be buried or cast into a river, but where wood is at a premium and the rocky ground hard the year round and frozen for six months of the year, sky burial is the usual manner of corpse disposal. After death, three days are allowed to elapse during which time the *Tibetan Book of the Dead* (*Bardo Thodrol*) is usually chanted to advise the liberated spirit to vacate the corpse, give up all attachment to it and the world that it has abandoned, and to progress through the intermediate state, the bardo. Then, after the joints of the limbs of the corpse have been broken to enable the legs to be tied up to the torso, the body is taken from the place of death to the sky-burial site, tied to the back of a relative if the distance is short, or on the back of a pack animal if it is greater. Here, at dawn, while the vultures wait uneasily at a distance, after shearing the hair, the butchers (*rogyapas*) open the body, remove the organs, amputate the limbs, cut up the flesh into small pieces and pound the bones to powder with a rock. Then, after the dismembered corpse is spread around, the vultures – small mountain vultures – are summoned to consume the flesh and bone. Dogs and other carnivorous animals devour the remainder. There are variations of this procedure from place to place. The butchers, the group devoted to this grisly task, are socially stigmatized, but take heart in their function of accumulating merit for the deceased: feeding one's mortal remains to other sentient beings – vultures and dogs – is an act of generosity.

The mystique of the sky-burial power place belongs more to tantric Buddhism than to the lay people and the mechanics of corpse disposal. The sky-burial site is the Tibetan equivalent of the Indian cremation ground, the most exalted of which are associated with the enlightenment of many of the great tantric adepts. In legend, rainbows link the eight great mythic cremation grounds of India, Silwaitsel (Sitarvana or Cool grove) near Bodhgaya being pre-eminent, to the great Tibetan durtro sites – Kang Rimpoche,

Drikung, Tsurphu, Bonri and others. This connection empowers the sky-burial site at the rainbow's receiving end through the yogi's visualization of the ambience and spiritual achievement of the great adepts, while in the yogi's meditative achievement there is a sense of transference to an Indian cremation ground which is a buddhafield, a pure-land. Certainly the bond between Indian and Tibetan sites of corpse disposal reinforces the sense of the durtro as the perfect place of meditation.

The great sky-burial sites are also consecrated by their identification with the tantric mandalas that have been constructed beneath them or metaphysically identified with them. Demchok (Samvara), whose yogi-followers are exhorted to meditate in sky-burial sites and cremation grounds, is the buddha-deity whose mandala is most frequently identified with the sky-burial site. The cremation of high lamas, Buddhas and adepts at these places has sanctified them to an optimal degree.

The meditation that is best performed here is, obviously, the basic contemplation of impermanence, the inevitability of death, death as a gateway to rebirth and the influence of karma in that relocation, and also meditation upon the fundamental reality of emptiness. But for the tantric yogi who wants to train himself in the discipline of transforming whatever arises in his mind into aspects of buddha-mind, then the durtro provides the necessary stimulant to his practice. The riff-raff of the spiritual realm gathers here – restless spirits or ghosts (*bhutas*), hungry ghosts (yidak), flesh-eaters (shaza) and the undead (*rolang*). The Dark Lords (*Gompos*), whose retinues consist of these various spiritual entities, also reside here. In the yogic process of emptying the depths of hell, these Dark Lords are evoked, and when the yogi can perceive their buddha-nature they are bound to his command. The closer the yogi comes to the perception of the clear light of the buddha-nature in all things, the more malignant and powerful are the spiritual forces that arise to impede him.

These sky-burial ground entities are utilized in a more direct manner by the *chodpa* yogi, whose practice it is to invite them to consume his 'body', or, rather, his ego, in an accelerated process of ego-loss. On the far side of the Khandro Tsokhang khorra circuit at Terdrom is a small isolated durtro still utilized by chodpas. And for tantric yogis the sky-burial sites are still the crucial source of bones for sacred ritual artefacts. Bones not only bear the associations of the sky-burial site, but also symbolize emptiness. Particularly, the thigh bone is required for a trumpet, and the skull for the skull-bowl to be used in rites of offering and sometimes as a dish. This tantric tradition is still alive – at the Drikung durtro in 1995, a chodpa was given the skull of a young monk who had died from disease and spent the morning cutting it into the shape of a skull-bowl and cleaning it.

The Drikung durtro is amongst the most renowned in Tibet. It is considered identical to the most famous of the eight Indian cremation grounds, Silwaitsel (Sitarvana) near Bodhgaya. Legend has it that a rainbow connects Sitarvana with this place and that the guardian deity Yibkyi Chang presides over both. An eagle's footprint in stone to be seen here is said to belong to him. Within a perimeter of chortens, lhakhangs and prayer-flags, a circle of rough boulders about 30 feet (10m) in diameter represents the mandala of Demchok (Samvara). A larger standing stone at the top and a flat stone near the centre are those employed by the rogyapa butchers. Another standing stone, painted red, is a self-manifest mani-stone. Behind the stone circle is a shrine-room with new paintings of the bardo deities, the 100 wrathful and peaceful deities, on its walls. Close by is a small room filled with hair shaven from the dead and further to the right is a chorten that marks the place of Drikung Kyabgon's throne.

# GAZETTEER OF POWER PLACES

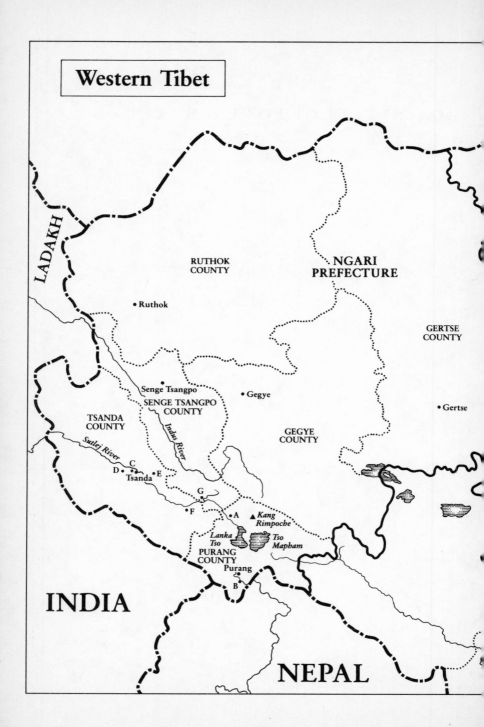

NAKCHU
PREFECTURE

Tsochen

TSOCHEN
COUNTY

SHIGATSE
PREFECTURE

NGARI
PREFECTURE

DRONGPA
COUNTY

*Tsamchok Tsangpo River*

*Karnali River*

•1

SAGA
COUNTY

R. •2

*DUNGLO
JONPA*

3

P

*Riwo
Pelbar*

*Kyirong River*

DZONGKHA
(KYIRONG XIAN)
COUNTY

*KUTANG*

Q

NEPAL

*PEMTHA*

*Trishuli River*

INDIA

Kathmandu•
Pharping•

CHINA

NGARI

NAKCHU

T I B E T

CHAMDO

SHIGATSE

LHASA

LHOKHA

NEPAL

INDIA

BHUTAN

BURMA

The Tibetan Autonomous Region

NAKCHU
PREFECTURE

Dangra
Yumtso

Targori

SHIGATSE
PREFECTURE

LHASA
PREFECTURE

NGAMRING
COUNTY

ZHETHONGMON
COUNTY

NAMLING
COUNTY

Ngamring
Kyemtso

•13

• 6

•11

D
•

E
•

rlung Tsangpo River  L •  K•

•14

14

G•

LATSE
COUNTY

A •  •12 •C

B•

12

15

S
•

•16

16

T•

•7 F•

SAKYA
COUNTY

H• •8

•15

U•

•V

W•

•17

KHANGMAR
COUNTY

LHOKHA
PREFECTURE

u Tso

Tsibri ▲  • 5

TINGRI
(SHELKAR)
COUNTY

ALAM
UNTY

9•

10•

J •  Labchi

TENKYE
COUNTY

KAMPA
COUNTY

Tashi Tsering
Chenga

Rongshar River

I

X•

DREMOJONG
SIKKIM

DROMO
COUNTY

Paro Taktsang
•

Nering
Senghe
Dzong
•

Bhote Kola River

KHENBALUNG

18•

Kyerchu
Lhakhang
•

Bumthang
Jampa
Lhakhang
•

Sun Koshi River

PADMAGANG

BHUTAN

Central Tibet including
Nepal and Bhutan

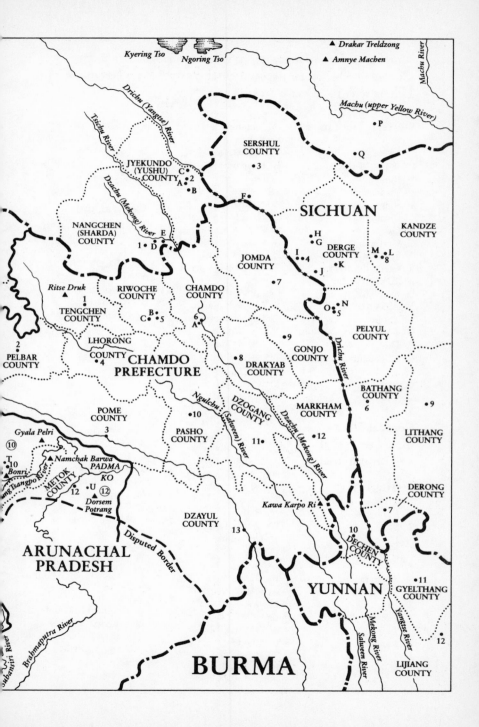

- Numbers refer to county towns where not labelled on maps.
- Circled numbers refer to counties where not labelled on maps.
- Letters refer to power places.

## Western Tibet map

NGARI
PREFECTURE
1. Purang
2. Tsanda
3. Senge Tsangpo
4. Ruthok
5. Gegye
6. Gertse
7. Tsochen
PURANG COUNTY
A. Tretapuri
B. Korchak
TSANDA COUNTY
C. Tholing
D. Tsaparang
E. Dungkar
F. Khyunglung Ngulkar
SENGE TSANGPO
COUNTY
G. Gurugam

## Central Tibet including Nepal and Bhutan map

SHIGATSE
PREFECTURE
1. Drongpa
2. Saga
3. Dzongkha
   (Kyirong Xian)
4. Nyalam
5. Tingri (Shelkar)
6. Ngamring
7. Latse
8. Sakya
9. Tenkye
10. Kampa
11. Zhethongmon
12. Shigatse
13. Namling

14. Rinpung
15. Panam
16. Gyantse
17. Khangmar
18. Dromo
⑫ SHIGATSE COUNTY
A. Narthang
B. Ngor Ewam Choden
C. Zhalu Gompa
NAMLING COUNTRY
D. Menri Gompa
E. Yungdrung Ling
Gompa
LATSE COUNTY
F. Gyang Bumoche
G. Phuntsokling Gompa
SAKYA COUNTY
H. Sakya Gompa
TINGRI (SHELKAR
COUNTY)
I. Rongshar
NYALAM COUNTY
J. Nyalam Dropa Phuk
NGAMRING COUNTY
K. Ngamring Chode
L. Chung Riwoche
   Kumbum
DZONGKHA (KYIRONG
XIAN) COUNTY
M. Gungthang La Pass
N. Tsalung
P. Drakar Taso
   Drubphuk
Q. Kyirong
SAGA COUNTY
R. Tradun Tse
⑭ RINPUNG COUNTY
⑮ PANAM COUNTY
⑯ GYANTSE COUNTY
S. Gyantse Pelkhor
   Chode
T. Ralung Gompa
U. Kyingkhor
   Trangdruk

KHANGMAR COUNTY
V. Nenying Gompa
W. Iwang, Yemar
TENKYE COUNTY
X. Chorten Nyima

## Central and Eastern Tibet map

NAKCHU
PREFECTURE
1. Shentsa
2. Pelgon
3. Amdo
4. Nyenrong
5. Nakchu
6. Trachen
7. Sokdzong
8. Driru

LHASA
PREFECTURE
1. Lhasa
2. Nyemo
3. Chushul
4. Tolung Dechen
5. Damzhung
6. Lhundrub
7. Taktse
8. Medro Gungkar
9. Kongpo Gyamda
10. Nyingtri
11. Menling
12. Metok
① LHASA COUNTY
③ CHUSHUL COUNTY
A. Drolma Lhakhang
B. Sangphu Neuthok
C. Kangri Thokar
④ TOLUNG DECHEN
D. Kyormo Lung
   Gompa

E. Nenang Gompa
F. Tsurphu Gompa
⑦TAKTSE COUNTY
G. Tsel
H. Drak Yerpa
I. Ganden Namgyeling
⑧MEDRO
GUNGKAR COUNTY
J. Gyama
K. Katse Gompa
L. Drikung Thil
M. Terdrom
⑥LHUNDRUB COUNTY
N. Reteng Gompa
O. Taklung Thang
P. Langthang Gompa
Q. Nalendra Gompa
⑨KONGPO
GYAMDA COUNTY
R. Draksum Dorje Drak
⑩NYINGTRI COUNTY
S. Buchu
T. Lamaling
⑫METOK COUNTY
U. Rinchen Pung

LHOKHA
PREFECTURE
1. Gongkar
2. Dranang
3. Tsethang
4. Chongye
5. Zangri
6. Gyatsa
7. Nangdzong
8. Lhuntse
9. Tsome
10. Lhodrak
11. Nakartse
12. Tsona
①GONGKAR
A. Gongkar Chode
B. Dorje Drak Gompa
②DRANANG COUNTY
C. Drak Yangdzong
D. Drathang Gompa
E. Mindroling Gompa
F. Samye Chokhor
G. Chimphu

H. Yamalung
③TSETHANG COUNTY
I. Trandruk Gompa
J. Sheldrak
K. Tashi Dokha
L. Lhakhang Keru
④CHONGYE COUNTY
M. Solnak Thang
N. Kings Tombs
⑤ZANGRI COUNTY
O. Densathil
P. Cholung
Q. Dzingchi Ling
⑥GYATSA COUNTY
R. Daklha Gampo
S. Chokhor Gyel
⑦NANGDZONG COUNTY
⑧LHUNTSE COUNTY
⑨TSOME COUNTY
A. Mawochok
⑩LHODRAK COUNTY
B. Khomthing Lhakhang
C. Kharchu
D. Sekhar Guthok
E. Lhalung
F. Guru Lhakhang
⑪NAKARTSE COUNTY
G. Lho Taklung
H. Samding Gompa
⑫TSONA COUNTY


CHAMDO
PREFECTURE
1. Tengchen
2. Pelbar
3. Pome
4. Lhorong
5. Riwoche
6. Chamdo
7. Jomda
8. Drakyab
9. Gonjo
10. Pasho
11. Dzongang
12. Markham
13. Dzayul
CHAMDO COUNTY
A. Ganden Jampaling
RIWOCHE COUNTY

B. Tsuklakhang
C. Takzham Gompa

QINGHAI
1. Nangchen (Sharda)
2. Jyekundo (Yushu)
P. Tarthang Gompa
Q. Dodrub Chode
JYEKUNDO
(YUSHU) COUNTY
A. Trangu Gompa
B. Benchen Gompa
C. Drogon Gompa
NANGCHEN
(SHARDA) COUNTY
D. Zurmang Dutsi Thil
E. Zurmang Namgyeltse


SICHUAN
3. Sershul
4. Derge
5. Pelyul
6. Bathang
7. Derong
8. Kandze
9. Lithang
SERSHUL COUNTY
F. Longthang Drolma
DERGE COUNTY
G. Dzokchen
H. Zhechen
I. Derge Gonchen
J. Pelpung Gompa
K. Dzongsar Gompa
KANDZE COUNTY
L. Kandze Gompa
M. Bongen Gompa
PELYUL COUNTY
N. Kathok Dorjeden
O. Pelyul Namgyel
Jangchub Choling


YUNNAN
10. Dechen
11. Gyelthang
12. Lijiang

The Tibetan Autonomous Region (TAR) is divided into six prefectures (*sakhul*), each prefecture into numerous counties (*dzong*), the county town of which is a *xian*, and each county into small districts (*qu*), the centre of which is a *qu*. The power places of the TAR are listed below under prefecture headings and their county is given. They are grouped according to geographical proximity, rather than alphabetical order. There is a separate section on Eastern Tibet – Kham (including Chamdo prefecture in the TAR) and Amdo. The power places of Tibet are legion, with thousands of gompas having some claim to power place status. Only those known to me as possessing some special source of blessing or especially distinctive feature have been included here.

## NGARI PREFECTURE

This is made up of the old province of Ngari Khorsum, including the ancient kingdom of Zhangzhung, the later kingdom of Guge, and also the vast expanse of the north-west Jangthang, the northern plains.

*Kang Rimpoche* (Gang rin po che), Kang Tise, Kailash, in Purang county, the great sacred mountain residence of Demchok. *See pp.153–65.*

*Tso Mapham* (mTsho ma pham), Manasarovar, in Purang county, the sacred lake to the south of Kang Rimpoche. *See pp.165–7.*

*Tretapuri* (Pretapuri), also Tirthapuri, in Purang county, 28 miles to the south-west of Kang Rimpoche. The power place is located on a ridge, the locus of power being the geyser and medicinal hot springs situated at the bottom of the ridge. The khorra path passes by the Tsogyel sky-burial site *en route* to the top of the ridge, then descends, past the Five Surrogate power places (*netsabnga*) and the

Drukpa Kagyu Tretapuri Gompa, to the meditation caves of Guru Rimpoche and Yeshe Tsogyel, the principal caves amongst many in this area. Tretapuri is one of the 24 major power places of the sub-continent, an abode of Demchok and particularly Dorje Phakmo where Heruka subdued Rudra. It is renowned for its sacred substances – the water of the hot springs, red lead from a cave site, ringsel from around the hot springs, and red and white earth. All are the sources of Buddha's blessings.

*Khorchak Gompa* ('Khor chags dgon), in Purang county, south-east of Purang Xian, near the Nepali border. This is a tenth-century Rinchen Zangpo foundation, known also as Kojarnath. It is a Sakya gompa, once the seat of one of the famous four Phakpa Lokesvara statues. The Lotsawa Lhakhang has survived with some original relics.

*Guge* (Gu ge), in Tsanda county, west of Kailash and to the north of the Indian border, in the Sutlej river valley. This was a kingdom that thrived from the tenth to the seventeenth century. The early Guge kings reintroduced Buddhism into Tibet and initiated the second period of dissemination of Buddhism, particularly through the invitation of Jowo Atisha to Tibet from Bangala. Invasion from Ladakh and a climatic change caused the kingdom's seventeenth-century downfall and along with it the decline of Western Tibetan culture.

*Tsaparang* (rTsa pa rang), in Tsanda county, in the upper Sutlej Valley. This was the capital of the old kingdom of Guge and its eleventh-century glory is still evident. The citadel, dating from the eleventh century, stretches about 200 yards (200m) along a ridge and is accessed by tunnels from below. It was abandoned in the seventeenth century after a massacre. The site has been ravaged by the Communists and only the finely painted Demchok Mandala Lhakhang remains. Below the citadel are three lhakhangs belonging to the palace gompa which have been preserved. The Lhakhangs Karpo and Marpo (the Red and White Temples) contain indifferently restored sixteenth-century murals and clay sculpture. The mandala murals that adorn the walls are derived from the

Namnang (Vairochana) yogatantra cycle. The third, the Jikje (Vajrabhairava) Lhakhang, has excellent murals from the seventeenth century.

*Tholing Gompa* (Tho gling dgon), in Tsanda county, in the upper Sutlej Valley, downriver from Tsaparang in the village of Tsanda Xian. This Rinchen Zangpo gompa dating from 995 retains three lhakhangs, two with their roofs intact. The assembly hall is painted with fine mandala murals of the Namnang (Vairochana) yogatantra cycle dating from the sixteenth century, brilliantly executed in the mature Western Tibetan style. Jowo Atisha taught here in the eleventh century. It was the most important gompa in Western Tibet until the Cultural Revolution, when it was destroyed. It remains unrestored.

*Dungkar* (gDung dkar), in Tsanda county, 15 miles (25 km) north of Tholing. Behind the village rises a scarp in which numerous meditation caves were excavated in the eleventh century and later, to create an extended area of cave hermitages. The principal cave at Dungkar is about 20 feet (6.6m) square with a lantern-style ceiling. It is entirely covered with fine murals depicting a Namnang (Vairochana) mandala deriving from the eleventh century and painted in the modified Kashmiri style of the early monastic period. The ruins of a Guge-period Sakya gompa stand atop the cliff face.

*Phiyang* (Phi yang), in Tsanda county, about 5 miles (8 km) west of Dungkar and in the same valley. This is a cave hermitage site dating from the Guge kingdom period with murals similar to those at Dungkar.

*Khyunglung Ngulkar* (Khyung lung dngul dkar), in Tsanda county. Near the ancient cave city of Khyunglung, which was the reputed capital of ancient Zhangzhung, is the Bon gompa of Ngulkar, founded in 1936 by Kagya Khyungtrul Jikme Namkhai Dorje, a Bon *rimepa*.

*Gurugam* (Gu ru gam), in Senge Tsangpo county, on the road to Khyunglung. This important Bon gompa, now rebuilt, is the home gompa of the principal Bon institution in India (Dolanji, near Simla). The meditation cave of Drenpa Namkha, a Bon disciple of Guru Rimpoche, is located in an extraordinary cave complex in a cliff face nearby.

## SHIGATSE PREFECTURE

This includes the old province of Tsang together with Lato and Mangyul in the west. It is divided into three sections: 1) Shigatse and Latse districts; 2) Tingri, Lato, Mangyul and Kyirong districts; 3) Gyantse and further west. ———

### Shigatse and Latse Districts

*Tashi Lhunpo* (bKra shis lhun po dgon), in Shigatse city. Alone of the four great Geluk gompas, Tashi Lhunpo survived Communist depredations. Only the 4,000 monks' quarters were razed. The fine examples of seventeenth and eighteenth century construction that remain form the splendid nucleus of this monastic museum. The abbot's palace (*labrang*) contains the Fourth Panchen Rimpoche's magnificent reliquary chorten (*kudung*). In the assembly hall (*tsokhang*) is the reliquary chorten of Gendun Drub, the First Dalai Lama, and several galleries where small bronze images are exhibited. The Jampa Lhakhang contains the Jampa Chenpo (Maitreya) image erected by the Ninth Panchen in 1914, standing 84 feet (26m) high and covered with 614 lbs (279 kg) of gold. The Tantric College and College of Logic are now functional. The most recent addition is the lhakhang built to contain the reliquary chorten of the late Tenth Panchen Lama. Tashi Lhunpo was founded in 1447 by Tsongkhapa's nephew and disciple Gendun Drub, who was retrospectively designated the First Dalai Lama. His successor moved to Drepung, which became the chief seat of Geluk power, but as the principal Geluk gompa in Tsang, Tashi Lhunpo regained its prestige when the Great Fifth Dalai Lama recognized his tutor as the fourth incarnation of Wopakme (Amitabha) in the line of Panchen Lamas and abbots of Tashi

Lhunpo. Since Wopakme is the spiritual source of Chenrezik, who incarnates as the Dalai Lamas, the Panchen Lamas are often considered spiritually superior to the Dalai Lamas, a relationship frequently exploited by the Chinese. The Fourteenth Dalai Lama and the Chinese have recognized different incarnations as the Eleventh Panchen. The outer khorra path (*lingkor*) circumambulates the entire Tashi Lhunpo compound and is a popular devotion for local devotees and pilgrims.

*Narthang* (sNar thang), in Shigatse county, 9 miles (14 km) west of Shigatse. A Kadam gompa, founded in the twelfth century, this became a Geluk foundation famous for its printing house, which has since been destroyed.

*Ngor Ewam Choden* (Ngor EVAM chos ldan), in Shigatse county, to the south of Narthang. The Ngor Gompa, the home gompa of the Ngor sub-sect of the Sakya order, was founded in 1429 by Ngorchen Kunga Zangpo, who was born and educated at Sakya and became one of the most successful of the Sakya missionary lamas. This gompa was renowned for its scholarship and tantric discipline, for its library, including a rich collection of Sanskrit manuscripts, and also for the Newar-derived school of painting that flourished in the fifteenth century. Of its 18 colleges and two assembly halls, only a single lhakhang, the Lamdre Lhakhang, has been restored and contains some significant power objects. Amongst the tulkus of Ngor are the exiled lamas Kangsa, Tartse, Tende and Lobdin Rimpoches.

*Zhalu Gompa* (Zhwa lu), Shigatse county, about 15 miles (25 km) south of Shigatse. In the history of Tibetan Buddhism, and also of Tibetan art, Zhalu is one of the most important gompas. Its chief buildings have been preserved, although their condition is precarious. Zhalu was founded in 1027, one of the original Lume establishments, but its assembly hall was not erected until the beginning of the fourteenth century, when the Mongol influence in Tibet was at its height. This explains its Chinese architectural influences, seen particularly in the roofs decorated with turquoise-coloured glazed tiles and mouldings. The religious renown of Zhalu was also achieved in the fourteenth century, when it became the residence of Buton Rimpoche, the great scholar who compiled the Tibetan Buddhist canon, the Kangyur and Tengyur. Thereafter it became the seat of the Butonpa, a school based on the lineage of Buton, derived from both Kadam and Sakya teachers. The murals of Zhalu are the only part of its treasure that remains today. But in quantity and quality this painting is incomparable in contemporary Tibet.

*Menri Gompa* (sMan ri dgon), in Namling county, east of Shigatse on the north bank of the Yarlung Tsangpo, in the Tobgyel Valley. The most important gompa in an enclave of three Bon gompas, this was an academy and school of logic that attracted Bon students from all over Tibet. Menri was founded by Nyame Sherab Gyeltsen, a native of Gyarong, in 1405. It was completely destroyed and only an assembly hall has been rebuilt, although the monastic community is again thriving. In Menri Lugari mountain behind the gompa there are various secret caves. Also in the Tobgyel Valley is Kharna Gompa, an important Bon gompa, founded in the nineteenth century.

*Yungdrung Ling Gompa* (gYung drung gling dgon), in Namling county, about 50 miles (80 km) east of Shigatse, on the north bank of the Yarlung Tsangpo, and on the eastern side of the Wuyuk Machu river. One of the three Bon gompas in this area and one of the largest in Tibet, founded in 1834 by Dawa Gyeltsen, Yungdrung Ling had 200 monks before it was completely destroyed. The assembly hall and the large Thongdrol Lhakhang have been rebuilt, housing the reliquary chorten of the founder. Kunzang Lodro Rimpoche is now in residence with 30 monks. Behind the gompa is the Wolha Gyelri mountain.

*Gyang Bumoche* (rGyang bu mo che) or Gyang Kumbum, in Latse county, on the Latse plain, near Drampa Gyang Lhakhang. This is one of the five great kumbum chortens, built in the first years of the fifteenth century by Sakya Sonam Tashi and Thangtong Gyelpo on a wide base and with less height than the other great kumbums and with flat-roofed lhakhangs. It has been severely damaged and remains unrestored.

*Gyang Lonpo Lung* (rGyang Lon po lung), in Latse county, on the Latse plain, to the east of the kumbum. A Guru Rimpoche cave is located here in a delightful miniature valley with trees and meadows on its slopes, above the ruins of a Nyingma gompa and a number of hermitages.

*Drampa Gyang Lhakhang* (gTsang Gram pa rgyangs), in Latse county, on the eastern side of the Latse plain, near Gyang Bumoche. This seventh-century missionary temple of King Songtsen Gampo subduing the demoness's left hip has now been restored. The fourteenth-century treasure-finder Zangpo Drakpa discovered the *Leu Dunma* treasure text here.

*Jonang Kumbum* (Jo nang sku 'bum), *see Phuntsokling Gompa.*

*Phuntsokling Gompa* (Phun tshog gling dgon), in Latse county, in the Yarlung Tsangpo gorge north of Latse. Now partially restored, this was the home gompa of the unorthodox Jonang order, to which the renowned Taranatha belonged, and which was proscribed by the Great Fifth Dalai Lama for its metaphysical heresies. In a valley near to the gompa stands the Jonang Kumbum, the earliest of the great kumbums, founded by Dolpopa Sherab Gyeltsen c.1330. Its lhakhangs were badly damaged during the Cultural Revolution although the solid pile remained, so that renovation, now completed, was not so difficult. No sculpture and only fragments of its murals have survived the restoration. This kumbum is named Thongdrol Chenpo, Liberation by Seeing.

*Sakya Gompa* (dPal Sa skya dgon), in Sakya county, 15 miles (25 km) south-east of Latse Xian. This home gompa of the Sakya order, once a large monastic town, was divided into northern and southern complexes. The oldest, northern complex, built around the meditation cave of Sachen, the first patriarch of the Sakya order, on the northern side of the Trumchu river, was all destroyed and only a small lhakhang on top of the cave has been rebuilt. The southern complex now consists of the Lhakhang Chenmo, a vast walled temple nearly 100 yards (100m) square, begun by Phakpa in 1268, finished in 1276 and restored in the sixteenth century. It is now an extraordinary museum containing a small portion of the wealth of sacred symbols and power objects of the old gompa. An internal courtyard gives access to the lhakhangs. The proportions of the principal lhakhang, the assembly hall, may be indicated by the thickness of the walls (11 feet, 3.5m), the height of the ceiling (50 feet, 16m) and the existence of 40 roughly hewn tree trunks (up to 6 feet, 2m, in circumference) supporting it. The altars on three sides support large buddha-images containing relics of the Sakya hierarchs, power objects such as the conch presented to Phakpa by Kubilai Khan, and innumerable images rescued from the northern complex temples, all made at different periods in different styles. It is perhaps the most amazing chamber in Tibet. The Great Library is adjacent to the assembly hall. Other lhakhangs are accessed from the courtyard and by the stairway to the first floor. The Glorious Sakya Gompa is again a functional monastery but a conservative commune at this administrative xian ensures that the reverence due to the remnants of Sakya grandeur and this gompa that once was the seat of the teachers of Chinese Emperors is restrained.

## Tingri, Lato, Mangyul and Kyirong

*Tsibri mountain* (rTsib ri), in Tingri county, north of the Tingri plain and to the west of Shelkar Dzong. The sacred Tsibri massif is encircled by a khorra path. Blessed by Guru Rimpoche with hidden treasure, the most significant power place on this circumambulation is Tsibri Gotsang, situated on a sheer cliff to the south-east of the range. This Drukpa Kagyu 'eagle's nest' was founded by the great yogin Gotsangpa in the thirteenth century. The hermitage gompa is in process of restoration.

*Labchi* (La phyi), in Nyalam county, east of Nyalam on the Nepal border and south of Tingri. The second of the great sacred mountains, the residence of Demchok. *See pp.167–76.*

*Chuwar* (Chu 'bar), in Tingri county, in the Drinchu Valley. *See Rongshar and p.212 and p.215.*

*Rongshar* (Rong shar), to the east of Labchi. Known to Westerners as the Valley of Roses, this area once provided the main route from Tingri down into Nepal. The Rongshar river meets the Gangchu several miles south of Labchi to form the Bhote Kola. The heart of Rongshar, or ancient Drin, is Chuwar at the confluence of Drinchu and Menlungchu rivers, although the political centre today is Chungmoche Qu. To the south of Chuwar is the Menlung Valley, the Menlungchu river rising on the south side of Tsering Chenga (Gaurishankar). The Menlungchu rises in the Latso Wokma lake, the Lower Lake of the Life-Spirit, and there are more lakes below the Menlung La pass, which crosses into Nepal. Jetsun Milarepa came first to Chuwar after attaining enlightenment in Drakar Taso near Kyirong. He returned frequently throughout his life, finally passing away here. *See p.213.*

*Drin* (Brin), *see Rongshar.*

*Tashi Tsering Chenga mountain* (bKra shis Tshe ring mched lnga), in Tingri county, south-east of Labchi, south of Chuwar and north of Rowaling on the Nepal border. This sacred mountain on the Himalayan divide is the abode of the Five Auspicious Long-Life Sisters, known as Gaurishankar to the Nepalis, who see Shiva Mahadeva embracing his consort Gauri in the dual peak formation. The Tsering Chenga are sky goddesses, sky dancers who are also mountain goddesses, and guardians of the Rongshar and Labchi regions. They are also called *lhamen gyelmo*, wild woman goddesses. They had several encounters with Jetsun Milarepa, who subdued them and brought them into the Buddhist tantric mandala as protectors of the tradition.

*Nyalam Dropa Phuk* (gNya lam Grod pa phug), in Nyalam county, near the village of Tashigang off the highway 6 miles (10 km) north of Nyalam (also Nyanang). This important cave of Jetsun Milarepa, excavated from the river bank, is now fronted by a shrine containing a new image of the master. The footprints of Milarepa and Rechungpa can still be seen within. Rechungpa's smaller cave is located above the lhakhang. Adjacent stands Phelgyeling Gompa.

*Ngamring Chode* (Ngam ring chos sde), in Ngamring county, on the shore of Ngamring Kyemtso lake, in old Lato Jang. Originally a thirteenth-century Sakya establishment, this place was blessed by Je Tsongkhapa and became a university town with numerous Sakya and Geluk colleges, now partially restored.

*Chung Riwoche Kumbum* (Cung Ri bo che sku 'bum), in Ngamring county, 50 miles (80 km) west of Kaga on the north bank of the Tsangpo, in old Lato Jang. The Riwoche Kumbum stands by the river at the bottom of a hill called Pel Riwoche (Glorious Mountain) upon which stands the ruins of a gompa of the same name. A many-doored, '1,000-image' chorten, it was built by the bridge builder, treasure-finder and great adept Thangtong Gyelpo and was consecrated in 1456. Although damaged since 1966, it has been renovated so that only the upper part of the spire is lacking. From its outer khorra path and peripheral wall the four terraces with five chapels on each side climb steeply to the dome which contains two levels of khorra path within it. Further lhakhangs are found in the 'box' and spire above the dome. Much of the mural painting within the lhakhangs, which never contained clay sculpture, has survived. The style of the painting is a provincial modification of that established at Zhalu, characterized by thick black outlines of both buddha-images and decoration. The term 'Lato style' has been adopted to describe this mode of painting. *See also Gyang Kumbum and Jonang Kumbum.*

*Tradun Tse* (Pra dun rtse), in Drongpa county, west of Saga Xian, in old Jang on the ancient trade route. This seventh-century missionary lhakhang of King Songtsen Gampo subduing the demoness's right knee, a place of hidden treasure, has been restored.

*Dzongkha* (rDzong kha), also Kyirong Xian, in Kyirong county. An ancient walled town overlooking the plateau at the confluence of the Sarong and Gyang rivers, this was the seat and castle of the Gungthang kings and the birthplace of Rechungpa.

*Drakar Taso Drubphuk* (Brag dkar rta so grub phug), in Kyirong county, Milarepa's enlightenment cave, *see p.212.* The Drakar Taso Gompa is located in the town of Kyirong.

*Gungthang La pass* (Gung thang la), in Kyirong county, to the east of Dzongkha, in the old kingdom of Gungthang, on the divide between the Kyirong Valley and the Pelku lake basin. Guru Rimpoche left Tibet and Dzambuling from this pass and flew on his magical horse to Zangdok Pelri, the Copper-Coloured Mountain.

*Pelku Tso lake* (dPal kud mtsho), also Pelthang Tso and Latso Sintso, the large kidney-shaped lake on the border of Kyirong and Tingri counties, in old Gungthang. This is the life-spirit lake of a sinmo demoness. To the north-west of the lake lies the Gungthang La *(see above)*, on its eastern shore Milarepa caves *(see p.215).*

*Riwo Pelbar* (Ri bo dpal dbar), in Kyirong county, old Mangyul, on the western side of the Kyirong (Trishuli) river, above Kyirong. The principal power-place mountain in the Kyirong Valley, this was blessed by Guru Rimpoche, who hid treasure here, some of which was discovered by Rikdzin Godem. The Riwo Pelbar Gompa and Milarepa caves are located on the mountain's flanks.

*Phakpa Wati Lhakhang*, in Kyirong county, Kyirong town. This four-storey Newar-style pagoda temple, now being restored, was the seat of one of the four sandalwood Phakpa Lokesvara images dating from the seventh century. It was taken to Dharamsala after the Chinese invasion.

*Jamtrin Lhakhang* (Byams sprin) in Kyirong county, in a village north of Kyirong, old Mangyul. This seventh-century missionary foundation of King Songtsen Gampo subduing the demoness's right foot is now a four-storey pagoda in the Nepali style, restored.

# Gyantse and Further West

*Gyantse Pelkhor Chode* (rGyal rtse dpal 'khor chos sde), Gyantse county. The town of Gyantse is dominated by the Dzong, a former seat of the Governors of Tsang, which was shelled and heavily damaged during its capture by the British in 1904, but restored afterwards. It was partially demolished after 1959 and again recently restored. The Dzong's lhakhang has been preserved and refurbished. The Pelkhor Chode, once a non-sectarian walled enclave protecting Sakya, Geluk and Kagyu gompas, was built beneath and on the side of a semi-circular ridge to the west of the Dzong. The only buildings that remain are the abbot's palace (labrang), a tower for displaying giant thangkas, the Tsuklakhang (the principal temple) and the Gyantse Kumbum. The Tsuklakhang is one of the most important monastic buildings in Tibet since all its murals, sculpture and power objects have been preserved. On the first storey are the Drubthob and Neten Chodruk Lhakhangs, containing murals and sculptures of the 84 great adepts and the 16 arhats respectively, all dating from the fifteenth century. The walls of the Utse Lhakhang, the topmost chamber, are covered from ceiling to floor with large mandalas of the Sakya tradition. The Gyantse Kumbum, the many-doored chorten of Pelkhor Chode, now unique in the Buddhist world, was founded in 1418 by the founder of Pelkhor Chode. The lhakhangs of the nine levels of the kumbum, decreasing in number at each level, are structured according to the compendium of Sakya tantras called the *Drubthab Kuntu*. Thus each lhakhang and each level creates a mandala, and the entire kumbum represents a three-dimensional path to the Buddha's enlightenment illustrated by increasingly subtle tantric mandalas. Its many lhakhangs, like many of the lhakhangs of the Tsuklakhang, demonstrate the mastery of mural painting in the late monastic period. The clay sculptures in the kumbum are mostly poor, new, substitute works, but many of the original murals are in good condition.

*Nenying Gompa* (gNas rnying dgon), in Khangmar county, 10 miles (15 km) south of Gyantse, just off the Gyantse–Yathung highway. An eleventh-century foundation, turned Geluk, this was where Je Tsongkhapa gave his first teaching. It was destroyed and has been partially rebuilt.

*Kyingkhor* (Jinka) *Trangdruk* (dKyil 'khor 'phrang drug), in Gyantse county, south-west of Gyantse Xian, near Kyingkhor Qu. 'Six-Tunnel Mandala', this Guru Rimpoche cave site is set in a cliff, with lhakhang-grottos, and inner caves reached by torturous tunnels with self-manifest rock sculpture and sacred springs. A day-long khorra encircles the power places of Kyingkhor.

*Iwang*, also Yemar, in Kangmar county, 40 miles (65 km) south of Gyantse, just off the Gyantse to Yathung highway. This small desolate structure contains the last of Tibet's remaining great clay sculpture from the twelfth century. Two of the three lhakhangs on the sides of a courtyard hold the sculpture; the northern lhakhang contains the Buddha Donyo Drubpa with three seated Jampas on either side; the western lhakhang contains 16 standing bodhisattvas. All these large sculptures have been leached of their colour and stand as the artists must have seen them before they were painted. This sad exhibition is transcended only by contemplation of the concept and fine lines of these masterpieces of Tibetan sculpture. It has recently been reroofed.

*Yemar* (dYe dmar) *see Iwang*.

*Ralung Gompa* (Rwa lung dgon), to the far east of Gyantse county, in the lee of the Jangzang Lhamo peak, a 4-mile (7-km) walk from the village of Ralung. This home seat of the Drukpa Kagyu was founded in 1180 by Drogon Tsangpa Gyare, a disciple of Drogon Pakmodrupa. The Drukpa Kagyu order, although renowned in Tibet for its great adepts of the ascetic meditation tradition of Milarepa, particularly at the mountain power places of Kang Rimpoche, Labchi and Tsari, is best known for its thriving, dominating, influence in Bhutan. The order is closely allied to the Nyingma order and there is a strong tradition of the ngakpa, the married adept, amongst them. The gompa is situated in a magnificent location on the plain beneath the snow peaks which contain innumerable caves and hermitages. It was devastated during the Cultural Revolution but a new assembly hall has been created within the colossal walls of the ruined Lhakhang Chenpo and a vibrant monastic community is resurrecting the Drukpa Kagyu tradition. This is the seat of the Drukchen, resident in Ladakh.

*Chorten Nyima* (mChod rten nyi ma), on the borders of Tenkye and Kampa counties, north of the Sikkim border, accessible from Tenkye or Kampa Xians. A geomantically spectacular cave power place, especially sacred to the Nyingmapas, blessed by Guru Rimpoche, Yeshe Tsogyel and Namkhai Nyingpo, this is the northern entrance to the hidden valley of Dremojong. To the west of the small restored gompa and Tamdrin Lhakhang is a scarp with the Great Guru's caves and on top of the ridge are the three chortens that give the place its name. To the east is a ridge with three renowned sky-burial sites. A two-day khorra loop into the mountains to the south includes the oracular life-spirit lakes of the Great Guru and his consort.

## NAKCHU PREFECTURE

Nakchu county lies to the north-east of Central Tibet and the prefecture of the same name encompasses the Jangthang, the northern plains, stretching far to the north and west to border Ngari prefecture.

*Dangra Yumtso lake and Targori* (Dwangs rwa gyu mtsho dang rTa sgo ri), in Shentsa county, south-western Nakchu prefecture. This lies north of the Nyenchen Thanglha range on the Jangthang, in the old Naktsang district, about 200 miles (350 km) north of Zangzang. This complementary lake and mountain site is an important place of Bon and Nyingma pilgrimage. Guru Rimpoche meditated and Shenrab Miwoche left his footprint here. Snow-topped Targori mountain is the abode of a Glacier Nyen deity. Khorra paths encircle both the mountain and the lake. The lake khorra circuit starts for most pilgrims at Ombu on the northern tip of the lake and takes up to 11 days to complete. The anti-clockwise circumambulation passes by the Bon gompas of Ombu, Serzhing and Orgyen, and at Khyungdzong, Eagle's Citadel, is a Bon cave hermitage site. Near Khyungdzong is a castle, indicating the importance of this secluded region to the ancient kings of Zhangzhung.

*Namtso lake* (gNam mtsho), on the border of southern Pelgon county in Nakchu prefecture and Damzhung county in Lhasa prefecture. Located beyond the Nyenchen Thanglha range on the Jangthang plains, this lake, the Sky Lake, is 45 miles (70 km) long and 25 miles (40 km) wide, shaped like a womb, ringed by Bon power places, and takes about 18 days to circumambulate. The principal power place is at the end of a promontory that protrudes deep into the lake in the south-east, giving it the sense of an island. This place of extraordinary power is called Tashido, Auspicious Rock, referring to the rock prominence that rises 600 feet (200m) at the end of the promontory. Namtso is the consort of the great mountain god Nyenchen Thanglha, whose mountain abode overlooks the lake. She is the daughter of the god-king Gyajin, who is Indra in the Indian mythology, and she is represented iconographically as a charming maiden. But here at Tashido, it is the stark elemental contrasts that inevitably intrude into the pilgrim's mind with withering intensity. The sacred multicoloured rock itself is sheer, bare of any vegetation; the calm frigid lake water lapping at the shore, slightly saline, can be whipped into breakers and whitecaps right across the lake in just a moment, the turgid hot air becoming a gale; the sun beats down with naked intensity on the bare rock; and the big sky of the plains overarches all. This is the elemental experience of the Tibetan plateau. On the south side of Tashido is the Tashido Gompa, a large walled-in overhang, the meditation cave of Guru Rimpoche, where he concealed several treasure texts. It is inhabited now by several Nyingma yogis. In the south-facing scarp are a dozen walled-in caves of varying sizes. It takes one or two hours to complete the main khorra circuit around the Tashido rock.

*Nyenchen Thanglha* (gNyan chen thang lha), the principal peak of the mountain range that stretches across southern Nakchu prefecture all the way to Kang Rimpoche, lies to the north-east of Lhasa, close to Namtso lake. This range separates the Yarlung Tsangpo valley from the Jangthang plains. It is the abode of the mountain god Nyenchen Thanglha, the greatest of Central Tibetan, if not all Tibetan, mountain gods. His name translates as the Great Nyen, God of the Sky-Plains, and he was so identified by the Bonpos from ancient times. The nyen are a class of ancient mountain gods highly malignant to human beings if not propitiated. The lesser nyen inhabit all aspects of natural phenomena. Nyenchen Thanglha is also king of the serpent spirits, who he spawned in the first place, king of the odour-eating sky gods, and a treasure-protecting god. He rules the 360 sky-plain gods whose abodes are the lesser peaks of the Nyenchen Thanglha range. Guru Rimpoche bound him to serve the buddha-dharma by flashing his mudra of threat at him when the mountain god, in the form of a serpent, challenged him on the way to Samye. Thus bound, he manifests as a white hero-human, dressed in silks, carrying a cane and a crystal rosary in his hands, and resting in meditation when riding a white horse through the three realms. When called upon by Buddhist yogis to chastise or execute oath-breakers and enemies of the buddha-dharma, he appears in armour, carrying weapons, covered by the skin of a black bear.

## LHOKHA PREFECTURE

This includes the Yarlung Tsangpo valley from Gongkar county in the west, through Tsethang county, to Nangdzong county and old Dakpo in the east; Lhodrak, north of the Bhutan border; and Monyul in the south-east. Lhokha prefecture is divided into three sections: 1) the Yarlung Tsangpo valley and tributary valleys; 2) the south and Bhutan; 3) around Yamdrok Yumtso lake.

### The Yarlung Tsangpo Valley and Tributary Valleys

*Gongkar Chode* (dGong dkar chos sde), in Gongkar county, south of the Yarlung Tsangpo. This well-preserved Sakya gompa contains the original sixteenth-century Khyenri murals that generated the ubiquitous style of Khyenri/Menri painting during the theocratic period.

*Dorje Drak Gompa* (Thub bstan rDo rje brag dgon), in Gongkar county, on the north bank of the Yarlung Tsangpo. Founded in the sixteenth century by the third incarnation of Rikdzin Godem and now rebuilt, this Nyingma gompa is the centre of teaching of Rikdzin Godem's Northern Treasure (jangter). The present incarnation of Rikdzin Godem is occasionally in residence.

*Drak Yangdzong* (sGrags Yang rdzong), in Dranang county, in the Dra Valley; a Guru Rimpoche cave complex. *See pp.206–7.*

*Drathang Gompa* (Grwa thang dgon), in Dranang county, on the south bank of the Yarlung Tsangpo in Drathang Xian, in the lower Dranang Valley. Yet to be restored from its state as a storage facility, this ancient gompa appears anything but a power place, but its history has consecrated it as one of Central Tibet's most sacred sites. It contains extraordinary remnants of twelfth-century murals of vital interest to art historians. The original assembly hall and lhakhang are in good condition, but the ancillary buildings have been destroyed. The gompa was founded at the beginning of the eleventh century, one of the four chief lhakhangs built during the lifetime of Lume. It was the residence of the important eleventh-century treasure-finder, Drapa Ngonshe, who revealed the Four Medical Tantras and to whom is ascribed the foundation of the gompa in 1081. At its inception Drathang was a Nyingma establishment, but it was usurped by the Sakya school early in the Sakya ascendancy. The twelfth-century murals found in the inner lhakhang, on either side of the aura that once surrounded the central Buddha, show strong silk-route influence, but are the only original murals remaining from the early monastic period in Central Tibet.

*Jampaling Kumbum* (Byams pa gling sku 'bum), in Dranang county, in the lower Dranang Valley, about half a mile (1 km) south of Drathang Xian. This kumbum, founded in the second half of the fifteenth century, was the largest in Tibet before its destruction during the Cultural Revolution. It is now under restoration. It stands within the compound of the ruined Geluk gompa Jampaling and both chorten and gompa are dedicated to the Future Buddha Jampa (Maitreya). The kumbum is called the Kumbum Thongdrol Chemo, the Great Chorten of 100,000 Images that Grants Liberation by Seeing.

*Mindroling Gompa* (sMin grol gling dgon), in Dranang county, 10 miles (16 km) up the Drachi Valley. Mindroling is the principal Nyingma gompa in the TAR, built in the seventeenth century by Padma Garwong Gyurme Dorje, the discoverer of the Southern Treasure (*lhoter*). It has now been rebuilt and restored, and is the vital centre of dissemination of the Southern Treasure.

*Samye Chokhor* (bSam yas chos 'khor), in Dranang county. The first monastery of Tibet, built by King Trisong Detsen, consecrated in 779 by the Abbot Shantarakshita, Samye Chokhor, after the Lhasa Jokhang, is the most potent gompa power place in Tibet. It is impregnated with the meditative vibrations of Guru Rimpoche and virtually every major figure in the Tibetan Buddhist tradition. Architecturally the elliptical walled compound represents the mandala of the Buddhist cosmos, with the Utse Temple in the centre representing Mt Meru, the four lhakhangs in the cardinal directions representing the four major continents, and the eight satellite lhakhangs the islands. The Utse has three floors, the original ground floor with its *sanctum sanctorum* enshrining the Jowo built in massive containing walls and surrounded by a passageway. The famous gomkhang is reached from the assembly hall. The second floor contains the Dalai Lamas' quarters which now serve as the treasury of Samye's power objects. The farming commune that inhabited the compound is being evicted and restoration is largely completed. Despite its presence in the administrative centre of Samye Qu, this is now a flourishing Nyingma gompa.

*Chimphu* (bSam yas mchims phu), in Dranang county, 8 miles (12 km) north of Samye Chokhor. A Guru Rimpoche cave site. *See pp.208–9.*

*Yamalung in Drakmar* (Brag dmar gYa' ma lung), in Dranang county, about 11 miles (18 km) north of Samye Chokhor. This Guru Rimpoche cave is one of the eight places of solitary realization. Guru Rimpoche taught his consort Yeshe Tsogyel the rudiments of the buddha-dharma here and gave her her first initiation. At the bottom of the site is a spring in a grove of trees, which flows with the water of long life, a gift of Guru Rimpoche, who also concealed long-life liturgies here. A little higher is the Orgyen Phuk, Guru Rimpoche's cave, which is a large enclosed overhang in the cliff. Within this cave lhakhang are several self-manifest phenomena, including the Great Guru's foot and hand prints. At the centre of the altar at the back is a new statue of Guru Rimpoche. Higher up the slope is the small meditation cave of the translator Bairotsana.

*Trandruk Gompa* (Khra' 'brug dgon), in Tsethang county, in the Yarlung Valley, 3 miles (5 km) south of Tsethang. This is an important seventh-century missionary temple of King Songtsen Gampo built to subdue the demoness on her left shoulder. The present, restored, wooden structure, built on the pattern of the Lhasa Jokhang, probably dates from the fourteenth century. This has been a Geluk gompa since the Great Fifth Dalai Lama's time. The new lhakhang in the south-east corner of the gompa complex enshrines the few images saved from the destroyed lhakhangs, together with several important images from other vanished gompas of the Yarlung Valley, including a Padmapani depicted in pearls and mother of pearl, stone sculptures of the Five Buddhas, perhaps from the seventh century, bronzes of a talking Menlha, the Medicine Buddha, and a talking Guru Rimpoche known as Ngadrama, affirmed as his own likeness by Guru Rimpoche himself, brought from Sheldrak Phuk. Guru Rimpoche consecrated this place and concealed treasures here.

*Sheldrak* (Yar lung shel brag) in Tsethang county, on the western side of the Yarlung Valley. *See pp.209–10.*

*Solnak Thang* (Sol nag thang), also known as Yarlung Thangboche, in Chongye county, on the east side of the Chongye Valley halfway between the confluence of the Yarlung and Chongye rivers and the Chongye tombs. This gompa was founded in 1017 by Drumer Tsultrim Jungne, a disciple of gelong Lume, and is one of the oldest sites in Tibet. Jowo Atisha's cell (zimphuk), the power place of the gompa, is located in an isolated spot on the north-eastern side of the site. Solnak Thang was an important Kadam gompa later adopted by the Gelukpas. It was totally destroyed after 1959 but a lhakhang has been rebuilt and several monks are in residence.

*Yarlha Shampori mountain* (Yar lha sham po ri), on the southern border of Tsethang county. This is the abode of the Yarlung Valley's mountain and territorial god, one of the four chief mountain gods of Tibet.

*Kachu Gompa see Lhakhang Keru.*

*Lhakhang Keru* (Lha khang ke ru), otherwise known as Kachu Gompa, in Tsethang county, on the northern side of the Yarlung Tsangpo, 9 miles (15 km) up the Yon Valley, near Yon Qu. The power of this geomantically and architecturally unassuming gompa lies in its antiquity. The style of the temple building is of the simplicity associated with very early construction, a few large undecorated beams, without supporting pillars, holding the roof. It was built in the middle of the eighth century after refugee monks from Khotan had been invited to Tibet. The beautiful 12 feet (4m) high clay sculpture of the Buddha in the lhakhang may date from this time. The clay sculptures of the bodhisattvas that flank the Buddha on both sides probably date from the eleventh century. In the north-west corner of the courtyard is the small room in which Jowo Atisha stayed for a month in 1047/8. The small chorten that contained some of his relics has vanished. Murals of Jowo Je and his principal disciples, Dromton and Naktso Lotsawa, can be seen there. Je Rimpoche Tsongkhapa also lived in this small room for some time. Next to it is the empty lhakhang that was associated with the Geluk tradition. The gompa is now shared between Nyingma and Geluk monks.

*Tashi Dokha* ('On bKra shis rdo kha), in Tsethang county, north of the Yarlung Tsangpo in the Won Valley. Some 5 miles (8 km) up the Won Valley, in a fold low on its eastern side, where a spring emerges to provide a rash of variant greens on the barren hillside, is the rebuilt hermitage and lhakhang of Tashi Dokha where Je Tsongkhapa stayed in retreat for two months in 1415. Here he met his disciple Gendun Drub, who became the first Dalai Lama.

*Densathil* (gDan sa mthil), in Zangri county, on the north side of the Yarlung Tsangpo valley, equidistant from Yon and Zangri. Densathil was founded in 1158 on a shelf in the upper reaches of a ravine high above the Yarlung Tsangpo Valley, where Je Gampopa's disciple Drogon Dorje Gyelpo had his hermitage hut. Dorje Gyelpo is better known as Phakmodrupa, the founder of the Phakdru Kagyu sub-sect and a family lineage that ruled Central Tibet during the fourteenth–fifteenth century. Amongst Dorje Gyelpo's 800 disciples who meditated here were Taklung Thangpa Tashi Pel (root-guru of the Taklung Kagyu), Drikung Rimpoche Rinchen Pel (root-guru of the Drikung Kagyu) and Ling Repa Padma Dorje (root-guru of the Drukpa Kagyu). Densathil is a place of extraordinary natural beauty, the ravine full of rhododendrons, wild roses and an amazing proliferation of other flowering shrubs. Under the limestone crags of the broad amphitheatre that forms the backdrop to the gompa is a forest of giant junipers. The remains of meditation caves pocket the cliffs to the west of the gompa at the same level as emerging springs. The gompa was in a state of decline before 1959, but still possessed immense wealth as the legacy of the Phakdru political ascendancy. It was completely destroyed during the Cultural Revolution and little restoration has been accomplished. The main power place is within the ruined walls of the Lhakhang Chenpo, the spot where Dorje Gyelpo first constructed his hut out of willow sticks, and pilgrims have placed a canopy of prayer-flags over it.

*Cholung* (Chos lung), Zangri county, in the Wolkha Valley, near Wolkha Taktse. This hermitage site, the place of Je Tsongkhapa's principal meditation retreats, is located by a stream falling from the slopes of Wode Gungyel. Tsongkhapa left the proof of his achievement in prints of his hands, feet and knees, and the six-syllable mantra OM MANI PADMA HUNG written with his finger in rock. Consecrated by the master's meditation, this power place became a major Geluk hermitage site. It was restored after complete destruction in 1982 and is now again a vital place of retreat for the Geluk order. Nearby is Chuzang, another hermitage site consecrated by Je Tsongkhapa's meditation. A new hermitage has been built here.

*Dzingchi Ling* (rDzing phyi gling), in Zangri county, in Dzingchi Qu at the top of the Wolkha Valley, jeepable from Tsethang. Je Tsongkhapa came to Dzingchi Ling to restore the main power object here – an image of the Buddha Jampa that had spontaneously manifested in the meditation of a tenth-century Khampa monk called Buddha Jampa. The feet of the old image are now the focus of devotion in the Jampa Lhakhang, which has been restored. The lamas of Dzingchi, the Gyeltseb Rimpoches, were incarnations of Gyeltseb Je Dharma Rinchen, one of Tsongkhapa's chief disciples, whose seat was in the Dzingchi abbot's palace (labrang). Buddha Jampa's meditation cave is found in the escarpment behind the village.

*Daklha Gampo* (Dwags lha sgam po), in Gyatsa county, old Dakpo, 8 miles (12 km), east of Gyatsa Qu, north of the Yarlung Tsangpo. This is Je Gampopa's gompa, founded in 1121. Je Gampopa Dakpo Lhaje was the scholarly disciple of Milarepa who formalized and institutionalized the great yogi's teaching. The gompa was built on high flatland in the lee of Daklha Gampo Ri. The khorra path encircles the gompa and the caves in the ridges behind it. The caves have a long and celebrated history and may be considered the principal power places of the site. Sewa Phuk is the principal cave, consecrated by Gampopa and his three main disciples – Dusum Khyenpa (the first Karmapa), Phakmo Drupa (founder of the Phakdru subsect) and Sagom Shatopa. The gompa has been rebuilt in part, and a lhakhang contains some notable images and power objects.

*Lhamo Latso lake* (Lha mo bla mtsho), in Gyatsa county, 25 miles (40 km) north of Gyatsa Xian, in old Dakpo. This oracle lake holds the life-spirit of the protectress Pelden Lhamo, which is identified with the life-spirit of Tibet and the Dalai Lamas. The small lake is viewed from the Dalai Lamas' stone throne on a ridge high above the lake, which is a mirror in which visions of the future can be seen. The gompa power place associated with the lake is Chokhor Gyel, where the day-long pilgrimage to the lake commences. Now in process of restoration, it is built within a unique triangular walled compound.

*Wode Gungyel mountain* ('O lde gung rgyal), on the border of Zangri and Gyatsa counties, in old Wolkha. The ancestor mountain of the nine chief Central Tibetan mountain gods and therefore the ancestral deity of the Central Tibetan people.

## The South

*Mawochok Gompa* (sMra bo lcogs dgon) in Tsome county, on a hill to the east of Tsome Xian. The seat of the great thirteenth-century treasure-finder Nyangrel Nyima Wozer, this has been partially rebuilt.

*Khomthing Lhakhang* (mKho mthing lha khang), in Lhodrak county, in Lhakhang village, near the confluence of three rivers, close to the Bhutan border. A seventh-century missionary lhakhang of King Songtsen Gampo subduing the demoness's left elbow, the two-storey lhakhang remains unrestored. It is a place of treasure texts consecrated by many Nyingma yogis.

*Tselam Pelgyiri mountain* (Tshe lam dpal gyi ri), in Lhodrak county, south of Lhakhang village. This hill contains a Guru Rimpoche cave with Tsogyel's cave and a spring nearby.

*Kharchu Gompa* (mKhar chu dgon), in Lhodrak county, near Lhakhang village. Built in a magnificent geomantic setting on a pine-clad ridge surrounded by snow peaks, this gompa has been partially restored. Here the great Kharchu khorra, taking one day, includes important power places most sacred to the Nyingma and Kagyu orders. The Namkhai Nyingpo Drubphuk meditation caves were sanctified by this disciple of Guru Rimpoche in exile here from Central Tibet in the eighth century. The Lhamo Kharchen three-storey hermitage was the meditation place of Phakmodrupa, the founder of the Phakdru Kagyu order, and Lhamo Kharchen itself is the great Indian power place Devikota transposed to Tibet. The most important power place here is the Chakphurchan Ri, one of the five Guru Rimpoche caves *(see p.209).*

*Phukring in Lhodrak* (Lho brag dPal gyi phug ring), in Lhodrak county, near Kharchu. This is Namkhai Nyingpo's main cave.

*Sekhar Guthok* (Sras mkhar dgu thog), in Lhodrak county, in the lee of Kula Khari mountain. This is the nine-storey tower that Jetsun Milarepa built to purify his karma in the eleventh century, now restored with a small gompa. A few miles to the south-east is the Drowolung Gompa of Milarepa's teacher, Marpa, unrestored. A half-day's walk away is Taknya Lungten Phuk, Milarepa's first cave hermitage.

*Kula Khari and Padmaling Tso* (sKu bla mkha' ri dang Padma gling mtsho), in Lhodrak county. The great mountain Kula Khari, King's Life-Spirit Sky-Mountain, on the Bhutan border, and the Padmaling Tso, Lotus Island Lake, on its north-east side, form a complementary pair. Kula Khari is one of the four great mountain gods of Tibet, an emanation of the hero-king Gesar and a very powerful force. The idyllic lake Padmaling, lying in its lee surrounded by snow peaks, has on its banks the ruined gompa of the great treasure-finder Padmalingpa and a Guru Rimpoche cave nearby. Khorra paths circumambulate both mountain and lake.

*Lhalung Gompa* (Lha lung dgon), north-west Lhodrak county, on the highway. An important gompa with a history of Drukpa Kagyu and Nyingma occupation since 1154, the sixteenth-century terton Padmalingpa blessed this place. It has been partially restored.

*Guru Lhakhang* (La yag Gu ru Lha khang), in Lhodrak county, above Lhalung Gompa. This was the seat of the major twelfth-century treasure-finder Guru Chowang. It has been partially restored.

*Tsari*, in the south-east corner of Nangdzong county, in the far east of Lhokha on the Indian border. Tsari is one of the three great mountains sacred to Demchok. *See pp.176–88.*


## Bhutan (Druk Yul)

South of Lhodrak county is the independent kingdom of Bhutan. Four of the most important power places of the Tibetan Buddhist tradition are located here.

*Kyerchu Lhakhang* (Lho sKyer chu'i lha khang), in the Paro Valley, western Bhutan. This seventh-century missionary lhakhang of King Songtsen Gampo subduing the demoness's left foot is built in the Bhutanese style and remains in immaculate condition.

*Paro Taktsang Phuk* (sPa gro sTag tshang phug), in the Paro Valley. One of Guru Rimpoche's 'tiger lairs', this gompa is built on a ledge on a high vertical rock-face, and reached by a long climb and finally over bridges fixed into the cliffside. The small Guru Rimpoche cave is covered by the main lhakhang of the gompa. This is the foremost place associated with Guru Rimpoche's emanation Dorje Drolo, Adamantine Fat-Belly, who in wrathful mode rides a pregnant tigress. Above is the site of the original Kathokpa Gompa, a Nyingma gompa founded in the late thirteenth century. The main gompa, administered by the Drukpa Kagyu order, has remained untouched by human hostility down the centuries and is in the usual pristine condition in which the Bhutanese maintain their power places. Milarepa meditated here and innumerable treasure texts have been revealed here, one by the great iron bridge-builder Thangtong Gyelpo.

*Jampa Lhakhang* (Byams pa lhakhang), in the Bumthang Valley in central Bhutan. This seventh-century missionary lhakhang of King Songtsen Gampo subdues the demoness's left knee.

*Nering Senge Dzong* (Ne ring Seng ge rdzong). *See p.210.*

## Around Yamdrok Yumtso Lake

*Yamdrok Yumtso lake* (Yar 'brog gyu mtsho), in Nakartse county. A powerful scorpion-shaped lake identified with the life-spirit of Tibet, this is the abode of one of the chief protectresses of Tibet, Dorje Gekyi Tso.

*Lho Taklung* (Lho sTag lung), Nakartse county, on the south-west side of Yamdrok Yumtso lake. This hilltop gompa was the substitute seat of the Taklung Kagyu order in Central Tibet *(see Taklung Thang)*, and then under the Dorje Drak Gompa. It was a previous residence of the late Kanjur Rimpoche and the Taklung Tsetrul Rimpoches. It was partially destroyed and is now partially restored.

*Samding Gompa* (bSam lding dgon), in Nakartse county, near Nakartse Xian, overlooking Dremtso lake. This twelfth-century foundation, belonging to the Bodongpa school, is the seat, now restored, of Dorje Phakmo Rimpoche, generally considered the highest female incarnation in Tibet, who is now resident in Lhasa.

*Noijin Kangzangri mountain* (gNod sbyin gang bzang ri), on the borders of Nakartse and Gyantse counties, south of the Karola pass. The abode of the mountain god Kangwa Zangpo, the territorial lord of Tsang, a bestower of wealth, one of the four chief mountain gods of Tibet, is coupled with the goddess of Yamdrok Yumtso lake.

# LHASA PREFECTURE

Lhasa prefecture includes the Tolung Valley in the west, the Kyichu basin up to Namtso lake in the north, the Drikung Valley in the east, and also the entire old province of Kongpo, including the Yarlung Tsangpo valley and Padma Ko, down to the Indian border in the south-east. This section is divided into four parts: 1) Lhasa city and environs; 2) the lower Kyichu river basin, west of Lhasa; 3) the upper Kyichu river basin, east of Lhasa; 4) Kongpo and the south-east.

## Lhasa City and Environs

*Lhasa Jokhang* (Lha sa jo khang). At the centre of Lhasa is the Jokhang, the principal power place of contemporary Tibet. It is the focus of all Tibetans' spiritual and national aspirations and the first place of pilgrimage. It is a lhakhang power place, the oldest in Tibet, which has been enlarged into a gompa and restored over the centuries. Its structure survived the Cultural Revolution unscathed, though with substantial loss of its sacred symbols and power objects. It was built by Songtsen Gampo in the seventh century to subdue the Tibetan demoness's heart *(see p.21)* and to enshrine an image of the Buddha known as the Lhasa Jowo. It has been blessed by every major figure in Tibetan religious history and the ardent worship of generations of devotees. Three khorra circuits circumambulate the Jokhang: the *nangkor* within the gompa precincts, the *barkor* around the entire complex, and the lingkor around old Lhasa city.

*The Potala* (Po ta la). At the core of the Potala fortress-palace is a meditation cave where King Songtsen Gampo sat in retreat and which was later blessed by Guru Rimpoche. The present massive structure was built in the seventeenth century by the Great Fifth Dalai Lama and has been the residence of the bodhisattva Chenrezik's Dalai Lama incarnations ever since. This power place is now an extraordinary museum.

*Dralha Luphuk* (Brag lha klu phug), on the north-eastern side of Chakpo Ri, near the Potala. This Guru Rimpoche cave predates Guru Rimpoche's presence here. It is the cave where the serpent spirits who infested the lake that was once Lhasa were imprisoned before the Jokhang could be constructed. The Emperor Songtsen Gampo himself is said to have meditated here. One of Guru Rimpoche's disciples, Nyang Tingngedzin, achieved rainbow-body here. The antiquity of Dralha Luphuk is suggested by its design. It was carved out of the living rock to leave a massive central pillar which was then sculpted with images of the Five Buddhas. Notable images carved into the cave's walls show Birwapa, Pelden Lhamo, and the Emperor Songtsen Gampo and his queens. All of this remarkable sculpture, said to have appeared magically from the rock, was damaged during the Cultural Revolution, but excellent work has restored it.

*Ramoche* (Ra mo che), to the north-west of the Jokhang. The Ramoche Gompa was built at the same time as the Jokhang and eventually enshrined an image of Mikyo Dorje (Manjuvajra) brought by Songtsen Gampo's Nepali queen Bhrikuti from Nepal. The gompa has been completely rebuilt since the Cultural Revolution.

*Drepung Gompa* ('Bras spungs dgon), 5 miles (8 km) to the west of Lhasa. Founded in 1416, Glorious Drepung was Tibet's largest monastic town, housing over 7,000 residents. It was the chief seat of the Geluk order until the Great Fifth Dalai Lama constructed the Potala. Thereafter it retained its premier place amongst the four great Geluk monasteries. About 40 per cent of the old monastic town has been destroyed, but Drepung's chief buildings – the four colleges, the Tsokchen and the Dalai Lamas' residence – have been preserved. It was one of the richest foundations in Tibet and its wealth is reflected in the decoration of these buildings. Behind Drepung is the mountain power place of Gephelri and on its southern side the hermitage of Gephel Ritro.

*Nechung Chok* (gNas chung lcog), to the south-east of Drepung. The gompa power place of Nechung derives its spiritual potency from the presence of the Nechung Chokyong, the dharma-protector Pehar, who was channelled by the State Oracle. Pehar is still in residence here but the State Oracle is in exile. Nechung is also called the Demon Fortress of the Oracle King. It was gutted during the Cultural Revolution, but the assembly hall, the gomkhangs of Pehar and Pelden Lhamo, and the Guru Rimpoche Lhakhang, enshrining a colossal image of the Great Guru, have been splendidly restored. Nechung is the seat of the Nyingma Nechung Rimpoches, now in exile; the Oracle is a Gelukpa.

*Sera Gompa* (Se ra dgon), 3 miles (5 km) to the north of the Jokhang at the edge of Lhasa city. One of the four great Geluk gompas, founded in 1419 by a disciple of Je Tsongkhapa, this housed more than 5,000 monks in 1959. Much of the original complex was destroyed during the Cultural Revolution, but the chief colleges and lhakhangs, along with their images and relics, were preserved. The gompa's three colleges are Sera Me, which gives fundamental instruction to the monks; Sera Je, the largest, reserved for wandering monks, particularly Mongols, with its marvellous assembly hall enshrining the buddha-deity Tamdrin and other extraordinary power objects; and the Ngakpa Dratsang, a school for teaching the tantras. The Tsokchen, the Great Assembly Hall, enshrines a colossal image of the Buddha Jampa and a powerful image of Thukjechenpo, the Great Compassionate One. Some 300 monks are now associated with Sera. The main Lhasa sky-burial site is located behind this gompa.

*Phawongkha Photrang* (Pha bong kha pho brang), 5 miles (8 km) to the north of Lhasa in a secluded valley. One of Tibet's most ancient power places, Phawongkha was already established when King Songtsen Gampo arrived in the early seventh century to meditate in a cave hermitage and to build a seven-storey tower upon an immense flat-topped boulder. Thonmi Sambhota finished his work on the Tibetan alphabet here. Guru Rimpoche and King Trisong Detsen meditated in the cave hermitage known as the Tsechu Lhakhang. In the eighth century the first seven Tibetan monks, the Misedun, lived at Phawongkha. The tower was truncated by Langdarma in the ninth century and the three floors that stand today, with a lhakhang on the second floor, have been restored several times through the centuries. The Great Fifth Dalai Lama absorbed Phawongkha into the Geluk fold and it became the seat of the Phawongkha Rimpoches, the greatest of whom was the tutor to the present Dalai Lama's teacher, the late Trijang Rimpoche. Phawongkha is also identified as the great Indian tantric power place Devikota, sacred to Demchok. The Pawong sky-burial site, Lhasa's most sacred, lies just to the east.

**The Lower Kyichu River Basin, West of Lhasa**

*Drolma Lhakhang* (sGrol ma lha khang), in Chushul county, Nyethang village, 10 miles (17 km) south-west of Lhasa on the highway. When Atisha came to Central Tibet in 1045 a gompa called Chodra Chenpo Dewachan in Nyethang became his base. The Drolma Lhakhang, which is all that remains of that complex, was built by Atisha's heart-son Dromton between 1045 and 1054. Atisha stayed here in meditation, studying, debating and teaching, and he died here in 1054. Several Geluk monks are the present stewards of the lhakhang, which is now a museum lhakhang. Its three chambers contain some of the best bronze images in Tibet, including the 21 large gilt Drolmas that give the lhakhang its name, and also relics of Atisha, Marpa Lotsawa and Je Tsongkhapa, who adopted this Kadam gompa for the Geluk order.

*Sangphu Neuthok* (gSang phu Ne'u thog), in Chushul county, on the east bank of the Kyichu below Lhasa, at the top of the Sang Valley. This was the principal centre of academic study in Central Tibet for 800 years. Founded by one of Jowo Atisha's closest disciples, Ngok Lekpai Sherab, in response to the master's dream of an academy where monks could gain a firm basis in logic and philosophy, it was originally a Kadam institution, then a non-sectarian establishment dominated by the Sakya order and later by the Geluk order. It has not been rebuilt.

*Kangri Thokar* (Gangs ri thod dkar), in Chushul county, on the east side of the Kyichu river, at the head of the Nyephu Valley. On the south flank of Kangri Thokar, White-Skull Mountain, is a ridge identified as the body of Dorje Phakmo, the Adamantine Sow, and the meditation caves on this ridge celebrate her psychic centres (chakras). The peerless master Longchen Rabjampa hallowed these caves in the fourteenth century through his Dzokchen meditation, his visions and textual revelations. Below the ridge is the Shukseb Gompa, a twelfth-century foundation associated with the Khandroma Machik Labdron whose image adorns the altar of this rebuilt and flourishing nunnery.

*Shukseb Ani Gompa* (Shug gseb a ni dgon). *See Kangri Thokar.*

*Kyormo Lung Gompa* (sKyor mo lung dgon), in Tolung Dechen county, 4 miles (7 km) north-west from the Dongkar bridge. Originally a Kadam school of logic founded in the twelfth century, this gompa is where Je Tsongkhapa studied and taught. The Geluk monastic buildings have been partially restored. Close by is Zhongwa Lhachu, an enclosed spring-fed pond surrounded by trees, a power place blessed by both Guru Rimpoche and Je Tsongkhapa.

*Nenang Gompa* (gNas nang dgon), in Tolung Dechen county, in the upper Drowolung Valley, near Tsurphu Gompa. This is the seat of the Phawo Rimpoches of the Zhamar Kagyu lineage. It has now been rebuilt.

*Tsurphu Gompa* (mTshur phu dgon), in Tolung Dechen county, in the upper Drowolung Valley. Tsurphu is the seat of the Karmapas – the Black-Hat Lamas – and the Karma Kagyu. Since the first Karmapa Dusum Khyenpa, a disciple of Je Gampopa, established this gompa in 1185, the Karma Kagyu have been at the forefront of spiritual life in Tibet and, until the Yellow Hats destroyed their power in the seventeenth century, also political life. The walled Tsurphu Gompa, built on the north side of the river, was destroyed in the Cultural Revolution, but much of it has been rebuilt and since the young Seventeenth Karmapa took up residence in 1994 it has become the most significant focus of Buddhist life in the country. The principal structure in contemporary Tsurphu is the residence of the Karmapa above the assembly hall, part of which is the sanctuary where a few power objects are kept. The new giant appliqué thangka (goku) is also stored here. Annexed to the labrang is the gomkhang, or rather the complex of several small lhakhangs in which the guardian protectors are propitiated, and also the monks' quarters. Behind is the Gemo Dratsang, the college founded by the First Karmapa; the Sidung Lhakhang, built within the walls of the old immense assembly hall and housing colossal new images of Guru Rimpoche, flanked by the late Sixteenth Karmapa Rikpai Dorje and Shakyamuni Buddha; and behind and above the old lhakhang the Gyeltseb Gompa, again built within the walls of the enormous ruins of the old gompa belonging to the Karmapa's regent. The remainder of the 300 square yard compound is filled with monks' quarters. A khorra path encompasses the compound, the sky-burial site where the Karmapas have been cremated, and also hermitages and caves, particularly Padma Khyungdzong, the Lotus Eagle Citadel, consecrated by the meditation of the Second and Third Karmapas, Karma Phakshi and Rangjung Dorje. The late Sixteenth Karmapa's disciple the venerable Drupon Dechen Rimpoche is the acting regent at Tsurphu, the spiritual director and abbot. Amongst the tulkus most closely associated with the present Karmapa are Situ Rimpoche, resident at Bir in India, Gyeltseb Rimpoche in Rumthek, Sikkim, and Akong Rimpoche at Samyeling in Scotland.

## The Upper Kyichu River Basin, East of Lhasa

*Tsel Gompa* (Tshal dgon Gung thang), in Taktse county, 6 miles (10 km) to the east of Lhasa. Established in 1175 by Lama Zhang, one of the Three Jewels of Tibet, this was the home gompa of the Zhangpa Kagyu order and possessed significant political power until it was converted by Je Tsongkhapa to the Geluk order in the fifteenth century. Not far away, to the south of the Lhasa–Sichuan highway, is Tsel Gungthang, a sister gompa to the main Tsel Gompa, also built by Lama Zhang and usurped by the Geluk order. All the buildings of these two complexes have been damaged and remain unrestored.

*Drak Yerpa* (Brag yer pa), in Taktse county, 10 miles (16 km) north-east of Lhasa. This geomantically superbly appointed cave and hermitage site, built into the natural amphitheatre of a limestone escarpment, was hallowed by Guru Rimpoche and became the hermitage adjunct to the Lhasa Jokhang. Guru Rimpoche's Dawa Phuk cave, where treasures were concealed, and Jowo Atisha's meditation cave are the main power places here. Several other caves are associated with different meditation masters. The grotto containing a rebuilt image of the Buddha Jampa is another important power place. Below the scarp are meadows where the Kadam gompa once stood, where Atisha taught the buddha-dharma and where Lume built his Neten Lhakhang. Many of the caves and lhakhangs at Drak Yerpa have been restored and the hermitages occupied.

*Ganden Namgyeling* (dGa' ldan rNam rgyal gling), Taktse county, 28 miles (45 km) to the north-east of Lhasa. Je Tsongkhapa's meditation hut formed the nucleus of this first and foremost of the Geluk gompas. Founded in 1409, it was built across a south-facing amphitheatre at the top of a high ridge that, to the north, overlooks the Kyichu Valley. It was shelled by Red Guard artillery in 1966 and then dismantled by monks. Many of the gompa's temples have been rebuilt since 1986. Of these the chief is the Serdung Lhakhang, housing the reliquary chorten of Je Tsongkhapa called Thongwa Donden, Meaningful to Behold, and other important relics. The Sertrikhang Lhakhang contains the throne of Je Tsongkhapa, used also by his disciples Khedrub Je and Gyeltseb Je, and the successively elected Ganden throne-holders. The residence of the throne-holders has also been rebuilt, although the present incumbent is in exile, with three lhakhangs constituting the ground floor beneath the living chambers on the first floor. The abbots of Ganden, the elected Ganden Tripa Rimpoches, have been scholars and also held high political office in the Geluk theocracy. The entire site is encircled by the lingkor, which takes an hour to complete and is replete with mystical side-shows in rock that engage and support the pilgrim's faith. The climax of the lingkor is Tsongkhapa's meditation cave Wozer Phuk, Cave of Light.

*Gyama Rinchen Gang* (rGya ma Rin chen sgang), in Medro Gungkar county, about 35 miles (60 km) north-east of Lhasa on the Medro Gungkar highway, south of the Kyichu, 6 miles (10 km) up the Gyama Valley. The fertile and prosperous Gyama Valley was home to three small Kadam gompas: Rinchen Gang, Dumburi and Trikhang, all built in the twelfth century by disciples of Neuzurpa, one of Dromton's chief disciples.

*Katse Gompa* (sKa tshal dgon), in Medro Gungkar county, in the Kyichu Valley near the confluence of the Medro Machu river with the Kyichu. A seventh-century missionary temple of King Songtsen Gampo on the demoness's right shoulder, the ancient Thukdam Tsuklakhang has been rebuilt in the original pattern. Other monastic buildings still lie in ruins. A new image of the Drikung Kagyu Apchi protects the lhakhang. At the back of the assembly hall is the lukhang, the residence of the serpent that Guru Rimpoche subdued.

*Drikung Thil* ('Bri gung mthil), in Medro Gungkar county, 87 miles (139 km) north-east of Lhasa, at the top of the Drikung Valley high on a ridge. In 1179 a disciple of Pakmodrupa named Rinchen Pel accepted some land from another of Phakmodrupa's yogi-disciples high on the brow of a ridge in the upper part of the Sho Valley. He became the root-guru of the Drikung Kagyu and Drikung Thil, one of the chief Kagyu gompas, which played an important role in the pre-theocratic phase of Tibet's political history. It has retained its significance as the principal monastery of the Drikung Valley, a fiercely independent ethnic enclave. Although destroyed in the Cultural Revolution, it has risen again as a vital religious institution. Two assembly halls on two storeys, containing some important power objects, form the nucleus of the gompa. Close by to the east is the lhakhang of Drikung's protecting goddess, Apchi Lhamo, and a highly sanctified hermitage. Strung along the ridge are innumerable hermitages occupied by monks, yogis and young men performing their three-year retreat. At the western end of the ridge is the Drikung durtro, Thil's sky-burial site *(see p.236)*.

*Terdrom* (gTer sgrom), in Medro Gungkar county, in the Drikung district. The 'Box of Treasure' is a geomantically superbly appointed power place at the confluence of two rivers where medicinal hot springs rise, a place hallowed by Guru Rimpoche, generations of adepts and the Drikung Rimpoches. The inner khorra path around the confluence, hot springs and nunnery includes the Elephant-Head Plain above the confluence where a Guru Rimpoche cave, the residence of an incarnation of Yeshe Tsogyel and the hermitages of nuns are located. The middle khorra path, a one-day circuit, encompasses the limestone massif to the north in which the Khandro Tsokchen Kiri Yangdzong cave is located in a towering peak. This cavern, 150 feet (50m) high, is the Assembly Hall of the Sky Dancers. A ladder reaches to the cavern roof, giving access to an ascending passage that leads to a cell enclosed even higher in the limestone tower that is Yeshe Tsogyel Sangphuk, Tsogyel's Secret Cave. Guru Rimpoche and his Tibetan consort, Yeshe Tsogyel, spent a period of retreat together in this cave, during which the Great Guru gave his consort the tantric initiations. A week-long khorra encompasses the entire Terdrom and Drikung areas and other hermitage sites.

*Khandro Tsokchen Kiri Yangdzong*, a Guru Rimpoche cave. *See Terdrom.*

*Reteng Gompa* (Rwa sgreng dgon), in Lhundrub county, in old Jang district, in the upper Kyichu Valley. Reteng is the pearl of Geluk gompas, founded by Jowo Atisha's chief disciple Dromton, the Kadam master, in 1056, and hallowed by Atisha's relics and Je Tsongkhapa's meditation. A forest of giant juniper trees, 'the hair of Dromton', constitute Reteng's power place mandala, 'a heavenly garden with its great divine trees'. The well-walked Reteng khorra encircles the entire gompa complex. The enormous tsokhang has been reconstructed to half its previous size and the important lhakhang within it contains the sacred symbols and power objects remaining of the dozen lhakhangs that have been destroyed. Beyond the restored buildings containing Dromton's meditation chamber is the tree which is identified with his life-spirit (lashing) and the spring which he conjured called the Dutsi Chumik

Ringmo, the Everlasting Spring of Ambrosia. Behind and above the gompa is the hermitage of Yangon where, in the fifteenth century, Tsongkhapa composed his *magnum opus*, the *Lamrim Chenmo*. The site is in ruins but is still the chief power place at Reteng. Reteng was the seat of the Reteng Rimpoches, the last of whom played a crucial role in the downfall of Tibet *(see p.83)*.

*Taklung Thang* (dPal sTag lung thang), in Lhundrub county, north of Lhasa and Phenyul in old Jang, in a valley on the north side of the Chak La pass. Taklung Gompa was founded in 1185 by Taklung Thangpa Tashi Pel, a disciple of Phakmodrupa, and also some notable Kadam lamas whose order had an establishment at Taklung before Tashi Pel founded his gompa and the Taklung Kagyu lineage. The old gompa site was dominated by the architecturally marvellous Tsuklakhang, the ruins of which today speak of a past glory. The new buildings, a residence and assembly hall, form the nucleus of the monastic compound built against the cliff to the west. Power objects of the Taklung lineage are again on a Taklung altar, including the Talking Drolma image. The Taklung Kagyu lost their independence after the Yellow Hats gained control of the gompa in the seventeenth century and the real power of the lineage moved to Lho Taklung, south of Yumdrok Tso, and to Riwoche in Kham. The throne-holder at Taklung was the senior of the three incarnate lamas Zhabdrung, Matrul and Tsetrul.

*Langthang Gompa* (gLang thang dgon), Lhundrub county, in old Phenyul (the valley north of Lhasa), on the bank of the Phenpochu river. This was one of the great Kadam gompas, founded in 1093 by Langthangpa and later adopted by the Sakya order. Only the fifteenth-century abbot's palace has survived and now functions as the assembly hall and lhakhang. Some power objects are to be found there.

*Nalendra Gompa* (dPal Nalendra dgon), Lhundrub county, in Phenyul, north of Lhasa at the base of the Phenpogo La pass. Glorious Nalendra, named after the ancient Indian academy of Nalanda, was the last of the great Kadam gompas to be built. Founded by the polymath Rongtonpa, a contemporary of

Tsongkhapa, in 1435, it was adopted by the Sakya order soon after Rongtonpa died. Amongst the ruins in the large walled compound, a lhakhang and abbot's residence have been rebuilt.

## Kongpo and the South-East

*Draksum Latso lake* (Brag gsum mtsho), in eastern Kongpo, Gyamda county. Draksum Latso, a drowned river valley between forested slopes, is the spirit-lake of Ling Gesar. Upon the Tsodzong island in the lake, blessed by Guru Rimpoche and his treasure-finding emanation Sangye Lingpa, is Tsosum Gompa, which was rebuilt by followers of the late Dudjom Rimpoche. On the khorra circuit around the island Ling Gesar is evoked in several rock formations. The mountains Ama Jomo Taktse, Namla Karpo Naphu Gomri and Darchenri overlook the lake from the north and east.

*Draksum Dorje Drak* (Brag gsum rdo rje brag), in Kongpo Gyamda county, just off the highway between Gyamda and Bayi. This was the birthplace of the fourteenth-century treasure-finder Sangye Lingpa. Jatson Nyingpo, a seventeenth-century treasure-finder, was born nearby at Waru Namtsul and died on the opposite side of the valley at the Pangri Jokpo hermitage.

*Bonri mountain* (Bon ri), in Nyingtri county, on the east side of the confluence of the Yarlung Tsangpo and the Nyangchu rivers. This is the greatest of the Bon mountain power places, consisting of three peaks and with a three-day khorra. *See pp.195–200.*

*Buchu Sergyi Lhakhang* (Bu chu gser gyi lha khang), in Nyingtri county, on the east side of the Nyangchu before its confluence with the Yarlung Tsangpo, 18 miles (29 km) from Bayi. This seventh-century missionary lhakhang of King Songtsen Gampo subduing the demoness's left knee has been rebuilt with its gilded roofs. It is a place of hidden treasure, particularly relating to hidden valleys and the opening of Padma Ko.

*Lamaling Gompa* (bLa ma gling dgon), also known as Zangdok Pelri, in Nyingtri county, near Bayi Xian and Buchu Sergyi Lhakhang. This gompa was the seat of the late Dudjom Rimpoche, head of the Nyingma order. The Zangdok Pelri temple has been rebuilt. The Pelri mountain, or Bayi Pelri, a Guru Rimpoche power place, once a lake and island with a Guru Rimpoche meditation spot on top, towers above the gompa.

*Padma Ko* (Padma bkod), has its centre in Metok county and includes parts of old Pomi, Poyul and Lhoyul, on both sides of the Yarlung Tsangpo. The great hidden land of Padma Ko includes power places such as Kundu Dorsem Photrang, the principal sacred mountain in Padma Ko, sometimes identified as Padma Shelri. *See pp. 20–23.*

*Namchak Barwa* (gNam lcag 'bar ba), on the borders of Menling and Metok counties, within the great bend of the Yarlung Tsangpo. This mountain, Blazing Sky-Iron, is identified as the right breast of Dorje Phakmo in the sacred geography of Padma Ko.

*Gyala Pelri* (rGya la dpal ri or sKya lha pad ri), on the borders of Nyingtri and Menling counties, north of the great bend of the Yarlung Tsangpo. This mountain is in the far northern region of Padma Ko and is identified as the head chakra of Dorje Phakmo.

## EASTERN TIBET: KHAM AND AMDO

Eastern Tibet (Dokham) consists of the old provinces of Kham and Amdo. Its political boundaries have moved backwards and forwards over the centuries. The first formal boundary between Tibet and China was set during Tibetan ascendancy in the ninth century and included all the Tibetan-speaking areas. When Tibet was carved up after 1959, the area of Kham west of the Yangtse was included in the TAR, while most of eastern Kham became autonomous prefectures of Sichuan province and an autonomous prefecture of Yunnan province. Amdo forms part of the new province of Qinghai and a corner of Gansu province.

# Kham

Kham is the area of the Tibetan plateau deeply gashed by the upper reaches and tributaries of the great rivers of South-East Asia and southern China – the Ngulchu (Salween), the Dzachu (Mekong) and the Drichu (Yangtse) and Nyakchu (Yalong). It is known as the region of the Chuzhi Kangdruk, Four Rivers and Six Ridges. The four rivers are those mentioned above, the six ridges are the areas of high plateau grassland, sometimes rolling and sometimes culminating in snow-peaked ridges, that separate the river valleys. The entire vast region is well watered by the wet winds blowing up the valleys from the south, so that the valley sides are forested and the grasslands rich in pasture.

The old province of Kham is now divided between the Chamdo prefecture of the TAR and western Sichuan, the Drichu (Yangtse) river forming the border, while northern parts are in Qinghai province and the southernmost parts in Yunnan province. Thus the divisions below are: 1) Chamdo prefecture, 2) Nangchen and southeast Qinghai, 3) Derge and adjacent counties, 4) eastern and southern Kham.

NB. In Eastern Tibet the consonants ky, khy and gy are pronounced ch and j.


## Chamdo Prefecture, TAR

*Ganden Jampaling* (dGa' ldan byams pa gling), in Chamdo county, Chamdo town. This great Geluk gompa, the first to be built in Kham, dominates the heights above the important town of Chamdo in the Dzachu river valley. Chamdo was the inauspicious place where the Tibetan army capitulated to the Chinese in 1951. The gompa has been rebuilt since the Cultural Revolution and now consists of an assembly hall, a gomkhang, a residence and the Lhakhang Nyingba. The important tulkus of the gompa are Phakpalha, Zhiwalha and Chakra Tulku.

*Kawa Karpo* (Kha ba dkar po). *See below.*

*Ritse Druk* (Khyung po ri rtse drug), in Tengchen county, off the Nakchuka–Chamdo highway near Tengchen town, in old Khyungpo. This Bon mountain power place of six peaks is an important pilgrimage place exclusive to Bonpos in the TAR. New Bon gompas are to be found on the khorra.

*Riwoche Tsuklakhang* (Ri bo che tsug lag khang) in Riwoche county, in the Dzichu river valley, 18 miles (30 km) north of Ratsaka (Riwoche town). In old Khyungpo district, founded in 1276 by Sangye Won, the Riwoche Tsuklakhang is the nucleus of an important Taklung Kagyu and Nyingma gompa. The fabric of the vast three-storey Tsuklakhang survived the Cultural Revolution in need of restoration, which is now in progress. It was the seat of Jedrung Rimpoche, who was a teacher of the late Dudjom and Kanjur Rimpoches and an important treasure-finder.

*Takzham Gompa* (sTag zham dgon), in Riwoche county, 12 miles (20 km) west of Riwoche Xian (Ratsaka). This seat of the great eighteenth-century treasure-finder Takzham Nuden Dorje boasts a temple in the Zangdok Pelri style.

### Nangchen and South-East Qinghai

To the north-west of Derge, the old region of Nangchen is now split between the three Chinese provinces of Qinghai, Sichuan and the TAR. Jyekundo is the capital of the Yushu Tibetan Autonomous Prefecture in Qinghai. The new county town of Nangchen is in the far south-east corner of Qinghai. Nangchen is north-west Kham, a part of the rolling plains cut through by the tributaries of the Dzichu (Yangtse) river valleys, the plains inhabited by nomads and the valleys shielding gompas and small fixed habitations. The Kagyu order has several significant gompas in the area.

*Benchen Gompa* (Ban chen), in Jyekundo county, about 20 miles (30 km) south of Jyekundo. Located in a sheltered valley, this important Karma Kagyu gompa was totally destroyed and is being rebuilt. The Sangye Nyenpa cave above the gompa has had its lhakhang facing restored. Benchen is the seat of three tulkus: Tenga

Rimpoche, now resident in Swayambhu, Kathmandu; Chimme Rimpoche, now resident in London; and Sangye Nyenpa, resident at Rumthek, Sikkim. Near Benchen is Bida Nampar Nangdze Lhakhang, consisting of two small houses, one against a rock-face containing a self-manifest Namnang (Vairochana) rock carving.

*Trangu Gompa* (Khra 'gu dgon), in Jyekundo county, 4 miles south of Jyekundo, close to the Nangchen–Derge highway. This Karma Kagyu gompa, once totally destroyed and now being rebuilt, is the seat of Trangu Rimpoche, previously tutor at Rumthek and now resident at Boudha, Kathmandu.

*Drogon Gompa* ('Gro mgon dgon), in Jyekundo county, near Zhiwu town. This is a Sakya gompa, though it was originally a Kadam establishment. The present chief tulku is Drola Jikme, the son of the late Dudjom Rimpoche and father of his present incarnation. The main buildings are in the process of restoration.

*Tarik Gompa* (Khra rigs dgon), east of Jyekundo. A Sakya gompa, now rebuilt, this is the seat of Tarik Tulku of Boudha, Nepal.

*Dilyak Gompa* (Dil yak dgon), east of Nangchen Xian. This is a Barong Kagyu foundation, now rebuilt with 150 monks resident, the seat of the late Dabzang Rimpoche of Boudha, Nepal, and the late Sabchu Rimpoche of Swayambhu, Nepal.

*Karma Thargye Chokhorling*, in Nangchen county, 30 miles north of Nangchen Xian. Destroyed and now rebuilt, this is the seat of Beru Khyentse Rimpoche.

*Kyodrak Tenying Gompa* (sKyo brag bstan snying dgon), north of Nangchen Xian. A rebuilt Kagyu gompa, the seat of Saga Rimpoche, who is now in residence with 308 monks.

*Labkyab Gompa* (bLa khyabs dgon), south-east of Nangchen Xian. A Baram Kagyu gompa rebuilt by Sonam Dechen Tulku, this is the seat of the late Tulku Orgyen of Boudha, Nepal.

*Zurmang Dutsi Thil* (Zur mang bdud rtsi thil), in Nangchen county, 60 miles (100 km) east of Nangchen Xian (Sharda), the former capital of the Nangchen kingdom. Founded in 1475 by Trungpa Kunga Gyeltsen, this is the Zurmang Kagyu gompa of the late Chogyam Trungpa Rimpoche. The magnificence of the gompa has vanished but an assembly hall is rising out of the destruction.

*Zurmang Namgyeltse Gompa* (Zur mang rnam rgyal rtse dgon), in Nangchen county, 40 miles (60 km) east of Zurmang Dutsi Thil. Founded by Trungpa Mase, this is the sister gompa of Dutsithil and has one reconstructed temple and 100 monks affiliated.

### Derge and Adjacent Counties

Derge may be considered the heart of Kham. The old independent kingdom was centred in the valley of the Drichu (Yangtse) river and its tributaries. It is a Red Hat stronghold with no Geluk monastic presence. Derge gave birth to the eclectic movement that has revitalized Tibetan Buddhism during the last 200 years. The Yangtse river now forms the border between the Chamdo prefecture of the TAR and the Derge county of Sichuan province, splitting the old kingdom down the middle.

*Derge Gonchen* (sDe ge dgon chen), also known as Lhundrub Teng (Lhun drub steng), in Derge county, Derge Xian. Founded by Thangtong Gyelpo in 1448, this Sakya gompa is the seat of Sakya Tridzin, the chief of the Sakya order, now resident in Rajpur, UP, India. It was the Ngorpa stronghold in Kham and a rimepa gompa. The Gonchen assembly hall has been rebuilt. Nearby is the Derge Parkhang, the most renowned printing house in Tibet, containing the wood blocks of the Kangyur and Tengyur and of numerous other cycles of Buddhist texts. It is a commercial concern which now prints to order. A cave of Thangtong Gyelpo, the fifteenth-century iron-bridge builder, is located above Derge on the eastern ridge.

*Dzokchen Rudam Samten Choling* (rDzogs chen ru dam bsam gtan chos gling), Derge county, off the Nakchu–Derge highway to the north-east of Derge, on the north side of the Rudam Kangtro range, with the Dzachukha region to the north. Founded in 1695 by Padma Rikdzin, this became a major centre of learning with 850 monks. The old Khamsum Zilnon labrang is amongst those buildings that were not destroyed. Behind Dzokchen Gompa, in the upper Rudam Kyitram Valley, a hidden valley, are hermitages and caves sanctified by renowned Nyingma masters, amongst them Patrul Rimpoche, who composed *The Words of My Perfect Teacher* there, and Mipham Rimpoche. The present Dzokchen Rimpoche lives in Karnataka, India.

*Zhechen Tenyi Dargyeling* (Zhe chen bsTan gnyis dar gyas gling), in Derge county, north of Dzokchen Gompa, in Dzachukha. Founded by the Second Zhechen, Rabjam Gyurme Kunzang Namgyel, in 1735, this was a rimepa gompa, previously with 200 monks. The main buildings are now in process of restoration. It was the seat of the late Dilgo Khyentse Rimpoche and of Rabjam Rimpoche, now resident in Boudha, Kathmandu. Above the gompa, on the flanks of Drolmari mountain, is a Guru Rimpoche cave and other meditation caves.

*Longthang Drolma Lhakhang* (kLong thang sgrol ma lha khang), in Sershul county, in Denkhok Sharma, on the eastern side of the Drichu. The Drolma Lhakhang is the seventh-century missionary lhakhang of King Songtsen Gampo, subduing the demoness's left hand, the missionary temple furthest to the east, a place of Guru Rimpoche's hidden treasure. It has been restored.

*Kandze Gompa* (dKar mdzes), Kandze county, Kandze town. The Kandze Gompa is the largest Geluk gompa in Kham, founded by the Qosot Mongols in the seventeenth century during their pacification of Kham. Its fine buildings have been largely restored.

*Bongen Gompa*, in Kandze county, east of Derge, in the Rongpatsa Valley. A fine new temple has been built at this the Zhangpa Kagyu gompa of the late Kalu Rimpoche.

*Kathok Dorjeden* (Ka thog rdo rje gdan), Pelyul county, south of Derge above Horpo. The chief Nyingma gompa in Kham, this was founded by Dampa Deshek in 1059 and ever since has been renowned for the meditation masters who practised the founder's meditation instruction here. Built on a shelf high on the valley side, it was expanded by Rikdzin Dudul Dorje and Rikdzin Longsel Nyingpo in the sixteenth century. An assembly hall and the Zangdok Pelri Lhakhang have been restored and although its monastic population has been reduced from 800 to 180, Kathok is still a vital force in the religious life of Kham. It is the seat of Kathok Drime Zhingkyong Rimpoche, now resident in Chengdu, and has been rebuilt and restored.

*Pelpung Gompa* (dPal spung dgon), in Derge county, to the south of Derge, accessible by horse or foot from the Derge to Pelyul road. Founded by the Eighth Situ in 1727, this is the principal Karma Kagyu gompa in Kham, a rimepa gompa. Partially restored, it is the seat of Tai Situ Rimpoche, now resident in Bir, Kangra Valley, India.

*Dzongsar Gompa* (rDzong gsar dgon), Derge county, east of Pelpung Gompa. Founded in 1253 by Phakpa, this large Sakya rimepa gompa, renewed by the great Khyentse Wangpo in the nineteenth century and Khyentse Chokyi Lodro in the twentieth, was perhaps the most vital gompa in Tibet before 1959. It was associated with the late Dilgo Khyentse Rimpoche and is the seat of Dzongsar Khyentse Rimpoche, who lives in the West. The assembly hall has been rebuilt and the gompa is now functional again. Above Dzongsar is the Padma Shelphuk, a Guru Rimpoche cave and a power place of hidden treasure. Rongme Karmo, another important site of hidden treasure, a tiger's lair, lies to the east of the gompa.

*Pelyul Namgyel Jangchub Choling* (dPal yul rNam rgyal byang chub chos gling), in Pelyul county, 30 miles (45 km) south of Kathok Dorjeden in the Nguchu Valley. An important Nyingma gompa built high on a valley side and consisting now of innumerable scattered hermitages and an assembly hall, this was founded by Rikdzin Kunzang Sherab in 1665. Previously with 600 monks, it has been partially restored. It is the seat of the Third

Drubwang Padma Norbu Rimpoche, the titular head of the Nyingma order, who has a new gompa in south India, and also of Gyatrul Rimpoche of Berkeley, California.

### Eastern and Southern Kham

*Lithang Thubchen Chokhorling* (Li thang Thub chen chos 'khor gling), Lithang county, in Sichuan province, on the road between Bathang and Dartsedo. Lithang lies in the highlands between the Dzachu and the Nyakchu Valleys. Founded by the Third Dalai Lama in 1580, it is a large Geluk gompa, the principal gompa of the Lithang district, formerly with 2,800 monks. It was completely destroyed by bombs following fierce resistance to the Chinese invasion of 1951. It has been quickly restored by the Lithang Kyabgon and now possesses a large assembly hall and the Tsuklakhang Kungarawa.

*Minyak Lhagang Gompa* (Mi nyag lha sgang dgon), in Dardo county. Lhagang is the principal power place of Minyak, which is part of the old Chakla kingdom centred in Dartsedo. The gompa complex, of the Sakya order, includes the famous Jokhang Lhakhang that contains the Minyak Jowo. The image of Shakyamuni Buddha that was to become the Lhasa Jowo was part of the dowry that Kongjo, the Chinese princess who became a queen of the seventh-century King Songtsen Gampo, was bringing to Lhasa. At this place the Jowo could not be moved until a substitute had been made and erected. It is uncertain whether the Minyak Jowo now resident here is the seventh-century original.

*Gyelmo Murdo* (rGyal mo mur mdo), the main peak of the mountain range covering several counties of Ngawa prefecture, to the north of Dartsedo and Dardo county. Gyelmo Murdo was the mountain power place of old Gyarong, or Gyelmorong, constituting 18 kingdoms in this far eastern region of ethnic Tibet. The people of Gyelmorong were never considered pure Tibetan stock and in recent history the area has been partially colonized by the Han. The Gyelmo Murdo mountain range and its principal peak form a major place of Buddhist and Bon pilgrimage. Gyelmo

Murdo is a nyen mountain like Amnye Machen and Nyenchen Thanglha, mountains of supreme elemental power. The mountain god Murdo is reputed to bestow fertility, which is a primary motivation for female pilgrims to visit the mountain. Until Communist puritanism intruded, unmarried girls and spinsters amongst the people inhabiting Murdo's western flanks wore only a tasselled belt below their waists, while awaiting the blessing of the mountain god. It was to this eastern extremity of the empire that the great translator, adept and Dzokchen practitioner Bairotsana was exiled in the eighth century. His meditation caves are located on both the north and south flanks of the mountain. The mountain range consists of 64 peaks, and there are several khorra circuits around the principal peak as well as a pilgrim path up to it. Within the inner circuit (nangkor) is the Senge Dzong Lhakhang and Senge Drak, Lion Rock, in the river. Senge Dzong lies to the south of the mountain and the ascent to the top of the central peak begins here. Easily accessible from Senge Dzong is Murdo Wangchuk, a rock tower representing Murdo's phallus, one of the principal power places of the area. A middle path (barkor) takes seven days to walk round, while the outer circuits (*chikor*) – for there are variations of the route – take up to three weeks. The major power places *en route* include Tsonak, Black Lake; Bairotsana's meditation caves, the principal being Barkham on the north side; the Bon peak of Yungdrung Ne, Power Place of the Swastika, on the east side; and numerous caves, amongst them the meditation cave of Yudra Nyingpo, the renowned eighth-century adept.

*Khawa Karpo* (Kha ba dkar po), on the borders of the far southern corner of Chamdo prefecture in the TAR and the Dechen Autonomous Prefecture in Yunnan province. This is the principal peak of the range of mountains lying between the Ngulchu (Salween) and the Dzachu (Mekong) rivers to the south of old Tsawarong. It is sometimes held to be Demchok's buddha-speech chakra instead of Labchi. It is one of the great mountain power places of Tibet, sacred to both Bonpo and Buddhist. The 11-day khorra path is considered very dangerous and pilgrims need to tie themselves to trees at night to prevent themselves from falling into precipices.

*Ganden Sumtseling Gompa* (dGa' ldan gsum rtse gling dgon), in Gyelthang county, near Gyelthang Xian in the Dechen Autonomous Prefecture in Yunnan province. This flourishing Geluk gompa, founded in the seventeenth century, completely destroyed and now rebuilt, serves both Gyelthang and the adjacent counties with colleges and lhakhangs for each valley. There are about 600 monks in residence.

*Bumishi Gompa* (Bu mi bshi dgon), in Balung county, near Lijiang, in old Jang Sadam, in the Naxi Autonomous Prefecture of Yunnan province. Bumishi was the capital of the Jang (Naxi) state that formed part of the Tibetan Empire between the seventh and the ninth centuries. This southern outpost of the Karma Kagyu is built in Chinese style. Also in Balung county is a cave where the Chinese Chan master Bodhidharma is believed to have stayed.

### Amdo

The old province of Amdo covers the Machu (upper Yellow River) basin in Qinghai province. It is a land of rolling pastures. The chief focus of its sacred geography is the mountain power place of Amnye Machen, which lies close to the borders of Kham. In the north-west of Amdo is the sacred lake Tso Ngon (Kokonor). In the far east are Labrang and also Gengya, which now lies in Gansu province. In southern Amdo the population is Tibetan, dominated by the Goloks. In the north-west, around Kokonor, Buddhist Mongols are dominant. In Tsongkha and the north-east, Muslims of various ethnic groups are in the majority. Only a few of the great power places of Amdo are mentioned here, beginning at Amnye Machen, then north to Tso Ngon, east to Kumbum and finally south to Labrang and Rebkong.

*Amnye Machen* (A myes rma chen), in Machen county. The great sacred mountain power place of Eastern Tibet rises from the range of the same name that stretches some 120 miles (200 km) on a north-west/south-east axis to the south-east of the twin lakes Kyering Tso and Ngoring Tso within the giant dog's-hind-leg-curve of the Machu river. *See pp.188–95.*

*Tarthang Gompa* (Dar thang dgon), in Jikdril county, in the far south of the Golok country. Tarthang Dongak Shedrub Dargyeling, founded in 1882, is a branch of Pelyul Gompa in Kham. It is the home gompa of Lama Kunga, better known as Tarthang Tulku, of Berkeley, California. This large, vital Nyingma gompa, with 1,000 monks, has been well restored and the Zangdok Pelri Lhakhang is a special feature.

*Dodrub Chode* (rDo grub chos sde), in Padma county, southern Amdo. On the Tsangchen plain in the Do Valley, the Dodrub Chode was founded by the Second Dodrubchen Rimpoche in the nineteenth century. It has remained a primary source of the Dzokchen Nyingthik tradition that emanated from Vimalamitra. The present, Fourth, Dodrubchen Rimpoche lives in Gangthok, Sikkim. The topography of the site is envisioned as the meditating form of Longchen Rabjampa. There is a Zangdok Pelri-style lhakhang on top of a hill in the plain.

*Drakar Treldzong* (Brag dkar sprel rdzong), in Tsigorthang county, directly to the north of Machen county, south of the county town Xinghai Xian. White Rock Monkey Citadel, a mountain power place, is a fabled power place of Guru Rimpoche and one of Amdo's best known pilgrimage destinations. The five-hour khorra circuit around the peak includes the Great Guru's meditation cave and his Dorje Phuklam cave that has a skylight formed by the passage of his dorje; his consort Yeshe Tsogyel's hermitage, called the Khandro Tsokhang, the Assembly Hall of the Sky Dancers; a renowned sky-burial site; a bardo thang passage to crawl through; several self-manifest images with magical properties; sites relating to Je Tsongkhapa's stay in the area; a vital Geluk gompa with 300 monks; and several inhabited hermitages.

*Tso Ngon lake* (mTsho sngon), in Kangtsa county, 60 miles (100 km) west of Xining, in northern Amdo. It is best known in the West by its Mongolian name, Kokonor, which, like Tso Ngon, means 'Blue Sea' or 'Turquoise Lake', and the surrounding lands are inhabited mainly by Mongolian Buddhists who have little affinity with Central Tibetans. The lake is the abode of a serpent spirit bodhisattva, a minister of the serpent king Anavatapta. It is a gathering place of beneficent mother goddesses and sky dancers and has been blessed by many saints and adepts. At the centre of the lake is an island sanctuary called Tsonying Mahadeva. The original legends of the lake and island tell of a time when the lake was a plain with a spring in the middle covered by a stone. So long as the spring was covered again after water had been drawn it was beneficial to human beings, but one day the spring was left uncovered and the water flowed out with such strength that it drowned 10,000 people. The demoness of the lake was thereafter called Trishor Gyelmo, the Queen who Drowned 10,000, which is another name of the lake. The spring was blocked by Guru Rimpoche who, in the form of an eagle, carried a mountain from India – some say from the top of Kang Rimpoche – which became Tsonying Mahadeva. Later the Dzokchen adept Bairotsana left 108 treasures here. Zhabkar Rimpoche, Little White Foot, meditated here from 1806 to 1809 and built a small lhakhang on top of the island's peak, enshrining Thukjechenpo, the Great Compassionate One, flanked by Mahadeva and Trishor Gyelmo. Today Tsonying Mahadeva is a paradisaical island, with good caves and hermitages, plentiful water and wood, wild flowers and wild vegetables like garlic and edible plants in abundance, birds in the trees, fish in the water and 'freedom from thieves, mastiffs and vermin'. In winter the lake is frozen, allowing easy access. A small gompa is located there with a few monks in residence. The khorra circuit around the lake is approximately 190 miles (300 km) long and the 12-year pilgrimage event occurs in the sheep year.

*Kumbum Jampaling* (sKu 'bum byams pa gling), in Rushar county, south of Xining. The Geluk gompa of Kumbum is one of Tibet's largest. It was built around a sandalwood tree that sprouted from the blood of Je Tsongkhapa's mother's placenta and marked the place of the master's birth. The tree is now enclosed within a chorten, but a tree grown from a cutting of the original shows self-manifest images of Jampelyang, the bodhisattva of wisdom, Je Tsongkhapa's protector, upon its leaves and bark. The gompa's name is derived from the many-doored chorten that Tsongkhapa's mother built here in 1379 and from the Jampa (Maitreya)

Lhakhang, one of the early temples built at Kumbum. The gompa was founded in 1560 and despite a chequered history has survived as a very large monastic complex, built in the Chinese style. The Serdong Chenmo, housing an image of the master, and the Jampa Lhakhang, the most important of the many temples, form the locus of power in the gompa. The monastic colleges and residences of the tulkus comprise a large part of the complex. Reflecting the ethnic mixture of this part of Amdo, half of the present complement of 400 monks are Tibetan and the remainder Mongul, Tu and a few Chinese.

*Jakhyung Gompa* (Bya khyung dgon), in Bayan Khar (Hualong) county, south of Xining and off the road between Kumbum and Labrang Gompas. Founded on the site of a Karma Kagyu gompa on a ridge overlooking the Machu river in 1349 by Lama Dondrub Rinchen, the first teacher of Je Tsongkhapa, this is the oldest Geluk institution in Amdo. Tsongkhapa was ordained and studied here until leaving for Lhasa at the age of 16. Furthermore, the gompa lies near the birthplace of the Fourteenth Dalai Lama and it was here that he had his head shaved in ordination after his discovery as an incarnation. The gompa was destroyed during the Cultural Revolution but has been rebuilt in fine style and now houses about 500 monks.

*Denthik Sheldrak* (Den thig shel brag), also Denthik Shelkyi Bamgon, in Bayan Khar county, accessible from Hualong Xian. This is the power place where a few monks from Central Tibet took refuge from the Bon revival led by the apostate King Langdarma in the ninth century. Here the tradition of ordination was maintained until Lume and his friends arrived from Central Tibet to reclaim the ordination that would revive the monastic tradition in Central Tibet at the end of the tenth century. The caves where the refugee monks lived are on the sides of a small valley with some monastic buildings below.

*Labrang Tashikyil* (bLa brang bkra shis dkyil), in Sangchu county, 175 miles (280 km) south of Lanchou, near Xiahe town, also accessible from Jakhyung Gompa. The Geluk gompa of Labrang was, and still is, Amdo's largest and one of the few spared by the Cultural Revolution. It was founded in 1709 by Jamyang Zhepa, an incarnation of one of Je Tsongkhapa's teachers, who is the third-ranking Geluk hierarch after the Dalai and Panchen Lamas. Labrang had the reputation of being the finest Buddhist teaching institution in Amdo. The walled compound, nearly 2 miles (3 km) in circumference, contains seven major lhakhangs, five colleges and the palace of the tulku of Jamyang Zhepa, who lives in Lanchou. The gompa has 1,000 monks attached to it and several fine geshe teachers, but, like the great Lhasa gompas, it has been partly reduced to a museum.

*Gangya Drakar* (rGan rgya'i brag dkar), in Sangchu county, about 30 miles (50 km) north-east of Labrang, now in Gansu province. At the base of Dagyel mountain is a high escarpment several miles in length. In a ravine against this escarpment is the entrance to a cavern that penetrates the mountain several hundred yards on several levels. The mountain is the palace of the buddha-deity Demchok and also the abode of King Dagyel Mangpoche, who died here in battle with the Chinese in 659. A Guru Rimpoche cave is located in the vicinity and the great seventeenth-century adept Kelden Gyamtso is associated with the power place through his meditation here and his abbotship of the local Geluk gompa. The essence of the power place is the cavern called the Khandro Nekhang Rangjung, the Naturally Created Power-House of the Sky Dancers. Deep within the cave is the Demchok Yab-Yum lake, where Shinje, the Lord of Death, also dwells. The cave and the lake are replete with spontaneously manifest phenomena. Mythic tunnels leading out of the back of the cave system lead to Pataliputra (Patna, in India), which links it to the body-mandala of Demchok, and also to Lhasa and to Drakar Treldzong *(see p.293)*. The presiding incarnation is the khandroma Kham Gungru Yeshe Khandro, a female incarnation, and the site and its gompa, Gengya Dratsang, are adjuncts of Labrang Gompa. Associated with the Dagyel mountain is the nearby lake called Dagyel Gyentso.

*Rebkong* (Re bkong), in the Huangnan Autonomous Tibetan Prefecture. Rebkong (Tongren) county forms only part of the fabled Golden Land of Rebkong, south of the Machu river and west of Labrang. This area of rolling grassland may be considered the heart of Amdo. The topography does not lend itself to easy structuralization, but Rebkong can best be defined by the mandala of its eight power places of great spiritual accomplishment in the cardinal and intermediate directions of the Rebkong plains. Here the great adepts of Guru Rimpoche's lineage attained realization and performed miracles, and the region's 50 small Geluk gompas also attest to the devotion of its people. Rebkong was a lawless area of feuding Amdowa bandits, but it has always been renowned for its Nyingma yogis, practitioners of the secret tantras of Guru Rimpoche's lineage, who lived in the numerous hermitages of the area, dressed in white, their long dreadlocks piled on top of their head. At auspicious ritual times up to 2,000 yogis would gather for meditation. Wenba Tashikyil, the Guchu caves, Rebkong Nyingon and Rebkong Sibgon are some of the Nyingma establishments of the area.

*Rongpo Gonchen* (Rong po dgon chen), Rebkong county, south of the county town Rongpo Gyakhar. Founded in 1301 as a Sakya gompa, Rongpo Gonchen became a Geluk establishment in the sixteenth century. It is now the largest gompa in Rebkong with 400 monks under the care of the young Rongpo Kyabgon. The Rebkong school of painting, founded in the fifteenth century, is still alive at Sengeshong Yagotsang and Sengeshong Magotsang, north of Rongpo Gonchen.

# TIBETAN TIME AND FESTIVALS

Tibetan time is structured according to the passage of the planets – particularly Jupiter – and the sun and moon. The 60-year passage of Jupiter around the sun determines a 60-year calendary cycle, each sixtieth year marked by apocalyptic ritual. The 60-year cycle is broken into five periods of 12 solar years and the auspicious conjunction of every 12 years is celebrated in purification. Each of the 60 years is named after one of 12 animals and one of five elements in combination. Thus 1996 is the fire mouse year. The annual passage of the sun is marked at the New Year (*losar*) by the most important ritual festivals. The solar year is broken into 12 lunar months and it is the phase of the moon that determines the major festival days. Particularly inauspicious days, and also months, will be dropped from the calendar and the following day or month repeated.

The 10th, 15th, 25th and 29th days of the moon are the most auspicious. The 10th day is dedicated to Guru Rimpoche, being the day when the Great Guru promised to return to Dzambuling from the Glorious Copper-Coloured Mountain. The 15th and 20th days are associated with Shakyamuni Buddha. The 25th day is dedicated to the Khandromas, the sky dancers. The 29th day is devoted to the guardian protectors. These are the days that determine the pilgrim's schedule – he is guided by the moon. The 24 hours of day and night are divided into 12 two-hour periods, dawn and dusk providing the most potent ritual periods and the two-hour period before dawn being the most fertile for meditation.

The calendar for the new year is calculated by the astrologers of the Lhasa Menzikhang late in the old year. The year begins, on average, six weeks after the Western New Year. Each major gompa has its own calendar of festivals. The festivals mentioned below are mostly Lhasa festivals. But apart from memorial days of the birth and deaths of great lamas, most gompas celebrate the same auspicious days.

## First Month

Losar, the New Year Festival: first three days of the new year, throughout Tibet, a lay family festival with gambling and drinking but also public dance and carnival.

Monlam, the Great Lhasa Festival of Prayer: after Losar, from the 4th to the 25th, particularly in the Jokhang in Lhasa, a monastic festival with lay pilgrimage to the Jokhang, concluding on the 25th with the procession of Jampa (Maitreya).

Gaton, Lama Feast: 16th–18th, in Lhasa; on the 15th day butter sculpture is displayed around the Barkor and lamps are lighted on the roofs and in the windows of houses.

Pelden Lhamo Festival, celebration of the goddess-protectress: 19th–21st, in Lhasa.

## Second Month

Lugong Gyelpo, King of the Ghosts: 29th–30th, in Lhasa, monastic procession around the lingkor.

## Fourth Month

Saga Dawa: Shakyamuni Buddha's Enlightenment, for three to five days climaxing on the full moon (15th) and also variously thereafter, in Lhasa, and at Tsurphu, Samye Chokhor, Reteng, Tashi Lhunpo and other gompas; cham dance and display of giant thangkas.

## Fifth Month

Samye Consecration Memorial Day: full moon (15th), at Samye Chokhor.

## Sixth Month

Padmasambhava (Guru Rimpoche) birthday celebration, 10th day.

Ganden Siu Thang: display of the relics and thangkas at Ganden monastery, 15th day.

Drepung Zhoton, the Yoghurt Festival: full moon (15th) at Drepung Gompa and the Norbu Lingka in Lhasa; cham dance, picnic and drinking; display of giant thangka at Drepung; now developed as a tourist festival.

## Seventh Month
Yerpa Tsechu: the Yerpa Picnic: 10th day at Yerpa.

Bathing Festival: especially at Terdrom, 27th day.

## Eighth Month
Onkor: Harvest Festival, 1st day.

## Ninth Month
Lhabab Duchen, Shakyamuni Buddha's descent from the Tushita heaven: 22nd day, pilgrimage to Lhasa, day of devotion.

## Tenth Month
Pellha Rirab, Propitiation of Pelden Lhamo: 10th day, in Lhasa, procession around the Barkor.

Ganden Ngacho, Memorial Day of Je Tsongkhapa, 25th day, procession of Tsongkhapa image and lighting of lamps.

## Twelfth Month
Nganpa Guzom, the Inauspicious Period: from 12 p.m. on the 6th day to 12 p.m. on the 7th day people stay inside.

Tsegu Tor, Purification of the Old Year: 29th day, at various gompas, with cham dancing.

# THE TIBETAN DIASPORA AND TIBETAN BUDDHISM IN THE WEST

Only 100,000 Tibetans left their homeland in the wake of the Fourteenth Dalai Lama in 1959. Thirty-five years later, small but flourishing Tibetan lay communities exist in most large cities of America, Europe and East Asia, hundreds of Tibetan gompas and temples have been built in the Indian sub-continent and around the world, and Tibetan Buddhism has become one of the fastest growing religions on the planet. The Dalai Lama himself, a winner of the Nobel Peace Prize, has international status as a man and politician of rare, if not unique, integrity, and has assumed a high media profile in his crusade for the survival of Tibetan culture and for the oppressed people of his country. He is the spiritual leader of the Geluk order and his name is well known, but performing the same quality of spiritual guidance are scores of other lamas with similar status within their communities of Tibetan, Asian and Western disciples. How has this tiny number of representatives of a nation of four million people achieved such international renown?

In October of 1959 the Lhasa valley was full of refugees from Eastern Tibet, mostly Khampas, who had fled Chinese persecution in their homelands. Fearing for the safety of the Dalai Lama, they attacked the occupying Chinese People's Liberation Army, whose artillery, positioned on the valley sides, replied by mercilessly pounding the insurgent concentrations in Lhasa. In the wake of the failure of the Lhasa Uprising those Khampas who did not take to the hills, joining the Chuzhi Kangdruk guerrillas, left for exile in India following the Dalai Lama himself, a large part of the Lhasa government, the abbots and many of the monks from the great Lhasa and provincial gompas, the land-owning families of Central Tibet and the faithful from all walks of life who heeded the Dalai Lama's warning of dire times to come under the heel of the rabid Chinese Communists. Over the next few years these refugees were followed by small bands of monks and laymen, frequently led by a lama, from communities all over the Tibetan ethnic region as far away as Amdo and eastern Kham. Travelling at night to avoid Chinese patrols, their routes led them over the Himalayan passes into India where Prime Minister Nehru had vouchsafed sanctuary. Many died on the way from starvation, disease and the vagaries of climate and landscape.

In the pacification or 'liberation' of Tibet, the Communists naturally targeted the ruling classes. These consisted of the secular land-owning nobility and the religious hierarchs – abbots and tulkus – of the gompas, who, accurately enough, were labelled the feudal leadership. The Chinese unleashed a revolution that was to turn society on its head and give political control to the impoverished serfs and peasants of Tibetan feudal society. Religious practice constituted evidence of reactionary thinking and anti-revolutionary activity and was suppressed mercilessly. Mao Tse Tung's Cultural Revolution stressed the Communist imperative to eliminate representatives of the old regime, and the application of doctrinaire policies, many of which were ill-suited to Tibet even from the pragmatic Communist standpoint, together with starvation, forced labour and imprisonment of 'class enemies', constituted a strategy of genocide. During the late 1960s a constant trickle of refugees from the Cultural Revolution arrived in India and Nepal.

Although Nehru opened India's doors to the Tibetans, as did Nepal and Bhutan, he could not condone the settlement of tens of thousands of Tibetans in the ecologically fragile and politically sensitive Himalayan borderlands. So the Tibetan refugees were herded into reception camps on the Indian plains, particularly in Bengal, where they died from tropical disease by the thousands. After months or years in the reception camps the refugees, according to their Tibetan communal origin, were allocated land in central and southern India. The Dalai Lama and his government were given an old British Raj palace in Dharamsala, where the Tibetan leader was kept as a tame mouthpiece for the Government of India in the propaganda war with China. The Sixteenth Karmapa, the spiritual leader of the Kagyu order, whose foresight had prepared a sanctuary and a cache of treasure in Sikkim before the Dalai Lama's flight, had the wealth and influence to establish an independent foothold in exile. Likewise, Dudjom Rimpoche, the head of the Nyingma order, was blessed by the support of the Nyingma community in the Darjeeling area of West Bengal, and remained independent.

While the mass of peasant refugees were sent to the camps in inhospitable Madhya Pradesh and south India, the lamas with their monks were permitted to establish religious bases wherever they could. They constituted a disproportionate number of the exiles, with a large proportion of the lamas being from Kham, so in just a few years there were Tibetan temples, or at least shrine-rooms, in old colonial style houses, in virtually every Indian hill station and at the major places of Buddhist pilgrimage on the Indian plains, particularly Bodhgaya and Sarnath. This was achieved through use of the treasure that some lamas had managed to bring out of Tibet, through international government aid funnelled through the Dalai Lama's government in Dharamsala, through Western refugee organizations, and also through a few sympathetic private Indians and Europeans. In this way the old religious traditions and the lineal teaching were given a home and the lamas some security out of which they could provide their refugee communities with the customary religious support and also offer the Tibetan Buddhists of the southern Himalayan slopes the kind of vital mainstream Buddhist attention that they had never known before.

It was from these bases that the lamas began an extraordinary relationship – or love affair – with Westerners. It was a reciprocal relationship in which their spiritual wares were exchanged for a place in the modern world. Their initial association with just a few responsive Westerners was to grow into a world-wide fellowship. The lamas who had the spiritual goods on offer were mature teachers, scholars, adepts in meditation and yoga, who had successfully undergone the full rigorous regimen of monastic and yogic training in their homelands and had deep experience in transmitting the fruit of their mystical experience to at least one generation of devotees before their departure. They represented all the religious orders of Tibet, and all had the initiations and powerful authority derived from lineal transmission originating with a buddha-adept who had lived hundreds if not thousands of years before. Their allure, perhaps, lay in their cheerfulness and humour, the happy acceptance and openness with which they had emerged from the physical suffering and mental anguish of oppression and exile. Even the humblest itinerant monk had this spontaneous warmth. But the most highly-charged magnets were the lamas of renown whose Tibetan devotees provided a structure and a conduit for Western devotees, like the Karmapa, Dudjom Rimpoche, Khamtrul Rimpoche and Drukpa Thuktse. Lamas of lower profile with evident spiritual qualities, like Lama Kalu, Kanjur Rimpoche and Abu Rimpoche, also attracted devoted Western disciples. All these lamas passed on many years ago and are now incarnate as children.

The original Western characters in this scenario were diverse in personality and nationality, in motivation and intent, but what they had in common was an admiration, or reverence, for Tibetan religious culture and the men who embodied it. There was the Indian Parsee *grande dame*, a devotee of the Karmapa, who founded a nunnery and a school to prepare young tulkus for admission into Western universities – from which Chogyam Trungpa, amongst others, graduated. There was the American bibliophile from the Library of Congress, who paid the lamas for the privilege of publishing the manuscripts that they had carried with them – rather than food – in their escape from Tibet. A French film-maker amazed by the sensory display of Tibetan ritual had an enlightenment experience while filming the lamas and gave European television audiences a preview of the experience that hundreds of his viewers would later experience for themselves. There were scholars like the American anthropologist who came to study the phenomenology of lamaism and stayed to devote his life to the tradition as a monk, and others like the Scottish anthropologist who spent 20 years translating the *magnum opus* of his guru-lama, obsessed with the task of translating the voluminous Tibetan scriptures. Diplomats like the Canadian ambassador played a crucial role in providing the keys to the locks of the refugee cage and offering the possibility of travel to the West.

Then there were the old-style hippie travellers who became fascinated by the lamas and caught in relationships with them. Many of these individuals had come to India to pursue the quest for psychedelic experience begun in the spiritual awakening of the 1960s in Europe and America and continued within the ambience of the Hindu sadhu tradition. When the Tibetans, laymen and lamas, appeared on pilgrimage in Benares and Bodhgaya, and in Kathmandu, an immediate rapport with the hippies led to life-transforming relationships, for the hippies had neither personal agendas nor attachment and were wide open to the existential experiences that attended such meetings. They had the time to spend in learning the language in order to recite the liturgies and speak with the lamas in their own tongue. They lived already the renunciate lifestyle necessary to stay with the Tibetans in their abject poverty. They already possessed a similar philosophical vision, either subconscious or articulated, that facilitated absorption of tantric metaphysics, and they had a psychedelic drug-induced responsiveness to the transmission of mind-to-mind and symbolic meaning. Some ex-hippies still remain in India or Nepal today, absorbed in meditation and study. But many more, after some years, returned to the West, carrying the lore of the lamas with them, some to establish Tibetan Buddhist centres in their own countries, some to enlarge Tibetan departments in the universities, and all to swell the popular support for the Dalai Lama and his political agenda and private promotion of the numerous lamas who later would travel to the West.

By the end of the 1960s each of the Buddhist orders had established at least one major centre on the Indian sub-continent. In the 1970s these evolved into vital teaching institutions and those lamas who were able, lamas of all orders, began to establish Indian replacements for their gompas destroyed in Tibet. By the end of the 1980s this had been achieved in either India or Nepal. Nepal had taken in about 10,000 Tibetan refugees; many Western Tibetans had crossed over the Himalayas on the western borders of Nepal and had been settled in camps on that side. Many others had come in bands, led by their lamas, from Nangchen in western Kham, and settled by the great stupas of Boudhanath and Swayambhu, both magnets for pilgrims from all over the Himalayan area. Mainly Red Hat gompas – Kagyu, Nyingma and Sakya – were established there, but there was also the Geluk Kopan Monastery of Lama Thubten Yeshe, which was to become the home gompa of one of the largest international Buddhist fellowships.

In India, Dharamsala was the headquarters of the Dalai Lama, the Tibetan Government and the Geluk order. The Tibetan Library there became a centre of study for both Tibetan and foreign students. The Drepung and Sera Gompas were replicated in south India. The Karma Kagyupas, led by the Sixteenth Karmapa, were a wealthy and powerful order established in Rumthek, Sikkim, until the Sixteenth Karmapa's death in a Chicago hospital led to a schism, rival candidates for the Karmapa's throne, and separate seats for their conflicting supporters – the Zhamarpa in Delhi on one hand, and Gyeltseb Tulku in Rumthek and Situ Rimpoche in Bir, Kangra Valley, on the other. The Drukchen and the Drukpa Kagyu were based in Hemis, Ladakh, and in Darjeeling. Sakya Tridzin and the Sakya order were established in Rajpur, Dehra Dun. The Nyingmapas, always a decentralized order, were based in Darjeeling, the Kathmandu Valley, Dehra Dun and south India. The Bonpos were blessed with a remarkable lama-savant called Khenpo Tendzin Namdak who founded the Dolanji Gompa, Simla, and more recently a gompa in the Kathmandu Valley.

The first lamas to travel to the West were young tulkus eager to escape from caste-ridden India. Amongst them was Chogyam Trungpa, who first attended Oxford University and then established a centre in Scotland called Samyeling before moving on to the US, where he was immensely successful in building a Kagyu empire. Lama Thubten Yeshe travelled from Kopan to Europe to teach and founded the Foundation for the Preservation of the Mahayana Tradition. Tarthang Tulku migrated from Sanskrit University in Benares to Berkeley, California, to found a popular Nyingma centre. Some of the old grandfather lamas, like Lama Kalu and Dudjom Rimpoche, followed this first wave of tulkus to the west and bestowed upon their serious students the authority and initiations necessary for prolonged meditation practice. The first meditation retreat centres were established and Western practitioners were ushered into three-year retreat programmes.

From the beginning of the close association of lamas with Western friends and devotees in India, the lamas had encouraged their students to make the basic commitment of refuge in the Three Jewels – Buddha, his teaching and the community – and, amongst the Red Hats, to practise recitation of fundamental tantric liturgies and their accompanying meditation exercises. But despite the old tried and tested adage that no Buddhist community can thrive without a monastic base, there was some divergence of opinion amongst the lamas as to the wisdom of ordaining Western monks and nuns. Those who had trust in the ultimate efficacy of the Buddhist institutional forms to function in any society had no qualms, and Western monks and nuns of all orders wearing the traditional maroon Tibetan robes were soon to be seen at the gompas, in places of pilgrimage in India and also in the West. Other lamas, perhaps those who were less sure of their complete comprehension of the nature of Western mind, were uncertain of the capacity of Westerners to maintain the life-long vows that ordination implied.

This divergence of opinion was to separate the lamas into two camps in regard to their Western disciples. The first was of a deeply conservative mould that felt that if Tibetan Buddhism was to take root in the West as the prophecies of Guru Rimpoche had foreseen ('When the iron bird flies the buddha-dharma will go to the West') then it would be in Tibetan form with Tibetan language, along the strictly defined graduated path of study and meditation, with traditional ritual modes, hats and all. Those lamas who were more fluent in cross-cultural communication, whose exposure to Westerners was more intimate and whose personal experience and vision of the tantric tradition allowed a more flexible approach tended to a more liberal agenda for the West. There were Western disciples, meanwhile, who were not ready even for the most indulgent attitudes of these lamas and who perceived the Tibetan tradition as a vast resource of spiritual largesse from which could be extracted, at no cost, elements that their impoverished Western consciousness required to regain its health or to enrich it with mystical experience. No lama could sanction this individualistic attitude and continue to give structured teaching, because tantric practice requires tantric commitment and the first commitment is obedience to the teacher. As more lamas travelled to the West and established dharma centres, whether they were of a conservative or liberal bent, their disciples organized themselves into social mandalas with the lama at the centre, those fully committed to him forming an inner circle, those with tentative commitment in an outer circle and those with a peripheral interest on the outside.

Within these community mandalas the lamas' teaching styles differed radically. One lama would make menial discipline the chief practice and index of commitment, in imitation of Jetsun Milarepa's mentor Marpa, perhaps. Another lama taught 'crazy wisdom', using psycho-drama and alcohol to break through the obstacles to buddha-awareness. Many others insisted upon the three-year retreat as the open sesame to spiritual realization. Some saw philosophical and metaphysical study of the Buddhist texts as not only a prerequisite for tantric initiation and practice but as an end in itself. Others bestowed frequent ritual empowerment as the means to imbue students with the basic receptive attitude to the lama's blessings and instruction. Some relied on traditional exposition on philosophical and moral topics. Each lama developed his own teaching methods and styles, aspects or combinations of the above, in response to the peculiar Western social and psychological base with which he was presented and to the needs of his disciples.

Now the old grandfather lamas have passed on, and there is a new generation of tulkus educated in India and Nepal who never knew the rigours of Tibet. They have grown up in gompas steeped in the old traditions, but in the materialistic social environment that is the contemporary Indian sub-continent. Funds have poured into the lamas' coffers, not only from Western disciples and sympathizers but also from the devotees in the newly rich countries of Malaysia, Singapore, Hong Kong and Taiwan, where the Chinese have continued in a modified manner the old relationship of priest-patron. The lama-priest performs psycho-magical rites for the layman-patron's longevity, health, wealth and success in any enterprise, in exchange for the large offerings that Western disciples usually are unable to afford. In Tibetan and Chinese society wealth is an indicator of spiritual power, but part of the post-Christian West is loath to accept conspicuous consumption as a sign of Buddhahood.

For the younger tulkus now teaching in the West, wealth is only one obstacle to continued growth of their fellowships that has arisen with the popularity of the Tibetan Buddhist cult. The number of nominal adherents to Tibetan Buddhism in Europe, America and Australasia is now counted in millions, their centres in many hundreds and the leaders of the movement naturally attract media attention. Their sexual activity has been under scrutiny, particularly what is perceived as the exploitation of female disciples by unscrupulous lamas, but what is better seen from within the tradition as a dereliction in skilful employment of psycho-sexual training methods. Schism within the Tibetan Buddhist orders has also received media attention, particularly the sometimes violent conflict between the rival supporters of the two candidates for the Karmapa tulkuship. The recent political polemics between a schismatic Buddhist fellowship in England and the Dalai Lama himself concerning the moral integrity of worship of a particularly virulent guardian protector, a god imported from the old Tibetan shamanic milieu, also gained international media coverage.

Nevertheless the lamas have come a long way down the road to acceptance as the high priests of the planet since their incarceration in refugee camps only 35 years ago. Despite accusations of charlatanism, commercialism, exploitation of the naïve, power-politicking, primitive shamanic practices and conventionally immoral behaviour, Tibetan Buddhism continues to thrive. Evidently the positive, psychologically beneficial elements of this complex, multifaceted religion continue to fill spiritual gaps in Western consciousness.

The tradition itself can attribute its success in the West to a compassionate core in the minds of its exemplars that facilitates a transformative relationship with their disciples. It can emphasize the basic sanity of its moral doctrine. It can point to the efficacy of its meditation techniques that produce a balanced quiet centre in a mind then capable of insight into the nature of reality. It can highlight the traditional methods that bring an integration of the unconscious depths of the mind, where images of archetypal power lie latent, with superficial conscious activity. And ultimately it can indicate the imperative of liberation from suffering achieved by the Buddhas of its lineages. Outside observers may stress an analysis that features the sense of social community in an exotic esoteric ambience, or an indiscriminate hunger for replacement of discredited indigenous religious forms. But no simple rationale appears sufficient to explain the diversity of benefits that seem to accrue to all kinds of adherents to the tradition.

The success of the Tibetan lamas in their missionary activity in the West has a parallel within the lay communities in India and Nepal. Particularly in the Kathmandu Valley, *laissez-faire* economic conditions are conducive to commercial success and for freewheeling trading the reputation of Tibetans was second to none in Central Asia. The carpet industry, along with less reputable trading activity, has been the source of capital that is now invested in legitimate commercial ventures throughout Asia. A significant percentage of profits go to the lamas. The Tibetan trading network includes representatives in cities throughout the world. This affluence affords a stark contrast with the relative poverty of the Tibetans still in the camps of central and southern India, but even here, where agriculture has been the basic source of survival, men leave the community to trade and bring back the elusive cash that raises their level of prosperity way above that of Indian villages. As in religion so in commerce: what is the secret of Tibetan success?

# GLOSSARY

| | |
|---|---|
| *bardo* | The intermediate state between dying and rebirth, during which the clear light and a series of visions arise. |
| *bodhisattva* | A spiritual or incarnate emanation of the Buddha devoted to the welfare of all sentient beings. |
| Bon, Bonpo | The indigenous shamanic tradition of Tibet and its devotees, reformed into a tantric order that differs little from the Buddhist orders. |
| *buddha-dharma* | The Buddhist tradition, the doctrine of the Buddha, the continuum of compassionate psycho-spiritual responsiveness. |
| Chakna Dorje | 'Wielder of the Dorje', the wrathful bodhisattva protector of buddha-body, Vajrapani. |
| *chakras* | The focal points of spiritual energy within the subtle body of the yogi. |
| Chenrezik | 'He who gazes upon the world with tears in his eyes', the bodhisattva of compassion, protector of Buddha-speech, Avalokiteshvara. |
| *chorten* | A monument or bronze of symmetrical design that represents buddha-mind; 'a receptacle of offerings' (*stupa*). |
| *chu* | Stream or river. A *tsangpo* is a major river. |
| Demchok | 'Supreme Bliss', a personal buddha-deity of the mother-tantra especially envisioned in the great moun-tain power places; described in the *Chakrasamvara-tantra*. |
| *dharma* | *See* Buddha-dharma. |
| *dorje* | The lamas' ritual implement symbolizing inde-structible empty awareness, a thunderbolt (*vajra*). |

| | |
|---|---|
| Dorje Phakmo | 'The Adamantine Sow', the khandroma consort of the buddha-deity Demchok. Vajra Varahi. |
| Dorje Phurba | 'The Indestructible Dagger', the buddha-deity described in the *Vajrakilaya-tantra*. |
| *drokpas* | The yak and sheep-herding nomad inhabitants of the Tibetan plateau. |
| Dukhor | 'The Wheel of Time', a personal buddha-deity described in the *Kalachakra-tantra* and worshipped by the Dalai Lama. |
| Dzambuling | The southern continent of Buddhist cosmology; our world (Jambudvipa). |
| *gelong* | A fully ordained monk (*bhikshu*). |
| Geluk, Gelukpa | The 'virtuous' order of Tibetan Buddhism and the Dalai Lamas, founded by Je Tsongkhapa. |
| *geshe* | A fully ordained monk who has passed the highest academic examination. |
| *gomkhang* | The secret chamber for propitiating the wrathful guardian protectors. |
| *gompa* | A monastery, 'a place of solitude'. |
| Gompo | A wrathful guardian-protector, particularly, Nakpo Chenpo, the Great Black One, Mahakala. |
| Guru Rimpoche | Tibet's Great Guru Padmasambhava who converted shamanistic Tibet to Tantric Buddhism in the eighth century. |
| intermediate state | *See* Bardo. |
| Jampa | The bodhisattva and future Buddha of 'Loving Kindness', Maitreya. |
| Jampelyang | The bodhisattva of wisdom 'Sweet Voice', wielding the sword of awareness, protector of buddha-mind, Manjushri. |
| Kagyu, Kagyupa | The order of Tibetan Buddhism with several sub-orders founded by Jetsun Milarepa, the principal of which is the Karma Kagyu of the Karmapas. |

| | |
|---|---|
| kaliyuga | 'The fag-end of time', the last phase of a cycle of universal creation, a time of degeneration, pollution and corruption. |
| *khandroma* | 'Sky dancer' (*dakini*), a female Buddha, or a wild celestial being, sometimes incarnate. |
| *khorra* | The devotional practice of walking around a power place or sacred person; circumambulation. |
| Kye Dorje | A buddha-deity described in the *Hevajra-tantra*. |
| *la* | A pass. |
| *lama* | Revered teacher, a tantric hierarch. |
| *lha, lhamo* | Gods and goddesses mainly from pre-Buddhist, shamanic, times, incorporated into the Buddhist mandala as protectors and protectresses. |
| *lhakhang* | 'God-house', chapel, a place of worship of the gods, sometimes a monastery assembly hall; a *gomkhang* is the lhakhang of the protecting deities. |
| *lu, luma* | Male and female serpent spirits dwelling under the earth and in rivers and lakes, protectors of minerals and treasure, source of various diseases (*nagas*). |
| *mandala* | A symmetrical diagram of buddha-mind depicted in art, visualized in the mind or perceived in the landscape. |
| *mantra* | A string of empowered syllables by which a Buddha is evoked in meditation practice through muttering. |
| *mudras* | A gesture or conventional hand sign symbolizing and evoking a particular state of mind, such as meditation or offering. |
| Namnang | The Buddha of the central station in the mandala, described in the *Vairochana-tantras*. |
| *nyen* | One of the more powerful types of mountain god, originally worshipped by the Bonpos and taken aboard by the Buddhists as protectors. |
| Nyingma, Nyingmapa | The 'old', original order of Tibetan Buddhism founded by Guru Rimpoche. |

| | |
|---|---|
| *phurba* | A sacred ritual dagger employed particularly in rites of transformation or destruction of demons and spirits. |
| *qu* (Chinese) | The administrative centre of a county division. |
| *ri* | A mountain. |
| *rime, rimepa* | The eclectic movement begun in Kham 200 years ago. |
| Sakya, Sakyapa | The order of Tibetan Buddhism founded at the place called Sakya. |
| *sinmo* | A shamanistic goddess, a mother goddess identified with nature and, incarnate, the original ancestress of the Tibetan people. |
| *tantra* | A synonym of 'Tibetan Buddhism', and also the Indian originated texts that form the basis of this essentially oral tradition. |
| *thangka* | A sacred painted scroll of cotton or silk usually illustrating the visionary form of a Buddha. |
| *tongpanyi* | 'Emptiness', the nature of reality according to the Universal Buddhist Tradition. |
| treasure texts | Texts (terma) that were hidden by Guru Rimpoche to be revealed by his treasure-finder emanations down the centuries. |
| *tso* | A lake. |
| *tulku* | A buddha-lama incarnate in a succession of rebirths. |
| Wopakme | 'Boundless Light', Amitabha, the Buddha of the western pure-land. |
| *yupa* | Inhabitants of the valleys, sedentary farmers, as opposed to nomadic drokpas. |
| *xian* (Chinese) | A county town, the administrative centre of a county. Tibetan: *dzong*. |

# BIBLIOGRAPHY

Arris, Michael, *Bhutan*, Vikas, New Delhi, 1980

Avedon, John, *In Exile from the Land of the Snows*, Wisdom, London, 1986

Batchelor, Stephen, *The Tibet Guide*, Wisdom, Boston, MA, 1987

Bernbaum, Edwin, *The Way to Shambhala*, Anchor Books, New York, 1980

—, *Sacred Mountains of the World*, Sierra Club Books, San Francisco, 1990

Buffetrille, Katia, 'One day the mountains will go away: Preliminary remarks on the flying mountains of Tibet', unpublished manuscript

—, 'The Great Pilgrimage of A-myes rMa-chen: Written Tradition, Living Realities' unpublished manuscript, forthcoming in *Mandala and Landscape*, DK Printworld, New Delhi

Chan, Victor, *Tibet Handbook*, Moon Publications, Chico, CA, 1994

Conze, E., *Buddhist Scriptures*, Penguin, London, 1959

Dalai Lama, *My Tibet*, Berkeley, 1990

David-Neel, Alexandra, *My Journey to Lhasa*, TBI, New Delhi, 1991

Dowman, Keith, *rNam thar Zangs gling ma* of Nyang ral nyi ma 'od zer, unpublished manuscript

—, *The Legend of the Great Stupa*, Dharma Publishing, Emeryville, CA, 1973

—, *The Divine Madman*, The Dawn Horse Press, Clearlake, CA, 1980

—, *Tilopa's Twenty-eight Verses*, Diamond Sow Publications, Kathmandu, n.d.

—, *Masters of Mahamudra*, SUNY Press, Albany, NY, 1985

—, *Power Places of Central Tibet*, Routledge & Kegan Paul, London, 1988

—, *The Flight of the Garuda*, Wisdom, Boston, MA, 1994

Dudjom Rimpoche, trans. Gyurme Dorje and Matthew Kapstein, *The Nyingma School of Tibetan Buddhism*, vols 1&2, Wisdom, Boston, MA

Epstein, Lawrence and Wenbin, Peng 'Ganja and Murdo', *Tibet Journal* 1994, XIX, 3

Ferrari, Alfonsa, *mKhyen brTse's Guide to the Holy Places of Central Tibet*, IsMEO, Rome, 1958

Goldstein, Melvyn C., and Beall, Cynthia M., *The Nomads of Western Tibet*, Odyssey, Hong Kong, 1990

Gyurme Dorje, *Tibet Handbook*, Trade & Travel Handbooks, Bath, 1996

Huber, Toni, 'A Pilgrimage to La Phyi: A Study of Sacred and Historical Geography in South-Western Tibet', unpublished MA dissertation in the University of Canterbury, Christchurch, 1989, forthcoming as 'A Guide to the La-Phyi Mandala: History, Landscape and Ritual in South-Western Tibet' in *Mandala and Landscape*, DK Printworld, New Delhi

—, 'What is a Mountain? An Ethnohistory of Representation and Ritual at Pure Crystal Mountain in Tibet' unpublished PhD dissertation in the University of Canterbury, Christchurch, 1993

— and Tsepak Rigzin, 'A Tibetan guide for pilgrimage to Ti-se (Mount Kailas) and Mtsho Ma-pham (Lake Manasarovar)'– *The Tibet Journal* 1995, XX, 1

Johnson, Russell, and Moran, Kerry, *Kailas: On Pilgrimage to the Sacred Mountain of Tibet*, Thames & Hudson, London, 1989

Lhalungpa, Lobsang P., *The Life of Milarepa*, Dutton, New York, 1977

Nebesky-Wojkowitz, René de, *Oracles and Demons of Tibet*, Tiwari, Kathmandu, 1993

Pal, P., *Art of Tibet*, LA County Museum of Art, 1983

Patrul Rinpoche, trans. Padmakara Translation Centre, *The Words of my Perfect Teacher*, HarperCollins, London, 1994

Ramble, Charles, 'Gaining ground: representations of territory in Bon and Tibetan popular tradition' in *Tibet Journal*, 1995, XX, 1

—, 'The creation of the Bon mountain of Kongpo' unpublished manuscript, forthcoming in *Mandala and Landscape*, DK Printworld, New Delhi

Rhie, Marylin M., and Thurman, Robert A. F., *Wisdom and Compassion*, Asian Art Museum of San Francisco and Tibet House, New York, 1991

Ricard, Matthieu, *The Life of Shabkar*, State University of New York Press, Albany, NY, 1994

Snellgrove, David L., *The Nine Ways of Bon*, OUP, London, 1967

Snelling, John, *The Sacred Mountain*, East-West Publications, London, 1990

Thurman, Prof. R., ed., *The Life and Teachings of Tsong Khapa*, Library of Tibetan Works and Archives, Dharamsala, India, 1982

Tucci, Guiseppe, *The Religions of Tibet*, Allied Publishers, New Delhi, 1980

Vitali, Roberto, *Early Temples of Central Tibet*, Serindia, London, 1990

Wylie, Turrel V., *The Geography of Tibet according to the 'Dzam gling rgyas bshad*, IsMEO, Rome, 1962

# INDEX